MW00861455

.

A TOUCH

ALLEN A. KNOLL, PUBLISHERS

OF CRAZY

THEODORE ROOSEVELT GARDNER II

Allen A. Knoll, Publishers, 200 West Victoria Street,
Santa Barbara, CA 93101-3627
© 2014 by Allen A. Knoll, Publishers
All rights reserved. Published in 2014
Printed in the United States of America

First Edition

19   18   17   16   15   14   5   4   3   2   1

Library of Congress Cataloging-in-Publication Data

Gardner, Theodore Roosevelt.
A Touch of Crazy / Theodore R. Gardner, II. -- First Edition.
    pages cm
Includes index.
ISBN 978-1-888310-79-5
1. Gardner, Theodore Roosevelt. 2. Authors, American--20th century--Biography. I. Title.
PS3557.A7146Z46 2014
813'.54--dc23
[B]

                    2014003542

Illustration credits

First house on Main Street, page 2 (photo by Audrey Racines)
Emmaus house for 58 Years, page 3 (photo by Abby Schott)
Kindergarten Class, page 4, (photo courtesy of Barbara Aten Leer)
Broad Street Hotel, page 10, (photo courtesy of the Emmaus Historical Society)
Cousins, page 36 (photo courtesy of Audrey Racines)
Cabin-mates from Nation's Gifted Youth, page 66 (photo courtesy of John Shroyer)
Publicity shot of author at 17 for *That's For Sure, page* 78 (Allentown Morning Call)
1948 convertible Studebaker, page 115 (stock photo)
General Hershey Bar, page 229 (photo courtesy of John Cavello)
The Piano House and The Book Building, pages 322-323 (photos by Stephen G. Schott)

For all my forebearers, offspring, relatives,
Friends and anyone who will take
The time to read this indulgence.

A TOUCH OF CRAZY

We are all, to some extent, crazy. If you come to know any human being well enough, you eventually gain access to the basement where the traumas and wounds and deprivations are stored:...The successful, reasonably happy people I have known are nuts in a way that works for them. Those who struggle and suffer fail to turn their preoccupations to some meaningful use.

—William Falk
The Week

TABLE OF CONTENTS

PREFACE

Talking much about one-
self can also be a means
to conceal oneself.

—*Friedrich Nietzsche*

Okay. Why?

Writing a memoir could be likened to lying on a psychiatrist's couch and, hopefully, telling the truth while lying…there.

Some people seem to fancy someone listening to them babble on. I never thought psychiatry helped people much, though I've never tried it myself. Our daughter Julia's husband Adam's father is a psychiatrist who gave up the schmoozing practice with the edict that it didn't work. He turned to prison psychiatry, said he loved it. Prisoners only had two questions of him:

Q: When do I get my meds?

A: They're not yours, they're the States. When the State decides to give them to you.

Q: When do I get outta here?

A: You've gotta ask the people who put you in.

It was easy and he made the same difference in people's lives as he did in private practice and didn't have to scrounge for and please the customers.

So I am currently more or less engaged in the quantifying of my memories.

Should anyone have a moment or two to escape the ubiquitous self-absorption to ask what I was doing, I could honestly, if not humbly, state I'm writing my memoirs.

It gives you an air of being an important person. It matters little what the memoirs say, no one really reads them anyway.

Is the real danger in taking ourselves too seriously? It's said it is better to keep your mouth shut and be thought a fool than to open it and prove it.

You might expect that in seventy-seven years one has had time to accumulate a significant amount of wisdom.

It ain't necessarily so.

Some of us just accumulate years and as the Pennsylvania Dutch say, we get too soon old and too late smart.

When you hear these sentiments expressed you may feel we are just apes, and the grandest mistake in evolution was granting us the power of speech.

I could call this the Autobiography of a Striver, in Service of the Ego.

Why?

Because it is so delightfully pretentious—plus I am immortalizing imperfection.

If this hasn't turned you off or tuned you out, there is more of the same ahead.

IN THE VESTIBULE

From the moment I picked your book up
until I laid it down I was convulsed with laughter.
Someday I intend on reading it.

—*Groucho Marx*

This minute is my last at age seventy-seven. I have always been intrigued by numbers and seventy-seven seems special. Two lucky sevens, back-to-back, or front-to-back more accurately. And we got this book down to precisely seventy-seven chapters. Who could ask for anything more? Less, perhaps, but not more.

I may not be exactly at death's door, but you could make a case that I was at least in the vestibule. If you work the percentages—how much time has passed and guess how much is ahead—you see I've already shot a good eighty percent or so of my allotment. Blessedly these are easier years. Even so, it may be best not to dwell on these percentages. Denial is a handy thing.

And I can say I started this exercise while I was seventy-seven. There is no book on when it will be completed. In my lifetime would be best.

Seventy-seven years. Fine time to begin a book of recollections, being so enamored of numbers and all.

It won't matter when it's completed, or indeed if it is completed at all. I have until 6:45 tonight, Eastern Standard Time, until I am no longer seventy-seven. I thought it only fitting to squeeze in a little bit more.

I have a potful of notes generated when I was seventy-seven. All I have to do is string them together so they make some sense, adding and embellishing as I go, doing my best to make myself come across as one swell guy—bright, personable, interesting, loyal, friendly, courteous, kind, thrifty, brave, clean and reverent—or thereabouts. Remind me to tell you my Boy Scout story—specifically the pursuit of the Eagle rank in record time.

Beethoven never wrote an autobiography. Nor did Leonardo da Vinci, Socrates or Shakespeare. So why me? Why a guy who if the word sneaked out I had written my autobiography the first question would be, "Who?"

I have enough experience writing books (I have written and published thirty-eight others) that I know snagging an audience of readers is a hard dollar. There are so many easily accomplished amusements available in modern life that it is a near miracle anyone will take the time, effort and expense to read an actual book.

So why write them—why specifically an autobiography of a "Who?"? Someone has suggested my reading audience is on par with those persons who write notes and place them in bottles which they launch at sea. Sometimes they are discovered washed up on some Pacific island shore...

Sometimes.

And when they are, the number of readers hovers around one.

Okay—so—why?

Why? Because I feel like it is why. I have discovered amid futile soul searching sessions writing is rather a selfish endeavor— there is no altruism involved. I write because I like to. Ben Johnson famously said anyone who writes for anything other than money is a blockhead.

I wasn't around when he was famously shooting off his mouth, but today anyone who writes for money is asking for two fates: poverty or disappointment. Perhaps a third: failure. So if you write for fun—because you enjoy it, suffering failure is remote— that is until you no longer enjoy it. Somerset Maugham arrived at that state in his late eighties or nineties.

Toscanini walked off the stage in mid-piece in his eighties

when he forgot the score. He had been conducting from memory all his life until he reached the juncture when his memory failed him. I too conducted my South Coast Choral Society from memory but I got out before my memory failed.

It is true I have written a memoir of my mother and father in celebration of the one hundredth anniversary of their births (2004). It is called *Momma Baby and Judgie,* and necessarily some of this material may have overlapped that a smidgeon. And that book credits another of my books, *Wit's End,* a second anthology of my newspaper columns. Recycling bespeaks patriotism?

Momma Baby and Judgie was, however, a limited edition of five hundred copies. Serious readers will want to read both but we have enough left of the five hundred to satisfy the handful of serious readers that exist for this folderol.

PRE-SCHOOL

The world's a stage. The trifling entrance fee
Is paid (by proxy) to the registrar.
The Orchestra is very loud and free
But plays no music in particular.
They do not print a programme, that I know.
The cast is large. There isn't any plot.
The acting of the piece is far below
The very worst of modernistic rot.

—Hilaire Belloc
The World's A Stage

MAIN STREET, EMMAUS, PENNSYLVANIA

The past is never dead.
It's not even past.

—William Faulkner
Requiem for a Nun

...is just like it sounds—the main street through Emmaus from Macungie and Alburtis to the county seat: Allentown. It was some kind of state highway. Was it Route 29?

The first house in my lifetime was on Main Street. In 1934 the traffic was not onerous, there weren't that many cars on the road—many roads were not paved. To go from our house to Aunt Verna and Uncle Paul's house—a distance of perhaps a mile or so—most of it was on a dirt road. This road was finally paved. I would say not much before the 1950s.

We lived in the Main Street two-story house until 1937 when we moved to a one story "bungalow" on the corner of 2nd and Seem Streets in Emmaus. It contained three bedrooms, one fronting on 2nd Street was connected with a door and small passageway to a second. Then a bathroom and the third bedroom. They

Main street Emmaus, PA. It seemed a lot larger to me when I was in residence at age two. The roof over the front porch caught most of the parents' clothes I disbursed out of the window to teach them a lesson.

were all small.

There are two notable memories about the house on Main Street which we left slightly before my third birthday. One of the memories is mine—the other my mother's of which I have no personal memory. Mine is of coming part way down the steps from my bedroom and seeing a peculiar ballet on the couch. Starring my mommy and daddy. They were sitting close to each other in a strange configuration of arms and bodies with their faces smashed against each other. I had never seen anything like it. My thought was it was some kind of violence.

I was discovered and hustled back to bed with the assurance that visual evidence to the contrary, everything was all right.

My mother's memory, which I don't share, was of my emptying her (and Daddy's) bureau drawers out the window and onto the roof of the front porch. I believe there was not so much wind that this malfeasance could not be completely remedied.

I just now wonder if this antisocial act didn't closely follow the smooching episode. My supposing is based on the window of my capabilities—I had not yet had my third birthday. But I have a memory of the physical embrace. I was old enough to leave my bed and make my way to the stairs. I also had the dexterity to open the drawers in my mother and father's bedroom, remove their clothing and throw it out the window, which may or may not have been opened. Wouldn't it be fun to think this was punishment I meted out to them for the violence of the night before? Or did I think I was a jilted lover?

My next memory of an attempt at affection was during mother's brutal bout with menopause and her emotionally estranged husband made an attempt to comfort her (on the advice of some physician or self-motivated). She was suffering in bed—hers, it was beyond the shared bedroom years. He put his knee on the bed and bent over with some term of endearment and I believe he attempted to hug her. I don't think she was receptive, though she may have been pleased. Was it too little, too late? Did she suspect as I may have he was doing it for my benefit since I was in the room to witness it? The malady, in any case ran its course.

Fortunately for all of us, my wife Virginia had a much easier time with that female nuisance.

Years later when said father had been moved to an euphemistically named "care facility" he was brought home to visit his wife who was in bed for the visit. Was she sick or just tired? Or did she fancy she needed protection from this feeble eighty-five year-old?

He looked from the foot of her bed at her with such worshipful eyes I must have been moved to tears. He asked her if she was sick. She made some deprecating response. I had always taken my mother's side in their arguments. Then I wondered if I had been wrong, or at least could have tempered my judgments.

There is no question they were both worthy combatants when pitted against each other.

401 North Second Street, Emmaus, PA--the family home for 58 years until the last parent (mother) went to glory in 1995. The adjoining lot was vacant and part of the homestead until the property was sold.

KINDERGARTEN

Kindergarten—Well, not everything I know I learned here.

(Standing): Larry Bisbing, Barbara Aten, (teacher: Beth Kratzer)
Nancy Willenbecker, Teddy, Patsy Iobst, (Kneeling): Evan Adams,
Lee Rahn, Joann Clewell, Jean Fretz

Larry is the only empty handed one in the bunch. All the girls hold dolls except Jean who was stuck with a cut out Christmas tree. Evan has a stuffed representation of a court jester. Lee, a patent attorney, a bow and arrow poised to shoot. I am holding a rather large model airplane which requires both hands. On my head is an aviator's cap.

Our teacher, Beth Kratzer, stands behind the two rows we formed. She is wearing a pillbox hat and a guarded, pleasant expression. All the girls are taller than us fellas, but we are evenly divided, four and four.

Left to right, top to bottom:

Larry Bisbing's father was an electrician. I have a faint memory of going to his house on Main Street to play, but he moved away soon after kindergarten, perhaps in a huff at not being given anything to hold for the picture. Barbara Aten had a happy smile and her doll was in the Pieta grip. She married a handsome chap from the bluegrass country and moved to Kentucky before her divorce. I took Barbara to a high school dance and after walking her to her door, I nervously tried to kiss her. She laughed at me.

Between Barbara and me was the older girl (a couple months? She ended up a grade ahead of the rest of us). Did I have a crush on her? I have an inkling I did but I can't be sure. I never saw her after kindergarten. She has the most wary expression of the bunch. Probably the age thing.

Then Teddy with his airplane who looks the most delicate of the bunch with a shyly, probing expression. One of the two boys with his lips closed. Did that airplane and aviator cap presage my brief, unlamented stint as a Navy pilot?

Next to me was Patsy Iobst, who became the valedictorian of our high school graduating class as well as associate editor of our yearbook. She seems the largest person in our class with a shy, engaging smile. Patsy asked me to a Sadie Hawkins dance (girls asked the boys). I clumsily declined and have felt poorly about it ever since. She was not a beauty and that was so important in those years. She was awkward, I was awkward. I had some sense about how gut wrenching it was to ask someone for a date (the fear never left me). Imagine how hard it must have been for a girl to ask a boy! I was by then president of the class and I stumbled on about how I would have to oversee many details of the dance and wouldn't have the freedom a date demanded.

What baloney—pure…unadulterated…

Patsy had three children, I believe. She didn't have more because after she delivered the third she jumped out of the hospital window.

Evan Adams in the front row has a pleasant, dimpled smile. I got my haircuts from his father and some years later from Evan himself who married and went on to be a hot shot salesman.

Lee Rahn next with the bow and arrow cocked for shooting. His thumb is on his lower lip and has the best smile of the fellas. He was a playmate in our early years—he was a year behind me in real school—though in this picture he might pass for my father. I remember him commenting on the relative portions of food we were served when he ate at our house, "He got more than I did," was his frequent mantra. He was an only child for eleven or twelve years.

He came to USC the year after I did and pledged the fraternity that tried to get me drunk after my seventeen-hour plane ride. About which, more later.

Lee worked for Bell Telephone after college and went to law school on the company, no strings attached. Bell's loss—Lee jumped ship on getting his law degree and returned to the land of his undergrad days and hired on to a Pasadena firm of copyright and patent attorneys. Lee sired a boy and a girl. The boy took the semester at sea program. Through some glitch the cruise administrator did not receive the parental written permission for him to go ashore. So he jumped off the ship ending his short life prematurely.

Joann Clewell was one of our buddies. A good sport, she participated with Lee in our sports rivalries though her heart could hardly have been in it. She is the only girl in the picture who is making a funny face—her mouth in the shape of a growling bear. She is the only one of the girls who is not clutching her doll in a loving embrace. Its legs straddle Joann's knee while her hand holds the doll indifferently. The doll is facing her, but she is not looking at the doll. She is crouched obliquely in front of the late Patsy Iobst. Joann's sister has an uncanny resemblance to Patsy and was sired around the time this was taken.

Joann is childless as her casual holding of the doll foretold. When asked on our fiftieth high school class reunion questionnaire what achievement after high school she was most proud of said, "That I never killed either of my husbands." Of course, there is still time.

Two incidents in kindergarten and first grade involving Joann do me no credit. Then why bring them up? These autobiographies are supposed to make you look good.

Perhaps it was first grade when I was walking home (one block from the school) with Terry Letterhouse who was stronger and more daring than I, when he grabbed Joann and threw her behind one of those large pine or spruce trees and pulled her underpants down. I'd like to report that I was seized with indignation and threw Terry to the ground where I pummeled him for this indignity to womanhood—but all I did was look. She cried. I certainly must have had at least a twinge of regret that this happened. I think I did. I hope I did. But you will notice this is one of the few things I remember from seventy-two years ago.

The second instance was my doing alone. Though I can picture another fella in our basement with Joann and me, I can't remember who. I was in possession of a camera, I don't know from where, and I asked Joann to pull up her dress so I could photograph her underwear. She resisted like I imagine any well brought up young lady would, and made me promise I wouldn't show the pictures to anyone. This I could readily and honestly do because there was no film in the camera.

Instead of being relieved that no one would see the nonexistent pictures of her underpants, she was outraged that I had deceived her.

Could my later use of nude models in my sculpture have had some weird genesis in this infantile experiment?

What I don't understand is where this puerile, lascivious behavior comes from in a six year old with a conservative, quasi-religious upbringing?

Jean Fretz on the right end of the front row has both her hands on her three-dimensional Christmas tree. Hers is a feline face with a questioning expression. Her parents and later her brother drifted into real estate and became quite successful. They were also very religious, but I don't know which came first.

In kindergarten in Mrs. Kratzer's basement (there was no "Ms." pretension then) the highlight of the day was the service of milk and cookies. The glasses were mostly adorned with flowers but there was one sailboat among them. I always coveted that glass. We took turns serving the milk and cookies and hence the glass with the sailboat. I remember many maneuvers to get the boat glass though the specifics have vaporized. Perhaps the coveting of the sailboat was a gender thing particular to the boys. And where did this interest in sailboats originate? I don't ever remember seeing an actual sailboat in our insular neck of Penn's woods. Perhaps we thought flowers were for girls and sissies and that left the sailboat as the last bastion of kindergarten masculinity.

At the time I think there was no public kindergarten. Beth Kratzer's operation was off the tax rolls and supported by the modest tuition she charged. Which made it, I suppose, an elitist operation.

HELPERS

In the early days on North Second Street, the house my parents occupied for fifty-eight years, there was only one bathroom.

One of mother's helpers came from a house where there were zero indoor bathrooms. It must have been a treat for her to take a bath or shower in our bathroom.

One day I heard my mother's voice, speaking in urgent tones indicating she had a dire need to get into the bathroom, ergo Fern Faust should forthwith get out.

This high school girl whom I expect helped around the house emerged forthwith holding a towel to cover her front. I, perhaps six years of age, not very sophisticated or mature in years watched as she passed through the hallway holding the towel lengthwise to cover her frontal secrets which did the job, but it left the back side of the comely young damsel unguarded.

God or Jesus or whomever it was that shaped her like that had done splendid work. It is a memory which, along with her name, has stayed with me more than seventy years. I don't remember anything else about Fern Faust.

How does this happen to a six year old? Where does it come from? How does it get in there pre-skin magazines and readily available pornography? Pre any sort of exposure to the prurient corners of life.

I think it was a girl named Helen Hoffman whom I wandered away from and made my way to my grandparents' hotel on Broad Street, perhaps a mile or so. Gramma called mother with the news of guess who just showed up on our doorstep?

When mother called home to inquire of Helen where I

was, she was assured I was out back playing in the sandbox.

"Will you check to be sure?"

"Gosh—he's not there—I don't know how he got away."

Another helper was a former ward of some social program for delinquents. She surreptitiously entertained a boyfriend on her watch. Another girl spirited me to the movies while she was at the helm.

The Broad Street Hotel (that cavernous fantasyland of my youth)

CANINE & FELINE

Real knowledge is to know the extent of one's own ignorance.

—*Confucius, Analects, Sixth Century, BC*

Dogs and cats, (fish and birds?) appeal to children and later, perhaps, the child in us all. Who is more powerless than a child? A condition that can be remedied with a being smaller than they are who, except for some early toilet training issues, doesn't give much grief.

My memorable pet when I was growing up was a dog we got—was it from Pennsylvania state senator Henry Snyder? At any rate, my father named the dog Senator in, I suppose, an attempt to curry favor with the political classes. Of course, we were Republicans and Senator Snyder was a Democrat so I was never sure how or why the influence flowed. My memory of the pooch is not strong, though I can visualize it: white with black and brown spots—fairly large spots.

I must have had a loving relationship with the dog because when I came home one day and discovered Senator was not there, I was inconsolable, howsoever briefly. I remember my father telling me that a boy in Allentown had a dog that had been run over. He was devastated so they gave this stranger my dog as a consolation.

Being a leisurely learner it took some time for me to wonder—what about me? I'm sad because I don't have my dog. Why was it more important to give my Senator to a stranger and exchange his broken heart for mine?

In the fullness of time I thought I caught on: the dog had been run over in the street and the innocent fiction would allow me to believe Senator was still alive.

When years later I asked my mother and father what really happened to the dog, neither could remember the dog.

I sometimes walked with my father in Allentown from the parking lot to his office. It made me feel grown up. We saw many people he knew on the way and I expect some he didn't know. He unfailingly tipped his hat to them. In those days men and women were naked without a hat—for men, usually a felt Fedora in the winter and a straw boater in the summer for sun protection. Women were fancier for the most part.

Working stiffs wore simpler haberdashery. Caps usually, woolen items in the winter that had the capability of keeping the ears warm, though the real machos often didn't bother with that nicety.

Senator Snyder was a fedora kind of guy. We were on the way on the sidewalk, to see him. I was six years old, having just welcomed into the family a baby brother, James Knoll Gardner, now a federal judge. I expect old Dad was doing his duty taking me off Ma's hands so she could do her duty to the newborn. Who knows, she could have still been in the hospital. One day when I saw Mommy nursing Jim, she tells me I said, "All that meat and no mashed potatoes." I have no idea where I would have gotten that. But my Uncle Barney was a good bet – it was his style.

I have a keen memory of these walks by my father's side. My father who knew everybody. My father who had run for congress unsuccessfully and was four years from running for District Attorney (successfully). But here he was laying the groundwork— tipping his hat to anything that breathed, paying a visit to state senator Henry Snyder—a political powerhouse in the state, albeit of the opposing party. No matter, you tilled the fields as you found them.

While I remember those walks, I have no real recollection of the psychology attendant thereto. I expect now I may have served as a mascot, even a puppy dog—often seen but seldom heard. Who knows, he could have genuinely liked me—before I got uppity. Before I saw myself as a guardian of my mother's wellbeing, and as such, my father's implacable adversary—often feeling like a football kicked back and forth by opposing teams.

Now, of course, I am reminded of Mark Twain's dicta about his father. He said, "When I was fourteen, I couldn't believe how stupid my father was. When I got to be twenty-one I was amazed at how much the old man had learned in seven years."

Senator Snyder figured largely in my young life. I have mentioned the Judge's kissing up to this local worthy in the hope, I suppose, of some political gain. I was in Senator Snyder's office with my father when this white-miened, august gentleman, almost southern in appearance—courtly, taking himself with due serious-ness—made an awkward attempt to bond with this kid facing him.

Politicians bond.

"How's that new brother of yours?" he asked.

I didn't have to think. "None of your business," I riposted.

Out of the mouth of babes…you can imagine my father was flabbergasted and livid. He tried to hide the latter feeling, but not the former.

When we left the senator's office and walked down the street back to old Dad's office he must have probed why I said such a thing. Where did I even learn such a crude arrangement of words—and how did I come by the rationale for using them in this circumstance?

This is all conjecture, of course. All I remember is my fa-ther (and now my brother Jim's father as well) being adamant that I apologize to Senator Snyder. I was just as adamant that I not. Why? Well, perhaps I thought what I said was absolutely accurate and carried the case in the circumstances. How my new baby brother was, was strictly speaking none of this old gent's business. I mean, why did he even care?

I'm sure I would have liked for Father to forget about the apology bit—but he did not. He kept up his mantra that I was going to apologize for my rudeness. I was just as adamant that I would not. This may have been the start of my ongoing conflict with my father.

In time, a compromise was reached. A short, terse speech was written for me by my father. I would agree to deliver it—as I recall: "I'm sorry I said none of your business to you."

How did he get me to agree to that what must have seemed

a compromise of my principles?

Bribery. A good, old fashioned, time-tested, effective if in the milieu of the courthouse crowd somewhat illegal method of persuasion—though in this case no argument would be filed. Indeed the bribee was not harmed or compromised in any actionable way.

In sum—he would buy me a scooter—this purchase to take place immediately after the apology was delivered. The sporting goods store was a block or two up the main street from the Senator's office.

It all came off without a hitch, and I remember the senator tousling my hair as though we had been old buddies all the time.

As agreed, we directly repaired to Witwer-Jones, the sporting goods shop up Hamilton Street, to the second floor whereupon I selected a scooter to my liking. I remember shooshing it onto the elevator and out on to the street. I'm sure the sales staff all thought I was cute as a bug in a rug.

A CHICKEN LOSES ITS HEAD

To be, or not to be. What's the big diff?

—*Dean Young*

Someone got the idea I should experience real time death — not just seeing an old relative in her coffin (for some reason the stiffs of my youth were all female. The male counterparts were long gone).

What did this six to ten year old boy think of the spectacle of the chicken held down by its legs with one hand of Grampop, while the other hand swung a hatchet expertly placed for a quick, clean cut? The chicken then released to scamper headless over the back execution grounds? I don't think I thought it fun or funny, though I can't recall exhibiting any sympathy for the chicken. Could any lesson about life and death — mortality — and immortality — have sunk, therein in? Could Grampop have said the chicken was now in chicken heaven, after the bird briefly pranced around as though searching for its head as for life itself. But the psychology, philosophy and emotions have escaped my memory bank. The RAM is full enough.

Could I have paused when we ate the chicken later that day? Paused to relive what finally brought the blissfully ignorant chicken to the plate at table in front of the blissfully ignorant boy? I don't know.

Perhaps there was some lesson about 'this is how we get food from animals.' In order for us to eat meat, this ritual in some way shape or form needs to be carried out by someone, somewhere. Since World War II was likely raging, if you wanted meat it behooved you to grow and butcher it yourself. Strict rationing was in place to keep the supply of meat slaughtered at home flowing overseas to where our brave boys were sent to slaughter the enemy humans. We are led to believe humans were not used for food by either side. I can believe we draw the line on human flesh for food. But would Adolf Hitler be so fastidious, or Joseph Stalin for that matter? The Russian winter can be brutal, with all out to shoot deserters on sight—and so many of them hankering to desert. There results a large pile-up of bodies which were left to the remaining starving soldiers to dispose of.

I remember my grandfather going out the back door of his large brick house to spit. It was a bit of a trip from the kitchen where the urge seemed to come upon him. He had to pass through an area that could be described as a closed-in back porch, down a few steps and past a bathroom to open the back door, down a few more steps—expectorate—and retrace his steps—on his way passing up opportunities to spit in his kitchen sink, the bathroom sink, or toilet for the great outdoors.

I think of him when I open my library or kitchen doors and spit. I'm sure it is not a condition unique to us. But what are we doing throwing this bodily fluid on the ground rather than in the plumbing to the sewer system?

There is some biblical reference to a man wasting his seed upon the ground. Could there be some relation to this and our spitting on the ground, however tenuous?

I am now a grandfather. Will some unconscious act of mine become an unpredicted legacy?

SCHOOL

ELEMENTARY – HIGH SCHOOL

If you wish in this world to advance,
Your merits you're bound to enhance,
You must stir it and stump it,
And blow your own trumpet,
Or, trust me, you haven't a chance!

—W.S. Gilbert
A Thought from Ruddigore

SANTA REDUX

Reason has a light, but
not a luminosity.

—Leon Wieseltier
The New Republic

How to explain my over-the-top Christmas rituals?

My mother went the whole hog—and it was magical. Of course, looking back is often achieved through magnifying glasses, which, when removed, are likely to yield a world rather smaller than remembered. Like going back to the Broad Street Hotel, that cavernous fantasyland of my youth, and seeing how tiny it actually was. It is, I suppose, natural for spaces to seem larger when we are smaller. Likewise, gestures and events. Hindsight has an unseen built-in stretcher. Perhaps likewise, those scenes that I orchestrated may seem more grandiose to me now than they actually were.

Was I in the first or second grade when I was playing across the street at my older friend's house? She was Merry Ellen Irwin whose father was the august

Charles Irwin, proprietor of the "ice plant" or frozen food storage locker. He was coincidentally a butcher as well, so if you delivered your deer, recently shot, to his plant, he would cut it up into steaks and whatnot and deposit in your own locker in the sub freezing walk-in room. I remember the biting cold of that "ice plant." In retrospect Charlie Irwin was a man of whom it could be said had ice water in his veins.

You could also buy blocks of ice at the ice plant, in case you had a real icebox at home and not one of those new-fangled Frigidaires that plugged into a wall socket and kept your goodies cold sans honest to goodness ice. I think Mr. Irwin supplied ice to people who delivered it, but didn't deliver it himself. I expect that might have been beneath him.

Later in life he was appointed to some minor office — could it have been justice of the peace? — to a vacancy caused by death or resignation. He was not elected when his vacancy term ended.

His wife, Ellen, seemed to delight in addressing him as "Squire," in public. And I wouldn't be surprised if that moniker applied in the privacy of their boudoir as well.

After all, we called our Judge, "Judge" and "Judgie" on all occasions and in all locales. How important any designation that sets us off from our fellows becomes. There are now seven billion of us and counting. And each billion is a thousand million.

One day in my early teens I was visiting Mr. Irwin while he was working outside his house and I must have said something flip as I was wont to do. He turned on me with that stern demeanor no one could better and said, "You go home and don't come back until you can keep a civil tongue in your head." The cause of this outburst eluded me then but it did serve to set the record straight about what a serious, important gent he really was.

Now I have no recollection of anything but his stern retort. But it has only been sixty-five years. Perhaps it will come back to me.

It is bizarre to me that the only other time I was redressed by an adult was in the same Irwin living room, at a party. The principals were Pete Leisenering and yours truly. I think I was home from college, engaged in a one on one tête-à-tête with Mr. Leisenering who had been a pillar of the community as owner of the *Allen-town Morning Call*, the county's premiere newspaper, which he lost in the depression—whereupon he was reduced to the status of an employee selling advertising. Had I any sense or insight I might have suspected I was talking to a fragile ego and should ergo tread lightly and mind my manners.

But the Leisenerings were old friends. We had been neighbors—two doors down I believe, and Helen, Pete's wife, and Edna Yoder (Ellen's sister) who had a debilitating goiter but was as good as gold, doted on me. Edna was childless. Helen had a grown daughter, and they would tell me Santa left some things for me at their house—perhaps he was lost or the load to my house was just too large to be dropped off at one locale. Whatever it was, I swallowed it. Why would a three year old look a gift horse in the mouth?

We visited them often and I adored their backyard which, as I recall, was fussily decorated with stuff I found melded well into my imagination. The man of the house, was, in my memory, never at home for those daytime visits.

The Leisenerings were family. So I expect in the Irwin's living room at the party while I was talking like a grown up to Mr. L, pillar of the community emeritus, I faked being a grown-up myself. College, after all, had to be indicative of *something* in this short journey from swaddle to shroud. Later I mention the big success I'd had employing the principles of Dale Carnegie as promulgated in his *How to Win Friends and Influence People*. So I expect while Mr. Leisenering was pontificating on some subject or other I threw in a little flattery. To be sure I followed the great Carnegie tenet, "Be lavish in your approbation and hearty in your praise." At the same time not being unaware of the edict to be honest and sincere.

Howsoever, Mr. Leisenering wasn't buying it. He stopped his monologue dead in its tracks and fixed me with an ever-so-stern countenance as if to telegraph the intelligence that he didn't suffer fools *at all*, and intoned, "*Don't patronize me.*"

Was it something in the atmosphere of the Irwin household that triggered these two stern dressings-down of this adolescent kid—perhaps three or four years apart? Or have I just forgotten other similar incidents which transpired elsewhere?

I promise to return to my original thought of Santa Claus just as soon as I am mentally able.

Merry Ellen (could it really have been *Merry* Ellen? That's the way we pronounced it) was an only child, and I believe three years older than I was. It must have been a terrible bore for her to play with me. In fact, we had zero interactions as the distance in ages seemed to grow.

She played the piano far better than I did. There were two piano teachers in town. Emily Schaeffer and Mary Deischer. I had the first, she had the other. For some reason Mrs. Irwin and I were discussing the merits of each and I lamented Miss Schaeffer wanted me to practice with the hands separately. I could easily accomplish the notes one hand at a time, but I couldn't put them both together very well.

With an I-told-you-so mien (but no less accurate) she said, "Then *that's* how you should practice," and somehow in the tone or further conversation Mrs. Irwin allowed as how that was why Mrs. Deischer was the superior teacher. I started practicing with both hands using a hymnal some seventeen years later, but I am, famously, a slow learner.

Okay. Santa Claus, where this palaver all began.

I was playing at Merry Ellen's house when she deigned to tell me there really was no Santa Claus. But how could that be, I wondered, I sure got a lot of presents from him.

Your mother and father give you the presents, she informed me. She did have a three-year edge in maturity, but we believe what we want to believe and I *didn't want* to believe that.

I went to her mother for corroboration. Not surprisingly, she came down on Merry Ellen's side. My recollection was that the Irwins were realists who never subjected their only child to such fantasy. This sort of dishonesty would be, well, dishonest and how could a child ever trust you again? Seems a little draconian to me. It is a fantasy life that gets a lot of us through the realistic vale of tears. Why, after all, is television watching so prevalent? Even reading has been called escapism. Where is the harm in good old Saint

Nick? Unselfish giving without a thought of gratitude or reciprocation?

My dear friend the Reverend Lloyd Saatjian did not let his two children believe in the fantasy of Santa Claus. It wasn't honest, he said, and he didn't want to deceive his children. How could they ever trust him again?

What about Jesus, I wondered?

Nobody who ever saw him wrote about him. I developed the theory that the Reverend Lloyd might have thought Santa Claus took the attention from the birth of Jesus. (Surely an undocumented myth—the stable, the manger, the hay, three wise men—the whole bit besides the biblical astronomical signs placed it in August, but who needs another summer holiday? What we all need is a pick-me-up around the shortest gloomiest day of the year. Voila! Jesus is born!) And his birth was of a virgin and he was resurrected after being crucified. Many religions in antiquity featured the same events.

I took this newfound Santa heresy home to my doting mother. My memory is she was shocked that the neighbor—senior in years ergo with an *obligation* not to spoil Christmas for a child—should not only resort to it (she's only a kid after all—if three years my senior, still a kid), but her mother? Why would she?

From another viewpoint perhaps mother was grateful someone else had done the dirty deed.

The same thing would happen about where babies came from, but I never let on…

THE FORTUNE TELLER

When I was a young kid, between seven and ten, I was at an occasion, I don't remember what, where a handwriting analyst held forth. He had us draw a picture of a person on one side of a letter-sized paper, and copy a paragraph on the other. He then looked at those and pronounced what our future would be.

I filled the paper with my rudimentary drawing and I was surprised to see some of my fellows used half a paper or even made tiny figures.

I'm sure the 'reader,'—a minor celebrity in our neck of the woods—had nice things to say about everyone as he went through all the submissions. You might not be surprised to learn I don't re-member what he said about anyone else, but I didn't forget the good stuff he said about me.

He said from my drawing I was a person who made the most of his opportunities (using the full page for the drawing). Somehow from my handwriting he drew this surprising conclusion: I was a person who was easily sidetracked by reading and I would read to the detriment of everything else. This intelligence was brought my way before or slightly after the sum total of my fiction reading was one (1), *Luke Larkin Looking Upward* in fourth grade. My second read was in college—*Great Expectations*.

Though I must confess I was an avid reader of newspa-pers—sports, politics, comics—not only the local Allentown paper, but also the *New York Herald Tribune* to which we subscribed.

Now my question is, did I attempt to fulfill the parts of this prophesy because they sounded impressive and I was at an impres-sionable age, or since I was slow to develop did this fortune teller just read into my future and predict what he was passing off as present tense?

I think I do make the most of my opportunities, but did I at nine or ten? Did anybody? Did I read to the exclusion of all else? I doubt it. Anyway, I thought it made me sound intelligent and who wants to disabuse anyone of that notion?

GOD AND JESUS

As a young fella I took my religion (protestant: evangelical and reformed, now—after "congregational"—the higher sounding United Church of Christ) very seriously.

I prayed every night in bed, prayers my father and mother taught me—the "Now I Lay Me Down to Sleep" classic and my father's contribution, "Dear Lord (always good to begin with a bit of flattery), keep me physically strong, mentally awake and morally straight." I wonder if I knew what "morally" meant at that age. I added personal prayers to them with, I thought, consummate tact. I had years of perfect attendance in Sunday school.

I subscribed to my share of bugaboos—self-controlling taboos. I'm not sure why I went so religiously to Sunday school. My parents didn't go—yet I had perfect attendance for five or six years (my brother still teaches Sunday school at age seventy-three). On Christmas Eve as I was struggling to go to sleep, I wrote with index finger on the sheet my prayers in longhand. Perhaps I was given the opportunity to go and just gravitated toward it. In time I joined the Sunday school orchestra, a ragtag collection of odd instruments and odder players. The oddest of whom was yours truly—wielding a cornet the operation of which was somewhat beyond my skill set.

At any given time we had a trumpeter (my cornet teacher who could play), a pianist (a junior high school teacher), and a violin or clarinet? There were sometimes one or two others, all of whom had the good grace in the Christian spirit not to badger me about my hopeless musicianship.

When I passed the church, which I did weekdays on my way to and from school, I employed self-discipline. In that era I had a sinus condition—perhaps allergies that only kicked in when I was outside—the manifestation of which caused in me an uncontrollable urge to spit. I developed the notion that this would be unacceptable (to whom is less clear—could it have been God?) so I kept the fluids in my mouth until I was clear of the church grounds. This was doable on the way to school. It was more difficult on the return because Poppa Hoffman, paterfamilias of a substantial brood, about which more later, was on his rocking chair on his porch watching (I surmised) my every move. I didn't think he would take very kindly to me spitting on his lawn. So even though I had taken to walking across his side street, I was inhibited by his gaze. This thought the epitome of self-centeredness to think a grown man would care two figs what a six or seven year old did. On the other hand, he didn't seem to have much else to do.

Later I found a framed picture of Jesus in a dining room drawer. How did we get that? And why was it in a drawer—out of harm's way? Could it have been a gift from a religious relative—I can't think of a likely culprit—or perhaps a friend who thought one or all of us could benefit with a touch of the holy? Was it in the drawer for a hasty retrieval in the event the donor surprised us with a visit? In which event it could be propped upon the highboy or buffet or whatever those dining room chests of drawers were called.

Somehow I got the idea it would be good form to kiss this picture whenever I thought it might be helpful to get something I wanted mightily—a baseball glove for example or a bicycle. I would commit in advance to the number of kisses I would give if the wish were granted. Then with success would follow through—religiously. I might even have proffered a number of kisses on speculation, to be supplanted with an additional number were the request granted.

Did it work? Well, I am fairly convinced that it was not detrimental—that those kisses (which were not required on the *face* of Jesus, just anywhere on the glass or frame) did not account for less success than if I had done nothing. Verily, we believe what we want to believe. So if the kisses didn't help, I don't think they hurt. And isn't that the way in life?

SIXTH GRADE CHILD ABUSE

Mr. Charles said some memorable things. He was the new principal of Central Elementary School. We were saddled with him as a replacement for our revered math teacher/principal, Floyd Laudenslager, who had a knack for making school fun—not an everyday occurrence in that serious neck of Penn's woods—you went to school to learn, not to have fun.

Mr. Laudenslauger married the third grade teacher who we thought was a serious prune—relatively late in life for both of them—or so it seemed to eleven year olds at the time.

I recall in retirement he opened a store out of his house on the main highway through town. The couple had a son who was one day playing outside the store, wandered into the street for a premature meeting with his maker.

We all thought Mr. Laudenslauger would make a perfect father and he never ceased to blame himself for the fate of their child.

They had no more children.

There was no fun with Mr. Charles, but he wasn't a half bad teacher. I learned some numbers. Could his name have been Ray Charles? It seems likely—especially since later revelations made me think Charles was a pseudonym—a first name at best, his last remaining a mystery.

When teaching us inversions of fractions he spoke thusly: "Now, do you know what inverting means? I might invert the girls in the class but not if they have skirts or dresses on." I must concede we got the picture. I recall in those days *all* the girls wore skirts.

Mr. Charles lived with an adolescent girl he said was his

niece. She seemed a serious sort, not unattractive, and I can still picture her walking to and from school clutching her books to her chest. The word was her parents were killed in an auto accident and Mr. Charles, being something of a humanitarian hero, took her in.

I can picture the girl who walked upright as though with blinders on, looking neither left nor right, from the house she shared with Mr. Charles, a block from my grandparents' hotel, to school and back. I don't remember seeing her any other time. The only mystery to me sixty-six years later is how old she was then. She was not in our class of twelve year olds and I had the sense she was not younger, and after the revelation I hope she was a lot older— but I'm afraid fourteen was about the outside limit.

One day in art class our latest project was spread out on a long table in front of the classroom. This was the class of Leila Neimoyer, a childless old crone given to sucking at her false teeth perhaps to keep them from falling out. And when her patience (not getting longer with time) was snapped she slammed the back of a hand to her mouth to prevent just such a calamity. I apparently was a champion at trying her patience. The product of our genius on this day was shellacked wallpaper cut in strips and curled to make beads which were strung into bracelets or necklaces.

Apparently at the time in question the beads were still wet with shellac and if Miss Neimoyer is to be believed, she told us not to touch them. Do you have to guess who touched them? I must plead inattention because it is so much less heinous than outright insubordination. I was just so fascinated with those shiny strips of curved wallpaper I couldn't resist touching them.

A student was dispatched to summon the principal, the self-same Mr. Charles, who responded forthwith.

Miss Neimoyer told him of my malfeasance. He exploded in anger, perhaps amid my denials of hearing her instruction to keep hands off this most tempting work of art.

Forthwith he grabbed my shirtfront and/or perhaps my ear (it was obvious the man in charge would give no quarter) and threw me out of the classroom door into the hallway outside of his room. Not a great distance. The walls were lined with empty glass-faced cabinets, the function of which eludes me. Our principal was so enraged, whether by Miss Neimoyer's recital of my crime or my possible smart mouth, that he threw me against the glass case to emphasize his omnipotence in the matter. It was with such force I expected my head—which struck the glass—would break that fragile surface which would then decapitate me.

Satisfied he had established his supremacy *vis à vis* physical strength, he sent me back to Miss Neimoyer's classroom where I trust I played the role of a wise guy kid who was suitably cowed.

It was some years later that the true story of Mr. Charles and his "niece" was made known. The young girl (statutory rape age) was not his niece after all. No! Indeed Mr. Charles couldn't be charged with incest. Since I received this intelligence second or third hand, I am left to creating the denouement myself from a combination of a sixty-six year memory and conjecture. How about this? He got her from an orphanage—or from a couple that didn't want her, and she being relieved to be free of the orphanage or abusive parents was satisfied to play house with the man somewhat older than her father, and let him have his way with her. Perhaps it made her feel grown up.

I don't remember the story of how the truth got out, but I think it might have been the girl coming to her senses or growing beyond trust in Mr. Charles.

At any rate, the school board must have been majorly chagrined at swallowing his story about being the custodian of his niece out of the goodness of his heart, of course, and hiring him to a position where he could beat the tar out of me and, I suppose, anyone else who displeased him (though I can't remember any).

BABYSITTING

My own babysitting career involved the care and feeding of my brother—six years my junior—and sister, ten years younger. There's little denying the parents knew how to space kids.

Jimmy carved my name in the living room desk. Sibling rivalry diminishes with a six-year age separation, but it doesn't disappear. He succeeded in having me blamed for the act, though I thought I was old enough to obviate my will to incriminate myself. I was saved from perdition when I recognized at that time of my life, perhaps twelve years old or so (Jimmy would have been six, more likely I was thirteen or fourteen and he was seven or eight) I wrote my name, TEDDY, with the top cross bar of the T connecting to the second D—all caps. Jimmy's version connected the *first* D. I was absolved, though I don't remember Jimmy spending any time in purgatory.

The first memorable freelance babysitting job was at the Lorbers.

Mr. Lorber owned and operated the lone movie theater in Emmaus, Pennsylvania, population in the day hovering around six thousand souls, most Pennsylvania Dutch (Deutsch—German) with a smattering of middle Europeans.

There were a handful of theaters in adjoining Allentown (population circa 100,000) where more current releases were shown. So it was not a booming business in Emmaus.

I recollect the Lorbers were the first Jewish family in town. I don't think there was a hint of discrimination among the populace. They may have moved in after the Second World War when sympathy for Jews should have been at an all time high. I personally have never experienced prejudice and I don't remember any among our family or friends.

The theater was adjacent to the railroad tracks. When a train went by there was a rumble in the theater.

The Lorber's home was two blocks from our house. They told me they would be home by eleven o'clock. Their living room walls were painted black. Also the ceiling. If my memory can be trusted, the carpet was also black. It was a black cocoon much like a movie theater. In my youth, while babysitting the one and only time at the Lorber's, I thought the black décor was a hip fashion statement. I have recently wondered if Mr. Lorber repainted the interior of his theater black and had some paint leftover. It was not conducive to a twelve year-old boy staying awake.

I fought off sleep until their ETA, but they didn't A. I must have succumbed to restful torpor when the phone awakened me. It was Mr. Lorber who said they would be perhaps another hour, would I be okay?

"Oh sure," I said reassuring myself more than him. "It's perfectly all right for you to go to sleep," he said. I was relieved to hear that since I had just woken up to answer the phone. I looked at the clock. It was a little after midnight. I fell blissfully into the sanctioned sleep, and was awoken shortly after two, perhaps to apologies, though I don't remember them.

I might have bagged five dollars for the five or six hours — a princely sum in those days.

SWIMMING

Dick Bell is the only competitor I remember. He was the one I couldn't beat.

His nickname was "The Whale" for reasons readily apparent when you saw him. So why could he beat me at every stroke (freestyle, backstroke) except butterfly breaststroke? It couldn't have been the superior buoyancy alone — I trained like a fiend — he didn't bother to train. He had "natural" ability. He did such things as consume a juicy hamburger between events at the meet. I never saw him train, but my mother was convinced he did at another pool — to throw me off — take him for granted.

Perhaps she was just making excuses for me. I was as I recall, in the range of ten to twelve years old, and one would have to concede, not a natural athlete. If I realized that, I thought I could overcome that deficiency with conscientious training. We overpaid a couple of the lifeguards, a coach and a competitive swimmer, to work with me to improve my technique and speed. Nothing worked. The Whale was unbeatable, except in the butterfly. He never beat me in that event. Perhaps because you lift your body out of the water in this stroke and perhaps his burden was too heavy for the task.

I expect my disillusionment about the will conquering a shortage of ability was foisted on me by my beloved mother who told me I could do anything I put my mind to. *The Power of Positive Thinking.*

In some areas it seemed to work, but not in others.

I suppose it was delusions of grandeur that caused me to enter the two-mile swim. I expect now I was fifteen or sixteen and if you've never done it, two miles is a long way to swim, even in a river (the Lehigh) going downstream. And cold. Could the English Channel have been any colder?

Mr. Lutte, the head lifeguard at the country club pool and swimming coach somewhere else, rowed the boat.

A guy named Carl Koch was in the race. He was a some-time boyfriend of my friend, Sally Backenstoe. He was a handsome guy some years older than I, and somehow I finished ahead of him. He said Mr. Lutte hit him on the head with his oar and knocked him off his game.

For years I had memorized my finish place in the two-mile swim, was it sixth? Twelfth? Something in between? Being the youngest participant I remember having an inordinate amount of pride in the statistic, but the fullness of time (sixty-three plus years) has dimmed the recollection.

With all that I was not exempt from taking the beginning swimming class at USC. Mercifully the instructor saw I could swim and I was excused. Mercifully? Perhaps not. Not after I saw the wool knit suits that were issued to the girls; and what happened when they got wet. I suspect the male coach had a hand in the selection of those suits.

We built a pool in Palos Verdes after we were in our house ten years. And another in Santa Barbara when we built the house. Both were enclosed. The Santa Barbara structure burned when the house did. On the rebuilding I covered half with solar panels. I swam laps in all three pools.

I don't kid myself that I could have outpaced The Whale, but by that time he had been dead for some years.

MY FOOTBALL CAREER

Politics is like football. The coach has to be
smart enough to understand how the game is played,
and stupid enough to think it matters.

—Eugene McCarthy

Football is a barbaric sport. It must be conceded I didn't always think so. Especially when I was playing it. My playing time was mercifully short—four plays, back to back.

I was in the seventh grade. The coach started me at left guard in our first game with an unremembered school.

Four plays—each running right through and over me for impressive gains.

Unsurprisingly the coach yanked me and I was so thin and the thinnest football pants were so large for I had to hold them up as I trotted off the field, never to return.

COUSINS

Grampop's back door (eating ice cream he probably made). Standing at left: Marva Kay Knoll Craig. Front row L to R: Audrey Ann Gardner Racines and JoAnn Knoll. Middle row: James Knoll Gardner, Audrey Jane Knoll, Byron Knoll, Jr (Corky). Back row: Teddy and Robert Knoll, Jr. (Nipper).

Cousins, it must be said, have their uses. The family familiarity can help ease you into the society of strangers.

Always the familiarity of family greases the skids for the otherwise shy, not to say backward little people trying to hold their own.

I had a bunch of these familiar cousins. The ones who had the most influence on me were older than I was. There were three of them: David DeWalt, Janice Trauger, and Pete Weiss.

Kay Knoll was slightly younger than I was, but a pal. After that I gained a brother and a sister of my own which seemed to fulfill any need I had of familial buddies.

My cousin, Pete, it must be conceded, never suffered malnourishment. There was a time he must have touched two hundred and fifty pounds. It wasn't all genetics, but I saw an early motion picture of Grampop Knoll. He waddled. Pennsylvania Dutch diet. Lived to ninety-one. Saw him touching TV with his nose to see the picture. Pete is eighty-two and going strong.

Pete's father, a large solid man, not as heavy as Pete, spent ten years or so bedridden under the care of his wife until the end when she took him to a home and he blurted out, "Don't leave me." His first and last words in ten years. Was it the fried potatoes and sausage that put him there instead of Pete whose diet was the same or worse? Another blow for the miracle (or curse?) of genetics.

As a kid, cousin Pete was picky eater. His mother decided she had to do something to get him to eat to keep his strength up. It had to be acknowledged, he was a scrawny guy. So she decided to experiment, reasoning, I suppose, that if the taste of food appealed to this fussy guy, he would eat it.

She put sugar in everything that touched his lips—milk, mashed potatoes, peas, corn, carrots, you name it.

And it *worked*. Pete grew and married a sweet woman named Jean who kept up with his eating habits, as did his five kids.

Pete was an only child for sixteen years.

He is three years older than I, and he was bigger and stronger. Some seventy-five years have passed since our first physical altercation and I still can't understand this animalistic macho rivalry. Perhaps if some contention for a female were involved—but at that age? Alas, boys at that young age continue to batter and bludgeon each other as though there were no other way to grow up.

I remember us sleeping at his house but not at mine. I suppose sleeping at your own house is not memorable.

I remember especially one laughing session as Pete was recalling the patter of one Pennsylvania Dutch auctioneer as he was huckstering a ceramic bed set consisting of a basin and a pitcher. "Fur washa, fur trinka und fur shissa." Which in spite of the sound of it translates to "for washing, for drinking and for pouring." But we were laughing to tears at the *phonetics*.

When I was twelve or so and Pete was fifteen or so, we spent the summer together working at Saylors Lake. Our grandfather had a cabin there and Pete and I occupied it during our labors of cleaning and renting rowboats, canoes and lockers—basic but indispensable chores.

We played pool in the pavilion after hours and were rewarded for our eight-week stint with $35 each, a royal sum to me in those days. The work was neither arduous nor long and I think we got some free food and free use of the pool table. At seven, five-hour days a week (or five, seven-hour days) that would be thirty five times eight or 280 hours. If my math is correct, that is 12 ½ cents per hour. And those weren't even the good old days.

David DeWalt was a prince among men. He was the only product of Ellis DeWalt and Ethel Gardner, our father's sister.

I didn't see him often. He was three or four years older and lived in Allentown—a daunting five miles from our homestead, and his mother—like all of my father's sisters—didn't drive. But when I saw him it was sheer pleasure. He was one of those rare pure souls without a nasty, combative bone in his body.

Worse then that I should break my collarbone while horsing around with him on the grassy hill of our yard.

He felt terrible and wanted to take the blame. I stoutly denied it insisting it was a complete accident; he was the last person who would try to hurt me. I suppose that mollified the elders somewhat, but the Gardners were a sensitive bunch and I'm not completely sure I dissuaded them.

David went into teaching in Easton, Pennsylvania where he coached sports and rose to be the principal of the school.

His wife is another delightful person—beautiful as only a former Miss Ephrata, Pennsylvania could be. Their children are also super—strike another blow for genetics. They told me David had his fatal heart attack a few pages short of completing his reading of my first book, *The Paper Dynasty*.

It should not be said the Gardners did not do their bit for population control.

9 children of Mary and Forest:
5 had zero children
2 had one each
1 had 3
1 had 5

5 children of Clara and Clinton Knoll:
1 had zero
1 had 2
2 had 3
1 had 4

So I had fourteen aunts and uncles (two died before I was born) leaving twelve. So we got twenty-two cousins out of fourteen couples—below replacement.

Before our basement was tricked out as a saloon with knotty pine walls and asbestos tile floors, it was a dark place with dirt floors. The minimal light trickled in from the small, high windows that outside, were below ground level in concrete wells.

On a day when the Traugers—mom, dad and Janice, my cousin—were visiting us, our neighbor lad, Stanley Mierhoff, came to call…on Janice. He was a young man, it must be said, who was not noted for his piety—his reputation not of celibacy.

The three of us were in our dark basement while the older, more levelheaded folk, were upstairs. I suspect Janice was thirteen or fourteen at the time, Mierhoff perhaps two or three years older, and I eight or nine, though anything but sophisticated in boy/girl matters. It soon became apparent to me that there was some rudimentary physical contact in the works and by mutual consent of the couple, I was persona non grata.

When I finally took the hint—just short of being carried out bodily—I made my way upstairs to the assemblage of adults and a visibly shaken Aunt Ida, Janice's mom.

"What are they doing down there?" she asked. I was given to understand it wasn't visions of sugarplums dancing in her head, but though I didn't understand it at the time, scary visions of an entirely different sort.

But the important thing to me was that my opinion was

being sought by adults—me, the ten year old expert on romance. I remember my chest swelling with pride. Carefully choosing my words to be accurate, yet not alarming, I allowed as there might have been some hugging and kissing going on but to my knowledge not progressing any further than that.

Aunt Ida didn't seem totally mollified. There was talk of her intervening. In the end, she didn't. I expect the discussion was of young people and their experimental urges—and what could happen with the parents upstairs?

Another near tragedy was apparently averted and I doubt the two ever met again, but I do remember a story told by Stanley Mierhoff's mother about a party in their basement where both sexes doffed their clothes, but Stanley was at pains to assure her that nothing sexual occurred—just kissing and "shimmying," a word I didn't understand at the time. But, notice I remembered it.

Janice went on to marry Don, the son of a big shot university scientist, and her mother, Aunt Ida, who took a back seat to no one in the worry department, expressed some trepidation that no matter what her new son-in-law accomplished he couldn't help but be compared to the old man—and no one could live up to that.

Perhaps ten years later Aunt Ida had a stroke and was parked in one of those facilities that looked after the lame and halt. My father and I went to visit her. She could talk, she just couldn't move.

Her brother, my father, sat with her, in her bleak, darkened room, held her hand and repeated the twenty-third Psalm with her.

In the car for our escape, my father told me it always tore him apart to see Ida like that. There were nine kids in his family, he was the seventh, and he was the only one to go to college, let alone law school. And Aunt Ida had worked to help him get through.

Janice and Don—alive in their eighties—have lived all over the country: Pennsylvania, New York, Arizona, Florida, the Carolinas. He was, as far as I know, a respected man in his own scientific field. His august father, of course, is long gone. Wherever they are, Janice writes long, thoughtful notes to me on her Christmas card.

The girl cousin closest to my age and heart was Kay Knoll—Marva Kay actually. She is one of those sparkling souls who seemed to be perpetually happy. Always a starry smile on her pretty face. If she had been able to patent her good nature she would have never had to work.

Instead she became a nurse. A perfect fit for her sunny disposition.

We complemented each other in our eating habits. She ate the yolk and I the whites of the hardboiled eggs—she the pickles and I the beans in that Dutch style chowchow. That is my recollection now; either or both, could have been the other way around.

In retirement, Kay moved to Florida. Some years later Kay and husband Bob Craig took Aunt Marva, in her nineties, from a skyscraper retirement home in Allentown, PA and installed her in their Florida home. There in semi-solitude Kay watched over her mother until several years into her tenancy she and her husband, Bob (also her father's name), had an opportunity for one or two nights out and all agreed it would be a nice change. They took Mother to a care facility where she died the next day.

Kay's forty or so year old son liked his home and mom and dad so much he decided not to leave. Oh, he tried to go out on his own once or twice, but he kept bouncing back.

Finally dad gave him an ultimatum. They would take him back this time, but it would be the last. That seemed okay with the young gentleman who didn't want to go anywhere else anyway. So he stayed. Can a home environment be too cozy? Kay has one sister, JoAnn, who recently moved to the same Florida community. JoAnn is attractive, yea vivacious woman who has managed to guard her single status. I tell her she should write a book on how to do it.

OCEAN CITY AND THE FIGHT ERA

Mother made friends. It was a talent I never grasped. One of these friends was a woman then married to a smallish town police chief—Chief Davis.

My only memory of him in their summer home in Ocean City, New Jersey, was of this strapping *man* vacuuming the carpet. I had never seen in my twelve or thirteen years *a man* wielding a vacuum cleaner. Some baffled inquiry of my mother yielded an explanation, but I don't remember what it was. Could it have been that she had a job as a schoolteacher and they agreed he would share in the housework in exchange for her sharing in the income yielding aspects of the marriage? More unusual then.

The Davis union produced one son named Donald. He was one year my senior and seemed to me at the doorway to my teens to be a pretty serious sort. Later he became a brain surgeon which I expect validates his serious bona fides.

My recollection is we became pals of sorts during my month or so stay in Ocean City, but with generous slabs of time by ourselves. This was a condition that seemed to suit me. I'm not sure how he spent the time we were apart. I burned a great deal of my time and energy in the ocean imagining I was a prizefighter punching the waves which of course fought back by trying to knock me off my feet.

At home in my front bedroom the walls were adorned with postcard sized pictures of prizefighters. Who knew what attracted me, this peace-loving kid, to such a brutal blood sport, another genetic conundrum. It was a fascination I mercifully outgrew.

During this time of my interest my father took me to the Allentown fairgrounds to see some honest-to-God human prizefighters. All I remember about the experience (my guess is I was between ten and twelve years old) was an episode before the fight. My father may have been the county district attorney which would explain why he was schmoozing with the police chief of Allentown (not to be confused with Chief Davis of Ardmore, Pennsylvania, my Ocean City, New Jersey host).

After I was introduced to the Allentown chief at the fairgrounds I noticed some kids around my age climbing a tall chain link fence to gain free admission to the fights. Ever the good citizen, I pointed out to the chief that these rapscallions were cheating the system — seeing the fights for free when others had to pay.

The chief put on a grim smile and noted he didn't see anything. So here was a guardian of law and order who was, if I understood correctly, condoning this blatant unlawful action. Surely my father, the district attorney would be outraged and would set the chief straight.

Didn't happen. When we were free of the chief I inquired of my father why these obvious lawbreakers weren't being stopped in their tracks, in light perhaps of the affront to the chief of police in his full view. The explanation I heard was something like:

"Those are poor boys who couldn't afford to buy tickets so the chief looks the other way when they climb the fence to get in free. They aren't keeping any paying customers from getting a seat."

The fairgrounds grandstand was a vast mountain of seats and the boys would slink to the rear.

I don't know that the logic snowed me at the time. I was a right is right kind of guy. And in that holy capacity while in Ocean City with the nascent brain surgeon, a memorable event occurred.

Don Davis had an interest in magic tricks. There was a store in town that catered to blooming magicians. Don had developed a technique whereby he would pocket the small, matchbox-sized tricks, then pay for a larger one that wouldn't fit in his pocket.

This morality-challenged action gave me a mildly sickened feeling. So, after he carried it off, I took the empty box back to the store and "bought" it so the store would not be cheated.

Why? Working up points for heaven?

But you see who became the brain surgeon and who the hack.

I never saw any of the Davis family after that summer idyll.

THE HORSE OPERA

In the second or third grade our teacher told us we would perform a reading assignment a day or so in the future.

I took the book home and read the story again and again, picking out a character I fancied. I expect it was the largest part. I don't know why it didn't occur to me someone else might get that part—but it didn't. On the performance date, the teacher assigned the parts. I was shocked when she named another boy for my coveted role. Rather shy at that juncture, I uncharacteristically blurted, "Oh, I want that part!"

To my everlasting surprise, the teacher gave me the part.

Did this harbinger my interest in drama leading to the lead in Harvey in our senior year and the writing and performing of a senior musical? I wouldn't be surprised.

Had the teacher taken shelter in her own ego and said, "No, I gave the part to so and so," would I have been devastated beyond reclamation?

I don't know.

It was around this time that I was horse crazy. I loved to ride a horse and my devoted mother took me early Sunday mornings to a riding group in Allentown. All the other riders were adults and it must have made me feel grownup to ride with them. My horse was named Tony—I was known as Teddy. One of the adult riders said, "There goes Theodore on Anthony." I was flattered to tears.

Aunt Verna and Uncle Paul had a barn at their house on the golf course. He was the greens' keeper.

For some reason they hosted an Arabian stud. Naturally I lusted to ride it.

It was not broken in; Uncle Paul said that would be dangerous.

Did I accept that and slink away? Or did I, rather, persist—not unlike my persisting with my father to buy me a horse—driving him to the point of proclaiming, "I don't care how often you say it, you're not getting a horse!" And I didn't get a horse, but I *did* get to ride the Arabian stallion housed in Uncle Paul's barn. I just now wonder how I wore him down. Was I such a nuisance—(as with my father)—that he said, "The hell with it. If he wants to get thrown off and suffer a concussion—or worse—let him. I'm sick of his nagging."

Well, I certainly had confidence in my horsemanship even if Uncle Paul didn't.

Uncle Paul, alas, was right. As soon as I mounted that spirited Arabian he took off like a shot. A cold, clammy, vise-like grip of fear took hold of me and no matter what rules of horsemanship I employed to control this rude animal, he just persisted in running a thousand miles an hour, spiriting me to the absolute depth of my fear while I tightened the reins, loosened the reins, pressed my ineffectual calves into his ribs—relieved the pressure.

The horse simply ran faster than I thought a horse could. This stallion would surely have left the winners of the Kentucky Derby in the dust.

I had not the slightest grasp of what to do to slow the horse or my fate if I couldn't. Shouldn't this wild animal tire and slow to a walk at some point? But time telescopes. A few minutes can seem hours when you fear your life is in danger. At some point after all my efforts to control the wild beast, I must have resigned my fate to the stronger beast and simply hung on for dear life. We seemed to be touring the entire golf course when in reality it was one or two holes.

The beast was not, as it developed, completely stupid. When the grassy golf course encroached upon a high-end residential section, he abruptly turned one hundred eighty degrees and headed back in the direction of the barn. And you know what a horse does on the homeward leg of his journey? He steps on the gas. But I was still on top.

Somehow I made it back alive realizing that I had not a modicum of control of this beast, but a ton of gratitude that he didn't throw me to the ground and trample me to death. In which case you wouldn't be reading this account of my hopeless horsemanship.

My interest in horses ended at some point. It could well have been then. Proving, I suppose, once again, the wisdom of my father.

PEYTON PLACE, PENNSYLVANIA

Suffer women once to arrive at an equality with you, and they will from that moment become your superiors.

—*Cato the Censor, 215 B.C.*

The revenge we hope for—dream about—almost never happens. If your nemesis gets his comeuppance it loses some savor if you miss out on it. So often retribution from a third party is so long after the crimes we have forgotten them. This was the case with Terry Letterhouse and Bernard Walters.

Terry was a chum—an early playmate in the first grade era (1940ish). He seemed to turn on me when that was in vogue in the neighborhood. His mentor in bullying was Bernard, somewhat older than we were—perhaps three or four years—and less inclined to mental nuance. Bernard was a dog heavy—a bully's bully.

In those formative years bullying seems to go with the territory. I too was a bully—mental though, not physical.

But Bernard got his comeuppance by dying young—in his twenties or thirties. But I was across the country and unable to savor the satisfaction I would surely have had had I been closer to the indignities and their sweet resolution.

Terry Letterhouse was another matter. He was brighter than Bernard, but younger, and (so I projected) influenced by the heavy.

By the time of Terry's comeuppance we were friends again, though separated by this vast country—Emmaus, Pennsylvania to Los Angeles was not a quick trip. A lot longer then, than now.

Terry had been 'going steady' with Martha Jane, a beautiful girl one year our junior. She was in the parlance of the time 'stacked,' as well as fair of face. Terry was a basketball star and stalwart of the baseball team, also a good-looking kid. Martha Jane was on the girls' basketball team and a drum majorette.

In those days the males of the species were drafted into the army, and so Terry was shuffled off to a training compound where he and his peers were trained in the killing skill needed, at that predrone time, to do battle for your country.

This left Martha at home. As luck would have it (or fate?) her family owned the taxi company in Emmaus which consisted of one or two cabs and probably two twelve-hour shifts of drivers.

One can imagine how sorely Martha must have missed Terry because they had been "going steady" for some years and suddenly he was no longer around to kiss and caress her. So in her loneliness, young hormones being what they are, she reputedly pulled what was called a one-nighter with one of the family company's drivers.

Bad luck for Terry: the reputed one shot resulted in a fetus carried to full term, and as was the custom in those days the new daddy was expected to make an honest woman of his prey. I can't remember if this actually happened, or if Martha actually preferred her new pal to Terry or if the driver was already terminally married, or if the driver married her and they lived happily ever after—or divorced—or he took over the family taxi company and drove it to a roaring success—or bankruptcy!

My memory of this hearsay was that Terry and Martha still pined for each other and Martha kept him in her heart for the rest of her life, where he surely would have been except for that one brief (perhaps drunken?) night where her loins wandered elsewhere.

Perhaps proof of the celebrity this caused was I was myself away from home when it happened and I got word through some forgotten gossip channel. I had been aware of the Terry/Martha relationship from high school. But after graduation Terry went to college in Pennsylvania, I in California and I don't believe I ever saw him again. Terry died before his time, perhaps of a broken heart.

Another shotgun marriage came up dry. At our fifth reunion I asked Morris Hoffman who attended the festivities with his wife

—to see pictures of his kids. It had reputedly been the *sine quo non* of his marriage.

"No kids," he responded which would have made me feel like a fool had I been given to those terrors.

Morris was a school principal when he showed up at the fiftieth reunion with a most attractive (slender in the land of heavy-weights) woman some twenty-five years his junior. She was a teacher at the school where he was top dog.

The wandering sperm theory figured in so many marriages when the first children were so often early. That's no big deal now. Couples have two or three children before they get married. They just want to be sure, I suppose. Then it was a minor disgrace.

The Hoffmans were a large well-known family in town—five kids—four sons and one daughter, I recall. She was touched on in the chapter "Helpers."

Père Hoffman had been a building contractor who was squeezed broke in the depression. His palatial two-story home with an attic and basement could have been the largest abode in town. Did I spend the night there with Morris, or just visit when he took me to his attic after dark to show me creatures I was ignorant of at the time? *Bats.* They scared the bejesus out of me.

Père Hoffman never worked after the depression laid him low. How he managed that with five kiddies I never understood. I expect he built his mansion with his own hands when times were rosier, and I expect it was paid for—and they grew a lot of their own food. Still…

One day three of the Hoffman boys decided they would fight me—one my age (Morris), one older (Howard), one a year younger (Arthur).

I opined I thought the odds a bit unfair and Howard said, okay pick one—we can all beat you. I picked the youngest but that didn't sit well with the majority so they all joined in with predictable results. I don't remember how old I was, perhaps nine or ten.

When I got home I spilled my tale to my sympathetic mother who forthwith telephoned the Hoffman household where-upon the offending troops were marched to our abode where they apologized like gentlemen.

So I wouldn't appear a hopeless sissy, I got my two cents in that I would have been happy to fight them one on one, which was not strictly true. I was an esthete, not a fighter, and would have been pulverized by any one of them.

Perhaps five or six years later when Jan Sachs came to town I was so smitten with her I wanted her to be my girlfriend, but I didn't have the slightest notion of how to go about it. Into the breech swoops Howard Hoffman, a handsome devil three years our senior in possession of a Ford with a rumble seat—dirty pool against a guy not even old enough to drive a car, let alone a car owner, an exalted state that was six or seven years in the future.

I managed to take Jan to some event—a dance? I can't remember what. But when I took her home, the ubiquitous Ford with the rumble seat was parked in front of her house in what I thought was a cheesy proprietary pretension.

Howard Hoffman had his grip on Jan until we went away to school—she to Gettysburg and me to USC.

At Gettysburg or after, when they worked for the telephone company, she met the man she married after graduation. She matched the Hoffmans with five children of her own. Her husband had a nervous breakdown fueled perhaps by the five kids and/or strong spirits. He died an invalid in a hospital with unending loving care from his children who religiously took daily turns seeing to his needs.

Jan herself fought several bouts with severe depression but licked it.

In later years I asked her what she had seen in Howard Hoffman. She said, "He treated me like a queen."

After I realized I'd lost her to Howard, I wrote her into my symphony number one, a dazzling arrangement of octaves and fifths with a heavy debt to Dvorak's New World Symphony, a melody based on my unwritten but heartfelt words, "Oh, Jan, you don't love me anymore."

BOY SCOUTS, SECOND PLACE

I promised the Boy Scouts, so I better deliver.

Before I was twelve, and old enough to join the Boy Scouts, I got my hands on the Boy Scout Manual and devoured it from cover to cover. The Webelos entity was not available then in our locale, nor was Cubs, the immediate forerunner of Scouts now. Four years later my brother was an exemplary Cub Scout and I was his "Den Chief."

I memorized the scout laws—a Boy Scout is friendly...etc., not only by title, but also the subsidiary verbage.

It was, perhaps, an early harbinger of achievement and I went at it mind, body and soul.

There were delineated steps to the pinnacle of Eagle Scout, beginning with Tenderfoot and advancing through Second Class, First Class, Star, Life on to Eagle. Each carried a minimum amount of time in which you could achieve each loftier rank, though I don't remember exactly what they were. Perhaps three months for Tenderfoot up through six months for Life—the whole enchilada requiring perhaps a year and a half to two years before the vaunted Eagle rank. Along the way you acquired merit badges which themselves accounted for part of the requirements—badges as diverse as camping, cooking, swimming, hiking, archery, masonry, music—something for everybody. Before I wore out I earned thirty-five or so of the suckers, giving me a sash full of the round embroidered medallions, and was it a silver cluster for my Eagle ranking?

And I must have had my eye on that Eagle (an eagle eye, perhaps) and I got right to work—didn't miss a beat. Nor did I miss a deadline for achieving each succeeding rank so I managed the feat in record time, not just for that year, but from the beginning of scouting in the Lehigh Valley.

The next step was an interview with the big shot adults of the Boy Scout Council. I was told it was just a formality.

I thought I breezed through that interview so imagine my surprise when I was told I was too immature and self-centered to get the award. Another six months cooling my heels should do the trick.

What they didn't say was a boy from an Allentown troop had done the same record time feat—and he was doubtless more worthy as a full page article with half the page a picture of this remarkable kid who had done this magical feat, never before to have happened in the Lehigh Council of Boy Scouts. No mention was made of me.

Apparently I had remarkably matured in six months because I got the award then without any competition.

UNCLE BARNEY WAS A CARD

Uncle Barney was a card. One of his favorite jokes was pretending to be a bra tailor measuring a woman for a bra. He drew "pockets" around the woman's breasts, whereupon she'd say, "What are you doing?"

He'd say, "I'm drawing the pockets."

In shock she would say, "I don't want pockets there."

He'd say, "Okay, no problem," then with both his hands he would erase the "pockets" across her chest.

Uncle Barney was a card.

He told this one after the war about the German air force:

A Pennsylvania Dutchman came home from the war and he was regaling his buddies about the terrors of air warfare. "I'm looking out the window of my plane and there they are, a bunch of fukkers diving at me, shooting their guns without stopping. (Pennsylvania Dutch pronouncing of Folker—the German warplane.) Just as I got clear of those fukkers another fukker comes at me from the other side. I'm doing hoops and loops but everywhere I look there's a fukker coming at me. Fukker here, fukkers there, and fukkers everywhere.

"And the scary thing about it was those fukkers were Messerschmitts."

You see what I mean about Uncle Barney being a card.

He was the youngest of the five Knoll siblings and the one who died youngest, perhaps twenty years younger than the others who all lasted from their late eighties to mid-nineties. Could his lack of longevity be attributed to his championship ribbon for producing the greatest number of kids?

He used to play a gagged up version of chopsticks on Aunt

Verna's piano—a duet with Uncle Clinton (the second youngest sibling).

Uncle Barney buried two wives. The first at a young age to a suddenly fatal brain tumor. She sat up with a brutal headache and died.

The second to cancer.

The surprising thing to all about Uncle Barney was the way he consistently attracted exceptional women.

He had a third serious girlfriend but when prodded to marry her he replied her daughter was living in sin (with a fella without benefit of clergy) and as long as that condition existed, he couldn't marry her.

Uncle Barney was such a card I couldn't believe this was a serious pronouncement, but it seemed to serve to get him off the hook as far as his own sinful living was concerned. The old adage, do as I say not as I do, held sway.

Uncle Barney's rendition of the "Midnight Ride of Paul Revere" in Pennsylvania Dutch was my favorite.

Ga-lup, ga-lup, ga-lup.
(sounds of knocking on the door)
(woman from within) Whos straus?
Eye da Paul Revere.
Was wit du, Paulie?
Da Brittisha cumma.
Ach, nay Paulie.
Yah, yah da Brittisha cumma, da gong in the Kirche, ein if by lund, und zwei if by wasser.
Ach, Paulie, come als rye. Hobt schnapps.
Nay, nay, musich gay, der Brittisha cumma.
Habt beer, Paulie?
Nay mus ich…ist der mann heim?
Nay, Paulie.
Der hell wit der Brittish.

Uncle Barney was such a card.
In his lifetime Uncle Barney had a passel of occupations.

During the war (he had flat feet or some other such nonsense) he worked at a defense plant (offense, actually) name Vultee. What they did was, I suppose, secret enough so I never knew what it was. Something to do with flying, I believe.

He bartended at his father's Broad Street Hotel, where he lived for a time until the result of his lust forced him to make an honest woman of Aunt Arvilla. No living in sin for him. The sin came first.

At some point Uncle Barney sold life insurance to folks who paid a modest stipend per week to keep it active. I went on his rounds to poor working stiffs who gave him what seemed to me meager amounts, fifty cents, seventy-five?

He was a chef's assistant at the Lehigh Country Club of which his sister, my mother, was a member. Perhaps he was a glorified dishwasher, perhaps he cut vegetables.

Then he elevated to a real cook at a barbeque joint on one of the highways, an extension of Allentown's Hamilton Street.

Then he bought a diner, I believe, one of those places that looked like a flattened railroad car, or more specifically like all those "diners" that dotted the countryside in that neck of the woods.

Luck was not with him and the diner went by the wayside. He cooked for another Allentown diner before or after this, it was hard to keep track of Uncle Barney. He was such a card.

Somewhere among this he was a freelance drapery salesman. Then he sold western rope ties, and shortie joke ties.

I expect I missed a number of his jobs, but you get the picture.

FOLLIES

The evil that men do lives after them.
The good is oft interred in their bones.

—*William Shakespeare, Act 3, scene ii
of Julius Caesar*

That Shakespeare had a lot of good ideas. So it is with our follies: we remember them more than our sanities.

Community Concerts (or something like that) was an association that took to communities not large enough to attract headliners, a collection of musical artists. My father was not that keen on this sort of thing. I suspect he thought it was for sissies, so Momma Baby took me. This particular afternoon or evening the attraction was a Scandinavian tenor named Jussi Björling.

Momma Baby always introduced me to everyone in sight.

At Björling's concert at intermission she introduced me to a Community Concerts Association functionary who was from the Big Apple, but for some reason was in Allentown, Pennsylvania attending our concert.

He was slightly built, smooth faced man of middle years who perhaps had genes orienting him toward males, but perhaps that was just a prejudice my father instilled in me. He was terrified I would become homosexual due to my interest in music.

Perhaps this gentleman asked me how I liked the concert. Treating kids as adults was good politics.

"He has good diction," I said, an eleven year-old music expert. But the gentleman didn't hear me and asked me to repeat it. That should have tipped me off to say, "Oh nothing," but I repeated the assessment of his diction.

He nodded. "Yes, very good diction," he said suffering this fool less than gladly.

I had read those words in the program. Did I think he wouldn't know where they came from? I now wonder if he hadn't written them. This was the fellow Momma Baby later had me play the piano for on the second floor of a music store. I resisted, said I wasn't that good a piano player. She pushed, said she'd already set it up and would be embarrassed if I reneged.

I played. Probably my grandiose but flabby techniqued Grieg's Piano Concerto, a lot of crashing chords to begin, then some simple melodies and harmonies before the real dexterity difficulty set in, before which I stopped playing.

"Well," he said appearing to give his opinion serious consideration, "it's sloppy." I still remember those words, seeing his scrubbed face and slender body relax as though he had performed an unpleasant duty without compromising his artistic integrity. Since I had been self-taught he recommended I take lessons. Years later, forty or so, when I replayed this scene for my mother, she denied it ever happened, and no amount of reminders could dissuade her. Verily, both memory and the lack of it are wonderful things. This assessment must include mine as well.

I expect I was somewhat younger when she took me to a performance of Hamlet starring the great classical Shakespearian actor, Maurice Evans. My guess is I was seven to nine, and only filled in for my father who chose not to go (an event that repeated itself as he became increasingly enamored of the relaxing qualities of strong spirits).

As you might expect, I didn't understand a word of the play, but I was mesmerized by the thoroughly enchanting rhythms of the speech of the ensemble.

I read later in my young adulthood that Maurice Evans was now considered a bit of a hambone, the tenor of the times favoring those Shakespeareans who spoke the lines more "naturally." Had that been the case when I was transfixed by his Hamlet, I expect I would have been bored to tears, since I didn't understand what he was saying and with the rhythms gone, all that was left would have been the words which I don't argue are often powerful if you understand them, which I at that tender age did not.

It was in the same way I got a dose of Richard Wagner's "Ring Cycle" via 78 rpm recordings in the third grade. These antique discs held about four minutes of music per side so I don't expect they taxed the interest spans of the nine year olds in the third grade. It certainly was an extracurricular activity inserted in the state mandated classes by our teacher. I can't speak for my classmates because I don't remember discussing it with them. I expect none of the others understood the German words either even though most of our ancestors were Pennsylvania Germans. But the music captivated me. I looked forward to the teacher producing those recordings to play for us. I expect I was sorry when this ended; I don't expect there was any announcement from the teacher, rather they just faded away or we moved onto the next grade and teachers who were less musically enlightening.

It was in this third grade class that I made my solo instrumental debut.

I had been taking cornet lessons from the undertaker who was the man who gave them in town. I had begun playing the bugle, which later stood me in good stead in the Boy Scouts ("Taps" by the river on Easter morning and assembly, mess call, and "Reveille" and "Taps" at Boy Scout camp). I remember my early lessons from Uncle Walter who was a trombonist and member of the vaunted Moravian trombone choir. He was married to my father's oldest sister, Helen. (Our oldest grandson, Jordan, is now an accomplished trombonist. He seemed to become accomplished at the instrument in a very short time.) I sat before a mirror on a door in our house practicing blowing into the coronet without puffing out my cheeks.

My solo repertoire in the third grade was not an inspiration to prodigies, but I was so far removed from that category that it hardly mattered. I chose for my debut, "Don't Fence Me In," a feature of which were note repetitions so I wouldn't tax my memory of fingerings. "Oh give me land, lots of land under starry skies above. Don't fence me in."

I was nervous as all get out—a condition that never left me

while performing on an instrument—I could sing or conduct our South Coast Choral Society from memory without a twinge of nervousness, but there was something about playing an instrument—brass or piano—in public that laid me low.

"Don't Fence Me In" being my world debut on the cornet must have been the height of nervousness (nine years old, remember) but I got through it, much to my relief. What I can't remember is *why* I did it. Rationale usually winds up in the lap of ego. Could I have been trying to catch the eye of some comely damsel? I wasn't knocking out anyone on the playground so this may have been my only weapon. Except for the bugling, I didn't repeat this kind of instrumental performance until I was in high school and improvised a piano piece for an assembly of students with heavy debt to bravura style. Since I was essentially faking it I don't remember being nervous.

Afterwards a girl who *could* play the piano, read the music, the whole bit, asked me if I made it up or had it written down. I faked my response to that also maximizing my feeble abilities to where I sounded like a near genius.

Amusingly our high school graduation yearbook pictured seniors in "best" categories—Best Athlete, Best Looking, Best Student, etc.—the girl who questioned my piano performance bona fides, Dolores Heiney and I were pictured over the caption

"Most Talented"

and I expect *she* was.

I saw her at our 50th high school reunion. Those years had not been kind. She was not upbeat about herself in response to the ubiquitous trivial question, "How are you?" She grumped out a response, not of the favorable kind, further probing yielded her opinion that her fondness for cigarettes had ruined her.

MARCHING BAND:
MR. GROSS NEEDS A PATSY

Perfection itself is imperfection.
—*Vladimir Horowitz*

Did he have visions, however fleeting, of leading a big-time college band on TV, at some nationally televised game? I didn't think of it then, but why couldn't a man leading a ragtag high school band have aspirations? It is said the cliché essay for college applications is "How the Band Changed My Life." I'm not sure my life was changed in the band, but it was certainly affected.

I recall being the never-ending butt of ridicule from the senior fellows in the high school band—guys who were actually *in* high school. I was in the seventh grade—a left-handed kid who had *beaucoup* trouble staying in step. I doubt my playing my trumpet was much better, just not as noticeable.

Insult to injury, a band director aptly named Mr. Gross was hired. He was a young man who found no greater pleasure than ridiculing me in front of the big boys with such endearments as Fleabrain and Chowder Head.

One occasion, a Halloween parade, when the big guys were harassing me on the march, my father must have been a witness. When I dragged myself home to bed I found a note and a $5 bill on the bed. The note said,

"To the best trumpeter in the parade."
I just now wonder why I didn't quit the band if it was so

onerous. Perhaps I'm not a quitter. Perhaps it never occurred to me. Perhaps I thought it gave me status—a thirteen year-old kid marching with high school kids four and five years older. Perhaps I liked getting out of my junior high school classes to go to the high school for band practice. Or was it because I was so smitten with a recent arrival in Emmaus, the saxophone player named Jan Sachs, super personable and very pretty too? She was a far better marcher (right handed?) and instrumentalist than I. I certainly don't think altruism was any part of my reasoning.

Parenthetically and mercifully, Mr. Gross lasted only a year. He was replaced by his antithesis a Mr. Rothenberg. A shy man whom I bonded with immediately. I even agreed to play that unwieldy sousaphone because he needed them. Was I the only one? Not impossible. I recall the instrument sank to better align with my abilities. It was pretty much um-pa-pa two or three notes per piece. The instrument was so rarely taken up I got into the district band and all state and awarded first chair in the Interlochen National Music Camp Band and orchestra.

One day on returning to class from high school band practice, Luther Souders, the principal, surprised us on the stair landing where three of us were fooling around with Jan's pencil. Silly, juvenile stuff. He hauled us back to the classroom, made us stand in front and demanded, "Now tell us about what you were doing to the girl in the stairway."

"Nothing," I said, beet-red with embarrassment at his obvious innuendo. I suspect if I had answered with something sexual or even innuendo that Mr. Souders would have been vindicated— his entire career as a junior high school principal capped with this accomplishment.

But nothing of the sort was taking place or implied. At that age and for many years beyond I had not the courage for anything close to what he was suggesting.

Jan's mother called principal Souders to assure him nothing like he so gleefully suggested went on in the stairwell.

I don't think he wanted to believe her.

THE NATION'S GIFTED YOUTH

Picture this: a fifteen year old kid stranded overnight in a big city (Detroit) airport, after his first ever flight, which must have been scary enough by itself. He rides a bus from the airport to downtown (never gets off) and back.

Did he consider getting a motel room? Or did his innate thrift forestall him? Or, since he had not ever done such, did he not know how to go about it?

It was by now perhaps midnight and he is surrounded for the first time in his life without the anchor of the familiar. He has sufficient rational fear not to get off the bus in downtown Detroit in the middle of the night. So he looks out of the bus window and chalks it up to sightseeing. There are very few people on the bus at this hour so he is able to get a window by himself—sitting with a stranger held a minor terror for him. The streets were for the most part, deserted—but the thought of missing the bus and having to wait hours for another inhibited his action. His ambition was to sleep—but his inhibitions held sway. What if someone robbed him while he was asleep? Took all his money *and* his plane ticket? Was the fear of homosexual predators in his mind? Not impossible.

So he sat up all night in the airline waiting room and somehow managed to board a plane for Traverse City, Michigan which put him in striking distance of Interlochen Music Camp. A camp counselor met him and a few others with a van.

That was the prelude to perhaps the best experience he ever had—and the last concert of the season featured Franz Liszt's "Les Preludes" signifying a commencement of sorts from fantasyland back to the real world.

"The Nation's Gifted Youth"

There was more to that slogan of the National Music Camp in Interlochen, Michigan, but I don't remember what it was. "Where the Nation's Gifted Youth Meet Under the Stars…"?

For sheer personal enjoyment, I still consider it the highlight of my life. Coming from a town of six thousand with a high school class of 123, you might imagine the music groups were short of world class. Since I was also short of world class I fit right in.

But National Music Camp was world class. It truly was a collection of the nation's gifted youth—I just didn't happen to be one of them. The first year I got a scholarship to play the tuba. As you can imagine, not a lot of people played the tuba, and if you've ever played the tuba, you know why. You probably wouldn't fall for the baloney about those handful of notes (in the band) laying the foundation for the ensemble. In the orchestra, the tuba notes could be more challenging—and interesting—there just weren't very many of them.

For my second year I played the French horn. Much more interesting and a lot more challenging. In the upper registers many of the contiguous notes required the same fingerings. Therefore it behooved you not only to *hear* what the note should be, but be able to screw your lips up in such a way that would produce the precise sound required. I was not one of them.

But I took lessons from the French horn teacher. I realized belatedly that my treatment at the hands of the tuba teacher was because I didn't take the pricey lessons he offered. I may have been the only one to shun that opportunity. But I fancied myself a composer and conductor and thought those lessons would be superfluous. And my second year, when I took the French horn lessons, I proved to be correct. My aptitude might be considered metaphorically in the lower register—of course I am persuaded that if I had practiced it might have made a difference.

I soon fell in with two of my cabin mates, John Shroyer, a violinist and violaist from Peoria, Illinois (where his father was a physics or chemistry professor) and Les Lisle, a trombonist from Charlottesville, Virginia.

Of the three of us, Les Lisle exhibited some sanity. John and I would "give people (especially visitors) the business." Making believe by pantomime and guttural emissions that we were retarded. A cruel and antisocial thing to do. But we did it. At the dining room table we would pretend to stab our meat with a fork and miss—sometimes I expect we did the dance with a spoon or knife—all the while making deranged faces with guttural groans. We seemed adroit enough at this to escape the detection of the faculty and staff.

Another of our staples was John acting as a blind man and me leading him by the elbow to the wishing well in the center of the camp entry—courtyard—whereupon John would intone, "Wishing well, wishing well, give me my sight back."

I suppose it worked because he was always able to see after those incantations.

In the orchestra we rehearsed and performed a symphonic program once a week. In the band, also weekly concerts. I suppose that was what ensemble playing was about—it was so good, you felt good playing music with your betters. We whipped through the symphonic (and band) repertoire for eight glorious weeks, performing as many great works as most college ensembles manage in four years.

The choir performed "Belshazzar's Feast" and the Brahm's "Requiem", but gave fewer concerts.

Based on my listing of works I had performed on the tuba, which I submitted with my application, I was awarded first chair in the band—perhaps second in the orchestra where there were fewer players, but they were better.

In our first rehearsal the section faculty leader stood behind me and kibitzed and cajoled making me mighty nervous. He was, I later surmised, out of joint that I was given the first chair and had not signed up for private lessons with him. No doubt that took a chunk out of the pay he hoped to take home.

Every week we had tryouts for seating in our sections. The first week I was unceremoniously dropped from first chair to last—or close to it. All the other stalwarts took lessons from this worthy and I just this minute wonder if he had given his pet students the part of the music he would use for the audition.

Whatever the reason, some of this seeming animosity spilled over to the orchestra where rather than eight or ten tuba players, we had four or five.

Mercifully, the faculty section leader was a different guy who simultaneously led the trombone section. So I thought I would fare better in the tryouts.

One of my favorite orchestral works was Paul Hindemith's *The Symphonic Metamorphosis of Themes by Carl Maria von Weber*. It had a tricky rhythmical melody that passed through the orchestra sections. Since I adored the composition, I was glad that was picked for the tryouts.

I must say, I played it flawlessly (the only time before or after that that I played so well). The others stumbled on the tricky rhythm. So did the vote for first chair go in my favor?

It did not. The vote was so egregious that the faculty leader berated the troops for the subjective voting.

I was so sure I'd won, yet must have been wary of prejudice from the band and faculty section leader, that I peeked during the vote. I didn't get the majority but was eager to see who voted against the only guy who played it right. (But then, if you didn't play it right, perhaps you couldn't tell when someone else did.)

The guy with a stammer who (I thought) was one of the few who was nice to me, voted against me — along with a few of the band man's favorite students. Enough to create a majority for the other guy — probably the one who played so well the week before.

It reminds me of the salesmanship slogan "Ability to do the job is 17th." So many (16) things are ahead of it…congeniality being close to the top.

That was the year my family drove west to pick me up and enjoy some of the end-of-the-year concerts.

The next year Les Lisle, trombone, did not return to camp. We sent him a collect telegram urging him to come.

He riposted with some mock (I hope) tirade about our audacity in the gesture without really offering an excuse.

The following year I went with Shroyer (violin — now an estates and wills attorney) to his house in Peoria where he then took me to the airport or train station for my trip home. His mother spoke to him from upstairs. I believe she was in a wheelchair and John was at pains to keep me away from her. Though I had introduced him to my entire family, I met none of his.

I expect he feared I would give them the business.

A cabin of the Nation's Gifted Youth. With not a smile among them, signifying the seriousness of the situation—Teddy is third from right, second row, struggling not to look deranged. Pals Johnie Shroyer, violin, third from left, first row, the geeky looking one, and Les Lisle, trombone, crouching far right.

SOME DATES
(OKAY, MOST OF THEM)

You have to be very fond of men to love them.
Otherwise they're simply unbearable.

—*Marguerite Duras*

Barbara Conklin: Junior Assembly

Gaga—stole away to Dundore's drugstore to get her a Christmas present. She was the quiet type, probably as nervous as I was, but I didn't know it at the time. Quiet often it is mistaken for sophisticated when it is just shyness. I was twelve years old—she was eleven.

With the help of a Dundore daughter given to *avoirdupois* I agonized but settled on a bottle of toilet water. I doubt I had any idea what it was, but was persuaded it was a bargain basement perfume, not as expensive and not as personal according to Miss Dundore.

I took it home and surreptitiously scrounged some giftwrapping paper, wrapped it and spirited it off to the Junior Assembly Christmas party at the Allentown woman's club where I presented it to the young lady.

December in Pennsylvania was cold, but I was warm with my loving gesture. You must understand the girl was pretty, there was a mysterious reservation about her that challenged me and piqued my interest and my imagined affection. The sum total of my relationship with her was the bi-monthly meetings of Junior Assembly and the imagination in between. We went to different schools. I think as a bonus we carpooled the several miles to and from the Allentown women's club.

I thought I had been clever in keeping the gift from my mother who would have doubtless proffered probing questions I was not capable of answering—no more than I had any desire to do so.

As you may well imagine, my wrapping job was shy of world class, in fact it was laughable. Well, sometimes it's the thought that counts.

Sometimes.

Barbara did a good job of concealing the toilet water (what an uncomfortable name) in her purse for the ride home.

The next day I heard from my mother who heard from Barbara's mother that I had given Barbara the gift. My mother seemed slighted that I didn't take her into my confidence about the operation. Perhaps she suggested she would have been able to help me get a more suitable gift.

I, of course, played blasé as any Lochinvar worth his salts was wont to do. As I can at this distance divine the purpose of mother's reaction, I think it was to let me know that any hanky panky perpetrated on the fairer sex would surely get back to my maternal watchdog.

Beware.

Silvia Shoemaker:

I remember her asking if her slip showed, if she had on too much makeup and if her perfume was too strong. How I was supposed to know the right answers to those inquiries, I've no idea.

I think she was my initiation into "Hold my earrings please."

I thought she was pretty, if a bit chunky. But all I knew of her was what I saw in the halls. She had a sparkle in her eyes and had an unfailingly friendly cache of greetings, but I had really never spoken to her. She was a year ahead of me. If I had spoken to her before I asked for the date, I could have saved us both a lot of awkwardness.

I held the earrings while she went off to do something else, I don't remember what—if I knew—I took her home and returned the earrings and that was that.

Barbara Aten I took to something and when I took her home I tried to kiss her. She was the one who laughed at me.

I reminded her of that at our fiftieth reunion from Emmaus High School, but she had no memory of it. I wonder if I had been successful with the kiss if she would have remembered. I doubt it, but I would have.

June Lyon:

Cello player, National music camp, from Missouri, was my first real kiss. I almost passed out from excitement. The locale was the girls' camp gate, crowded with aspiring campers, notorious for this kind of carrying on, but it was my one and only shot at this minor intimacy. She did not return to camp the following year and this must have been our last opportunity. Of course the area was crawling with camp counselors to assure that nothing happened that might besmirch the upright (uptight?) reputation of the camp.

We went through receiving lines each year and shook hands with Joe Maddy, the founder, a Michigan educator with spunk and mannerisms. Beside him was his down-to-earth wife, who when I told her in my first receiving line my name was Gardner she replied, "That's my middle name."

Due to the misconstructions of youth, the next year I introduced myself as Gardner, her maiden name. She seemed perplexed. No, her maiden name was something else, I forget what.

I refreshed her memory about the last year's receiving line when she told me Gardner was her middle name.

"Oh," she said, "I *love* to garden. That's what I meant."

Miriam Deutz:

Our mothers taught school together in East Orange, New Jersey before we were born. Her father was an importer of paint pigments.

One Sunday in the summertime in our later high school years, we drove from Emmaus, Pennsylvania to the Deutz manse in Maplewood, New Jersey. In the car en route my father opined it was a long way to go to make the match. I remember being surprised at the sentiment since the voyage had not been sold that way.

For her part, mother had been shocked. Shocked! that father could *think* such a thing. It was a perfectly innocent meeting of the families to renew old times. As I recall she protested too much.

Miriam was tall, blonde and attractive and in time I invited her to our senior ball.

The Deutzes returned the visit when I took Miriam to a party in a country barn. Were these events meant subliminally to put one in the frame of mind of animals? I couldn't say. But in this instance I knew one or two people slightly and it was not magical. Rather it was stilted and Miriam and I agreed we should go home so the Deutzes could head back to Maplewood, New Jersey at a reasonable hour.

I made several visits to Maplewood (perhaps two hours from home). I believe I bunked in a room that shared a bath with the mom and pop of the family. I remember having to relieve increasing pressure on my bladder in the nighttime, but being inhibited to inactivity by the fear of them hearing my water hitting their toilet's water. I trust I resolved the matter before I wet the bed which I must have realized would hardly be preferable to a little tinkling sound—they might even well have been asleep.

The same trip, or another, I remember driving all over the countryside with Miriam, trying to workup the nerve to kiss her.

In vain.

We went our separate ways. She to school in the east somewhere, I to Los Angeles and USC. She married an Annapolis graduate, foaled several of his children and accompanied him to his various postings.

On one of my trips east I arranged to visit Miriam and her husband Jack Strachan. In Palos Verdes we had a neighbor named Strachan. He had, as I recall an attractive and not shy wife. At their home for some kind of gathering I asked—Strachan not being a garden-variety name—if he was by any chance related to Jack Strachan in the east. This is the kind of question asked the world over, a question which always meets with a negative response.

Except this time. "That's my brother," he exclaimed. It was around eleven or twelve at night but my neighbor insisted on telephoning Miriam and Jack though I protested it was two or three in the morning where they lived. Miriam apparently answered the phone and her brother-in-law after a suitable (or un) introduction handed the phone to me. She sounded sleepy, no surprise, but was a good sport about it; though I can't imagine how she could have been.

In New Jersey in an attractive eastern country-house the Strachan's graciously sported me to a fine lunch—shrimp salad and whatever was needed to round out the repast. We spoke of Jack's Navy experience, and his retirement project which involved some engineering shenanigans which were beyond my sophistication.

Within a few years Jack was dead and Miriam moved to Connecticut to be a more frequent help to her grandchildren.

I still get nice notes on Christmas cards from her in exchange with irreverent notes on mine.

I should perhaps regret we had never kissed, but I'm too old now. Everything ends.

COLLEGE

(FIGHT ON FOR OLD SC)

Is there any reward?
I'm beginning to doubt it.
I am broken and bored,
Is there any reward
Reassure me, Good Lord,
And inform me about it.
Is there any reward?
I'm beginning to doubt it.

—*Hilaire Belloc*

YALE REGRETS—
BUT NOT VERY MUCH

In great attempts,
It is glorious even to fail.

—Longimus,
On the Sublime
(First Century, AD)

I am in the somewhat embarrassing position of no longer having to save money.

But old habits don't only die hard, they don't die at all. At least while we are alive. It is those habits which induced this horn of plenty in the first place.

How did I do it? I don't really have a good idea. I had many youthful aspirations, making a lot of money was not among them (most were associated with music and show biz).

My (sainted) mother taught me to do the best I could—always. "I don't care what you do for a living, if you want to be a garbage man, be the *best* garbage man." It should be noted that in that day, automated garbage trucks did not exist in Emmaus, Pennsylvania. Rather a four-sided, open-top truck patrolled the streets with a driver, a pitcher who threw the newspaper wrapped garbage onto the

truck, to the human compactor who stomped on the neat packages
of garbage to make room for more. One can conjecture a wide variety of wrapper efficiency. I always thought when my mother was
extolling the virtues of being the best garbage man you can, she was
referring to this particular job description.

She needn't have worried. And at that impressionable age,
I thought I was cut out for better things than garbage stomping.
Though a few people who have read some of my books might not
agree.

So, then what? I got elected class president after failing all
my attempts to get elected *something*—even eraser clapper in Mr.
Bear's science class. I'd like to report that the class finally recognized
my superior talents, but it was rather the result of my sending birthday cards to the other 122 members of the class. If you had the option to vote for the guy who sent you a birthday card or the guy who
didn't, wouldn't you be at least tempted? And I went at it like I
wanted to be the best. We ran functions that raised more money
than any other class. We donated it to the landscaping of the new
high school grounds along with a planted bronze plaque that stated:

First Landscaping
of High School Grounds
by the Class of 1952

The bronze bit of braggadocio was swiped in a matter of days. I suspect it fell prey to a member of the class of 1951 or before whose accomplishments, let it be said, paled by comparison. The school
administration recommended it not be replaced, being such a
demonstrative target for vandalism (and jealousy?).

Then for my senior year I wrote and directed a musical titled *That's For Sure*, a nod to a Pennsylvania Dutchism. Mother
wrote the lyrics, and the words and music to the song, "Little Wedding Bells." (Ring in my heart whenever you pass by. They ring for
me, they swing for you, oh what is your reply?...)

I made a speech of thanks—gratitude for all who helped
make this show possible. I thanked Errol Peters, the music teacher,
the English teacher, the drama teacher, the students and all the

teachers. I wouldn't be surprised to learn I thanked the school jan-
itors. In short, I thanked everyone—*every*one except my mother.

I thought under the circumstances she was extremely tactful when she pointed that out to me. Did she wait until the next
day so it wouldn't tarnish the glow from the minor triumph (as opposed to my father delivering the news of my failure to get into Yale
on the way to my last performance)?

In response to this egregious *faux pas* I stuttered something
to the effect that she was recognized on the program so I thought
she was on my side and I didn't speechify about myself. She was in
essence a partner in the noblesse part of noblesse oblige. It was a
nice try but I don't think it cut a lot of mustard.

Another memorable sideline to the musical performance
was the lead character who, with perhaps two weeks remaining
until opening night, the first performance in a two performance
run, disappeared. Nobody knew where she was. She wasn't at
home—her mother was either unreachable or feigned ignorance
herself.

Mild panic set in. Mary Lou Herman was her name and
she played the lead girl who became the prom queen who led her
court of three to five attendants down the aisle of the auditorium
and back to the stage and her throne—center stage.

Mary Lou had an older boyfriend whose name escapes me.
I didn't really know him. And older boyfriends of young girls can
mean trouble—as in this case it apparently did. As luck or fate
would have it, Mary Lou's pregnancy was beginning to show—and
by skipping school, except for the dress rehearsal and the perform-
ances, I expect she sought to minimize the chit chat, perhaps because she didn't want to upstage the show with her scandalous (in
that time and place) condition.

Perhaps her motives were not one hundred percent altruistic. At any rate she returned in time for the dress rehearsal in her
pregnancy smock and her condition did not affect her glorious
voice nor her performance as our prom queen.

The show, after all, must go on.

It is no secret I aspired to go to Yale. I expected all this extra
curricular glory along with my super grades (even if they were

largely encouraging gifts from a benevolent faculty—in the fall I was the lead in *Harvey*, in the spring I did a musical—how much time could I have had for schoolwork?) would pay off.

And it was the SATs done me in. In verbal and math I hauled down a combined score under seven hundred. Perhaps 335 and 350 when seven hundred each might have been smiled upon. Word was you got two hundred each for writing your name—a skill I was fairly accomplished at by that time.

It never occurred to me that Yale would be so snotty about this lack, and my high school guidance counselor told me not to take it again for they only considered the lowest score. I didn't fight him because I didn't see how I could do any better with that bunch of questions which were light years beyond me.

Six years later my brother got into Yale on his second SAT scores.

Do I regret it?

Not now. I realize as a Yale graddy I might have landed a coveted spot in a publishing company with an eventual goal of one-hundred-ten dollars a week. And with my lead-footed knack of schmoozing and politics, I would still be there, perhaps at three hundred per week in my prime. Not enough to rent a pad within a one-hour radius of Manhattan Island.

"If you don't smile, people will think you are intelligent." The author, seventeen years old, putting on airs for a publicity still to flog his musical *That's for Sure*.

DEFAULT "EDUCATION"

Musick hath charms to sooth a savage breast...

—*William Congreve,* The Mourning Bride

After Yale College decided I was not of their caliber, I was left with no options. Foolishly, as it turned out, I had applied to no other college. Why should I, I reasoned, I didn't want to go anywhere else. Paul Hindemith, German composer, was teaching there and I adored his music. That was the ticket for me.

Wrong.

A site visit to the office of admissions, Edward Noyes, *Chairman* (like that name? NO — YES. What else did he need in his trade?), disabused me of my dream. My SAT scores were so low he probably had serious doubts that the person responsible for those dismal numbers was a sentient being.

I made my pitch. I echoed my mother's belief that I could do anything I put my mind to. I laid heavily on my boundless ambition, soft-pedaling the standard test results.

The old guy—gray hair, craggy face, blue blazer with a Yale patch over his bosom (*Lux et veritas*) shed his *lux et veritas* on my case:

"Mistah Gahdner—I like to compare student applicants to automobiles. You can no more run a car with a large engine if you have no gas, than you can run a car with all gas and no engine."

Composer and Yale Professor, Paul Hindemith abandoned ship the next year—probably in a huff at my rejection. Edward Noyes' career came to an abrupt end the next year, probably for the same reason.

Transfer at the end of my freshman year somewhere was a possibility, but the immediate task was to get into a college. The elites were surely full up—it was the end of March.

My father had an acquaintance, George Shorpe, a stockbroker, who was a USC booster. He thought SC was the ticket. He didn't seem disturbed at my subterranean SAT scores. His say-so would get me in.

Columbia, in New York City, had a well-known musical show—was it called Varsity Show? I recall Richard Rodgers had written it in his time. I applied to Columbia—after interviewing with someone who said I would be a natural to do the varsity show.

Tempting. Was there a better entrée to Broadway? But plopped in the middle of Morningside Heights, which had at the time the highest crime rate in the *world* with its ninety-mile proximity to my home (would I not be expected and shovel snow on weekends?), I decided against...

I had never been west of music camp in Michigan, and USC offered a tantalizing prospect. I went.

On to SC who at the time had one question on the application: "Can you pay?"

My father could and perhaps because his father couldn't, he paid for college for his three kids—and law school for the talented two-thirds of the offspring.

When I got off the plane I was met by a bunch of fraternity boys bent on getting me drunk so I would "pledge" to join their group. I believe the coast-to-coast experience from Emmaus, Pennsylvania was seventeen hours or so and though jets were not in currency then, I was indisputably lagged. The imparted intelligence that I didn't drink baffled them. Someone should have told them. Perhaps the Emmaus place kicker who must have sicked them onto me, though he was not in attendance—but how would he have known? He was a class or two ahead of me and I barely knew who he was.

Somehow I got free of these pushy undergraddy salesmen, but not until after I spent the night at their frat house—the free, introductory offer that I supposed was meant to seal the deal.

Willard Hall was my pre-arranged residence dorm for the

semester. It was an old brick structure of three or four stories which was demolished soon after I graduated.

When I checked in my roommate had not yet arrived. But I had been assured that roommates were carefully paired to compliment each other for compatibility.

Unbelievable. I wondered how this canard could have taken root at Willard Hall after I met my roommate—perfectly nice fella, but if we had something—anything in common it sailed over my head. This was an early nail in the school's coffin from my standpoint. Why should they make a fuss about this careful pairing if they didn't do it? I had gotten expectations up without foundation.

It was some fifty years later that I discovered the truth from this roommate himself (an engineering student who spent his life working for the water company in Los Angeles). According to Nick Friesen, said roommate and life-long Porsche car buff, he was too late in checking in. There had been some mix up, I don't remember what, but he took the room (mine) that was reserved for a Friedman. Since I never met Mr. Friedman, I can't assess our commonalities. Do you suppose Friedman might have wound up at Yale?

It was Nick Friesen who introduced me to my lifelong friends John Callos and Lloyd Saatjian (the Reverend). The three of them had gone to high school together in Long Beach, California.

Registering for my classes took eight hours. Yes, no exaggeration. Eight hours of standing in line after line, making selections based on zero knowledge of the relative merits of the offers.

The course "Man and Civilization" was a requirement. I had it with five hundred others in Bovard Auditorium. I don't remember who Bovard was, but it would be in character for the institution if he gave them a lot of dough. Did I select the teacher because he had written the text (with a couple of other chaps who weren't teaching at SC) because I thought he would be best qualified to teach a course for which he had written the text—after all, it is some distinction? Or was it a random, chance thing, or perhaps I was given no choice.

At any rate, calling him a teacher was a merciless stretch.

What he was, was a reader. He read his book to us in the dullest, most monotonous voice imaginable. Was this SC's idea of wowing the new arrival with celebrity?

At some point in the arduous registration process a kindly older guy—a grad student—offered to help me out. I can imagine I looked lost. How could I not? I was lost.

He gave me tips on teachers to take and avoid—courses offered. The only one of his tips I remember was to take the physics course with a guy this physics major touted as having almost won the Nobel Prize—not a common thing at USC in those days. He really knew his stuff, this guy said, and knew how to make it clear for the novice.

I took the course and found nothing special about the teacher. It was true he didn't talk over our heads, but I found him dull. I had no aptitude for science to begin with and this near-miss Nobel laureate did not kindle any interest in me. Now I wonder why a guy of his scientific brilliance was teaching the introductory course.

Frank Baxter had two uniforms for teaching his English course. Blue blazer, grey flannel pants, white shirt and regimental striped tie—my guess is blue and grey stripes. That was one of his outfits and the second was exactly the same. I suppose he had to have something when one of them was being cleaned. He was the closest thing sartorially at SC to Yale's Edward Noyes.

Baxter was famous for his TV show on Shakespeare. It might have been a national offering. 1952 was early for television and the format was rudimentary. Baxter had an engaging way about him—a twinkling enthusiasm for his subject that was infectious.

His English class was, not surprisingly, full. I went to beg that he admit me. He was most gracious about it and I expect he swore me to secrecy lest the whole school would ask for a waiver.

But the first day of class a horde of students showed up. He said there were unfortunately more than the room would hold and he would be compelled to pare the class down to fit the room. His method was arbitrary—either alphabetical or where we stood in the room. I was, alas, in the eliminated group.

As the other failures were leaving in various states of disappointment, I reminded him of our meeting where he said I could join the class.

"Yes," he said, "fool that I was." And I squeaked over the line.

Here I read *Great Expectations*. All I remember him saying was "smells are better than sights and sounds."

It was the only novel I read at SC.

Was it SC we were supposed to call the school or USC? The administration made a point of calling it one or the other. It does me no credit that I don't remember which.

The rah-rah stuff left me cold. I lusted for intellectual stimulation. I was beginning to wonder if I was at the right place for that.

One of the handful of good classes I took was in Philosophy. The subject of the day was peoples' untoward reactions to frustration.

After the class I spoke to the teacher positing I didn't experience those reactions—expecting I suppose for him to pat me on the head and say "My, what a good boy you are." He did the next best thing and said, "Perhaps you have an unusual resistance to frustration." This tidbit remained with me for sixty years. What else could he say? "Oh, then my theory is wrong." Or, perhaps, "Oh, son, you are deluding yourself."

But no, he gave me an out while boosting my pride so much I couldn't wait to write home that my philosophy professor said I had an unusual resistance to frustration. Now I wonder why I made such a fuss about that string of words—enough to remember them. It must have been the "unusual" part. I must have coveted being unusual at eighteen, when I expected most of my contemporaries lusted to conform.

But now sixty years on, through the fires and adversities of life, I still don't wear jeans, but evolution has taken a toll on my resistance to frustrations. For now the smallest hindrance in my simple routines will set off my temper in a torrent of cursing. If I bump an elbow on a refrigerator door, drop my fork twice or suffer the ineptitude of some fellow driver on the public streets, I become a ferocious, if short-lived volcano.

I sometimes wonder what that philosophy professor would say now—Watson—I think his name was, believe it or not—Watson

(I was no Sherlock). And I wonder if my mother lived up to my expectations of praise—though my expectations in that line were abnormally high.

✻   ✻   ✻   ✻

The USC music school was small, perhaps one hundred fifty students. They were in the business of grinding out music teachers. The small size of the school was something that attracted me to 'SC.

Of course, I was naïve in not looking beyond that when those stats enchanted me from across the fruited plain. As far as I could tell, every single member of the music faculty was…alive. Much more than that, I couldn't swear to.

Pauline Alderman, my advisor, looked to be in her eighties with a hearing aid attached, taught the required course in music appreciation. Of course I already appreciated music or I wouldn't have signed up for a music major. After a semester with Dr. Pauline my music appreciation diminished appreciably. She sported enough weight to account for another person which was quite a feat at her age.

Something Woodward. Same age bracket as Dr. Pauline but rail thin so she looked the part of an octogenarian. To round out the picture she sucked on her teeth in frustration. I expect they were false. She'd earned it.

She taught solfeggio—or music dictation. She played the notes (one at a time) on the piano and we were obliged to write them down—pitch and rhythm. A deadlier occupation I can't imagine. As far as I know she didn't teach any loftier subject.

At this activity I was abjectly hopeless. It didn't help my cause that she reminded me of that forehead slapper Miss Neimoyer my fifth grade teacher but, instead of opining that I had no home training, Woodward went on about my nervous jiggle of my legs. "Mr. Gardner, I broke Mr. Gilmore of that last semester and I'm going to break you."

Did she? Or did I henceforth take a seat in the back row where my nervous tic might not bother her?

Ellis Kohs taught harmony. He was a guy in his fifties, sad and distracted looking, and who could blame him? Doubtless he fancied himself a great composer who was prostituting himself teaching rudimentary harmony to a bundle of snot noses. He had to live, didn't he? It was Mr. Kohs (a PhD would have been superfluous for a man of his ambition and talents) famously told me I would never be a composer. Now I wonder if I should have riposted, "Are you one?"

I saw Mr. Kohs on Hollywood Boulevard late at night and he looked so forlorn I speculated he was trolling for a young—or not so young—boy to pick up. He didn't seem to be having any success. I decided it would not be in my interest to greet him.

Halsey Stevens was a specialist in the music of Béla Bartok. I recall him being a decent teacher if a bit morose—like his idol Béla Bartok who Stevens said weighed ninety pounds and seemed a sad sack. I was not aware of depression then, but in hindsight that could have been right on the money. I can't remember what he taught, I don't think it was composition—perhaps the music of Béla Bartok—whatever it was, I didn't detect much enthusiasm for it.

Leon Kirchner was a composer. Could he have taught composition? He was a super teacher—the difference being he had a knack for people—the others were submerged in academia and might have shone at faculty meetings, but Kirchner was a guy who seemed to genuinely like music and his students. The next year Harvard got him. Lucky Harvard. He was a fish out of water at 'SC.

The head of the music department, Dean Kendall, had been a YMCA band director. This was the word on the street. I never verified it—though his yearbook write-up was vague and uncertain, it omitted this info which would in no way have distracted from what was offered.

Perhaps thirty some years later I met a young Harvard music student. He was reviewing musical events for the *South Bay Daily Breeze*, and worked up some generous assessments of our South Coast Choral Society. He had recently graduated from Harvard (the USC of the East Coast Ivy League?) and studied with Leon Kirchner. His opinion if I recall, was that Kirchner was a good guy who suffered angst. Like he said, I don't know why I'm alive—that, I recall, was the sentiment, if not the words.

Before long I discovered I could take any music course I wanted to without being a music major—and I wouldn't have to suffer the requirements of the Music School.

So I changed my major to Communications. All three of our daughters chose this college major.

The first unrequired music course I took was the best. It was the film music class I had with Miklos Rosza, the film composer of *Ben Hur* (Academy Award), *The Lost Weekend* (nominated), and a passel of other period costume pieces. He was an engaging teacher, the kind of guy from the real world who enchanted the class with anecdotes and practical suggestion for writing film scores.

The film we scored for was given to us from another class. There were perhaps eight to twelve of us in our class—a rare exclusive experience at SC. We were each assigned a section of the film to score. We each manned an instrument or two so we also provided the orchestra. As I recall I was the percussionist—my talents as a real instrumentalist being somewhat wanting. The upside of playing the French horn or trumpet was that you had a lot of notes, whereas the percussion was predominantly rests. So it behooved me to count like crazy—never my forte. Shades of my wandering mind while being read to as a child.

Further rumination makes me think I played only peripheral percussion—woodblocks, cymbals, chimes, gong, marimba perhaps. But the incessant counting of rests made me edgy, and God knows how many cues I missed. I have a dim memory of the teacher cuing me—he was the conductor—but the same God knows if I came in (timidly to be sure) at the right time.

AUNT JEAN (& UNCLE CLINTON, OF COURSE)

Aunt Jean was my favorite. An aunt, certainly, but a pal nonetheless.

And I done her wrong.

And she almost killed me.

The scene of the crime (hers, not mine) was Saylors Lake, up country Pennsylvania—a car ride of thirty-five miles, perhaps an hour and a half in those days—before World War II—in the thirties car, and on the rudimentary roads which were barely kept up.

My crime was later, during the war, at Aunt Jean's gas station in Emmaus. It was Uncle Clinton's gas station too, but he was off in Uncle Sam's navy.

When I do the math now, I realize Uncle Clinton and Aunt Jean were nineteen or twenty years older than I was. But when you are four or five years old that doesn't register. They are full-grown just like any garden-variety adult.

Sailor's Lake itself was glacier cold. I don't remember the temperature specifically, but I figure it just had to be cold, fifties or so. As an adult I drove by the "cabin" we all stayed in for those summer family outings. It belonged to Grampop Knoll, Mother's father and Clara, her mother, though there was little community property nonsense in those days in Pennsylvania. Of course Gramma Knoll worked like a slave for her joint enterprise with her husband in the Broad Street Hotel in Emmaus, and she worked like a slave cooking for the multitudes at the vacation cabin in the woods outside Stroudsberg. Some vacation.

When I was small, the cabin seemed large. But when I drove by it as an adult it looked tiny. In those days we must have packed from fifteen to twenty people in there and I can't see how that was possible. I can only imagine three bedrooms at the most, no attic or basement. There was a decent sized living room, a long kitchen and eating area the length of one side—an outdoor privy—indoors; no running water or electricity. Nighttime illumination was by kerosene lamps and water was fetched at a community well, a half block or so from the cabin. Yet, I don't ever remember being crowded or uncomfortable. It remains a mystery.

Aunt Jean and Uncle Clinton had no children. Uncle Clinton was not modest about his escaping three marriages without the burden of progeny. In retrospect Aunt Jean was able to indulge me with her maternal instincts.

She had diabetes, a mysterious malady to me at the time. I knew she had to be careful what she ate and had to inject a mysterious medicine called insulin into herself, and if she ate sugar bad things might happen. But I dearly loved Aunt Jean and I didn't want her to die. Her life expectancy was at that juncture was about thirty-six or ten years more.

The folklore has it that Aunt Jean's parents laid all this out for Uncle Clinton as a cautionary tale about what was in store, and, subtly or not, recommended against the marriage. Uncle Clinton is reported to have said, "I don't care, I love her and I want to marry her."

And marry her, he did. I don't think he ever regretted it.

And Uncle Clinton was a gentle, loving soul at home—though I imagine he was a terror in his work—management and labor union battles were his bag. I remember being surprised in his telling of visiting the Nevada legislators with a bag of money. The sums given to each seemed unrealistically modest. One or two digits. Perhaps it was an age/memory glitch.

I expect I was four or five when Aunt Jean, amazed that I didn't know how to swim, took it upon herself to teach me. We walked the block to the lake and I must have been excited, if not a little fearful of how I would learn. If I had ever been in a body of water larger than a bathtub, it was probably no deeper than my knees.

What was sweet, loving, loveable Aunt Jean's method of teaching a four year old to swim? She threw me in and hoped for a miracle.

It didn't happen. I was terrified I was going to die. I had no idea how to get my head back above water.

None.

I thrashed and grabbed for Aunt Jean's arms but they weren't there. If I got any closer to her, and I have no thought that I ever did, she backed away. She was—for this eternity—always beyond reach.

Since I am apparently at least partially alive to tell this tale, she must have fished me out in the nick of time. I must have sputtered something about her letting me die, to which she responded there was no danger of that. She seemed so sure. I with my lungs bursting was far less sure.

After that she taught me in a more civilized fashion, hands under my belly as I lay on the water paddling and kicking per her instructions and begging her not to let me go.

My recollection is Aunt Jean and Uncle Clinton lived at the Broad Street Hotel for a while, then moved a few blocks to the town triangle in an apartment above the bank.

I visited there (I suppose I was being babysat) and she gave me lettuce with mayonnaise and I thought I was in heaven. I kept asking for more and apparently she had more because she never seemed to run out. (The same gluttonous performance was played out with Grampop Knoll and chicken noodle soup.)

When World War II came Uncle Clinton went into the navy. His older and younger brothers were somehow exempt. Flat feet? Partial deafness? Uncle Clinton was the second of three boys. Mother and Aunt Verna were older.

Shortly before the war Uncle Clinton and Aunt Jean bought a gas station on the main street in Emmaus. It was perhaps one block from our former Main Street house. This was a town of six thousand souls, give or take, and there may have been one other gas station at the time.

When the war came gas rationing came with it. Books of stamps were issued to car owners who couldn't exceed the amount of gas covered by the stamps.

The station was a short four or five blocks from home and it was a real treat for me to go there because, among other things, Aunt Jean sold candy bars. Being the saint that she was, she would give me a candy bar when I went to visit. This contributed in no small way to the "treat" of visiting her.

Now I expect I am eight or nine years old and given to excess as I was, and a penchant for sweets, just one candy bar didn't seem enough. So I did the next best thing—I helped myself to one or two more. Perhaps one at the start, then escaping detection made a bolder snatch at two.

Of course, the inevitable happened. Aunt Jean was no dummy. She must have had a sense of how the candy stock was diminishing beyond the sales. So the confrontation, "What's in your pocket?"

Face flushing to red, "Nothing."

"Let me see," she said.

Clever kid that I was I pulled out the empty pocket.

She was *more* clever.

"Let's see the other one."

Now a fire engine would look positively pink next to my face color.

I fumbled around—put my hand in the offending pocket and announced with maximum trepidation, "There's nothing in there."

She looked at me skeptically. She knew better. She knew I knew. May she be blessed for all eternity, she let it drop.

I never stole another thing.

After the war Uncle Clinton and Aunt Jean sold the gas station and moved to San Francisco where he became head of the California/Nevada Employers Council representing employers in labor disputes. And he *lived* the job. Soon thereafter they moved to Reno.

I found a guy my first year at USC who lived in Reno and I hitched a ride during a break—Thanksgiving or spring? I took a share of the driving while the Reno car owner went to sleep. Before long I had burned out the engine. We were in the heart of the Mojave Desert. I've always remembered the equanimity with which the car owner received the news. To be sure there was a touch of aspersion about my driving too fast (undeniable) but he focused on getting us out of the mess. We had to hitch a ride to town some considerable distance from the car, then negotiate with a garage to tow it and fix it, then I caught a bus to Reno while he nursed the car back to health. I never saw him again, a condition I don't think he was at any pains to lament.

I believe the trip from USC to Reno was the last time I saw Aunt Jean. My memory is not as firm as I would like — perhaps because I had no idea it would be the last time.

She got eight or ten years more than those first dire predictions. On that last meeting I recall riding an inner tube down a Reno irrigation ditch behind their house. It got quite scary (a revisiting of my drowning scare when Aunt Jean let me sink in Saylors Lake?) but now I was a bigger guy and somehow I survived the turbulence.

Sadly I do not remember anything further of Aunt Jean. She was a giant figure in my childhood who faded with the increased distance between us.

Toward her end, Aunt Jean lost a good part of her eyesight. She learned Braille, and typed letters that were not perfect, but decipherable.

What must it be like to feel the imminence of death and soldier on in the midst of certain uncertainty?

Uncle Clinton had a rebound marriage to a woman he claimed was very high up (a pit boss, perhaps?) in Harold's Club — a legal gambling den in Reno — the largest, I believe. It was the site of my first foray into institutional gambling. I liked to say I doubled my money in three hours — as indeed I had. Perhaps playing the red or black in roulette or Black Jack? Whatever, there was no doubt I had doubled my money — I started with one dollar and went home with two. I think I wagered twenty-five cents at a time.

(My prior experience with games of chance was a stint at pulling the one arm of the bandit in an upcountry Elks Club. I was seven years old. Lucky seven. I kept winning money so I thought I was the cat's pajamas. On the way home my father disabused me of this childish fantasy, telling me I took far less out of the machine than those affable club members gave me to put in.

We left the club shortly after we heard a radio broadcast of the news the Japanese had bombed Pearl Harbor. It was December 7, 1941.)

Uncle Clinton's rebound marriage rebounded on the rails in short order. I expect he quickly discovered Aunt Jean was one of a kind, not to be replicated. He later told me his betrothed was a sex fiend who had been married *eight* times before their marriage. I of course expressed my doubt about that, four or five, I said, perhaps the others were just cohabitants.

"No," he insisted, "*eight times*!"

"Nine with you?"

"Nine with me! In those days you had to marry…"

What better place to get divorced than in Nevada, where they happened to live? The sexual romp disguised as a marriage lasted short of a year I believe. I never met this love machine—more's the pity.

Uncle Clinton married his third and final wife, Betty, a good soul, widowed mother, shy with the slightest glitch in her speech, around the time of Virginia's and my marriage.

We met them in San Francisco (we from perhaps Manhattan Beach, California, they from Reno, Nevada) and Uncle Clinton took us to his favorite Italian restaurant where he raved about the spaghetti which we found heavy and barely edible.

Vive la différence.

When we said goodbye outside his hotel, Uncle Clinton turned to Aunt Betty and said, "See, that wasn't so bad, was it?"

I visited them in their Reno home a number of times before and after Uncle Clinton had his stroke. He moved haltingly with a walker. His speech was impaired through his twisted cheek but he was still *compos mentis*. What must it be like to be invalided and live without hope of restoration? Resilience in adversity must be one of man's more miraculous traits. He was always so grateful for my sporadic visits of a day or two or three. Musing how blood was thicker than water.

True. Blood is also more colorful.

As is the lot of man, Uncle Clinton died and in my last phone conversation with him he indicated he was ready to welcome the reaper. He surprised me by telling me he was no longer able to do a bodily stimulation which had heretofore offered him pleasure. He was in his late eighties, crippled from his stroke and I told him I expected he'd gotten more out of it than most.

THE FRAT

We are brothers, now and ever, until the day we die.
—*Venerable Fraternity Drinking Song*

Alas, I must confess, I had a devil of a time getting into a fraternity at SC. This in an era when there was serious glut of fraternities on the campus. Those that seemed to want me held little appeal, while the one I seemed to have some chemistry with couldn't have been less interested (like the boy-girl thing) even after the second visit prompted by the interfraternity coordinator, a funny guy named Ken Shanks. In this case I expect the frat ΔTΔ had the more persuasive argument. I would not have been a "good fit" for a bunch of fellas who got their kicks getting drunk, hazing pledges having them smoke cigars under a wet blanket. But they seemed to have a lot of fun doing it.

At any rate, they had more success than I did in understanding that would not have been the place for me.

I "pledged" the house next door, on West Adams Boulevard. Both houses were the furthest from the campus of any living groups.

ΔTΔ being a frat of BMOC's (Big Men on Campus) and at the forefront of SC's social standing, they produced the Yell King, the head cheerleader for sports events. As I recall it was an elected position. While I had little contact with members of the Greek community after graduation, one did cross my path perhaps twenty-five years after graduation.

It was the former yell king—stellar member of Delta Tau

Delta who it will be recalled rejected me twice. (Yale still holds the record at three rejections.) We were resurfacing the walkways on our office building with a fairly new product—it was colorful pebble sized aggregate which was mixed with bullet-proof epoxy. That turned out not to be that bullet-proof after all, but that's an uninteresting digression.

And who else but our yell king installed the product—on his hands and knees?

I asked him if he enjoyed his work. He said oh yes. He was his own boss, had flexibility and just loved to work outdoors.

Besides, I expect he would never forget the triumphs he had at SC, which had surely prepared him intellectually for his vocation.

Being a member of a fraternity was an experience not to be forgotten nor repeated.

Lambda Chi Alpha, my choice, was so small they were not in a position to be fussy nor unreasonable about the hazing that went with the fraternity pledge territory. To wit: no smoking cigars under wet blankets.

I have modestly left off my resume that I was elected president of our pledge class. We began the semester after rush week with five members of the pledge class. The active member roster perhaps hovered around eighteen or twenty at the time.

In the new pledge class:

John Callos to this day a dear friend who was booted out of school for his activism on my behalf, e.g. flying an airplane over the campus and dropping leaflets that exhorted the landlubbers to vote for me for sophomore class president. It was an ill wind that blew them to Watts, where zero of the students resided.

But the *coup de grâce* was his stringing of a banner across a central campus street from the student union building to the Bovard Auditorium. And it was verily that that done him in.

Those big shots in charge were horrified, HORRIFIED at such anti-social behavior unbecoming a lad with aspirations to being a member of the Trojan family. So there was nothing for it but to remove him for a spell from the academic environment where he was obviously destined to pollute the delicate minds and souls of the innocent students. He took this opportunity to unencumber himself of his obligation to the military, where he acquitted himself sufficiently to lasso an honorable discharge whereupon he returned to the frat just as I graduated. And he, unlike I who shucked the whole thing on graduating, became a motivating force in the frat, the alumni association, the housing corporation, you name it. A credit to his pledge class.

Joaquin Gil del Rio: from Panama. Not only did he see the pledge class through to membership, he graduated from old SC and plied the prodigious knowledge gained therein to a career in Panama City as a stockbroker.

Les Biller: was a kick in the pants. Not a guy to take anything too seriously, he dropped out before pledge hell week. Showing once again not everyone is without judgment. He decided he was an artist and indeed painted a prodigious number of canvasses with blobs of color and riots of shapes, the understanding and appreciation of which were far beyond my comprehension.

UCLA thought he was the cat's pajamas and hired him to teach art—some feat I suspect, without the bother of advanced degrees. Our frat brother Tony Ward, attorney at law, loved Biller's paintings so much he actually *bought* a bunch of them. I hope he got a frat brother discount.

Tom Kornegay: a guy in the Navy ROTC who actually made it through to graduation as a Marine officer.

There were three votes cast for president of this mélange, and since I either abstained or voted against myself, I won the post. Coasting, perhaps on my two high school presidencies. I'd like to say the other two recognized my innate leadership talents, but I expect neither of them wanted to be bothered either so they ganged up to dump it on me.

The hazing of the pledge class was called Hell Week for obvious reasons. They kept us up all night doing ridiculous chores, gave us each a verse to spout about ourselves whenever bidden— mine had one phrase I remember:

"Whose sophistry stupefies all."

I expect I had to look up sophistry, but found it surprisingly and enormously flattering. I remembered it, didn't I? And I remember something about being lower than whale shit on the East Coast of Siberia when the tide is out and the wind is favorable.

The appeal of the frat after all was said and done was that it was a cheaper living alternative than a dorm or an apartment off campus. Of course there were downsides—you began rooming in the attic with perhaps six others. The hotshot rooms on the second floor were given over to upper classmen. There was a single room off the kitchen that was occupied by our resident weirdo, Elmer Post (may he rest in peace—and thank goodness). He was a graduate student transfer from some Podunk institution and it is from this remove not clear to me that we had an option of not taking him. Of course, we were so desperate for members we would have taken an elephant—which coming to think of it, Elmer resembled.

He smoked like a chimney and meddled in all his "brothers'" affairs—e.g. he would spirit away the mail and parcel it out if and when it pleased him. This after he had read it. He always seemed to be around, I wonder if he actually took any classes? He could have been a total con—I doubt anybody would look a gift horse in the mouth to ask for proof that he actually was a λΧΑ member.

I am as certain as I can be that Elmer was the cause of the disappearance of my high school yearbook—with personal notes and signatures of everyone in my class (one hundred twenty-two others). It was in his nature to disdain this kind of attention to anyone else. There is no doubt he roamed the premises looking for mischief.

While I was a pledge, there was a hush-hush meeting of the actives. An accusation from Elmer cost us a dearly needed member named Don Rocco who was on to Elmer and not the type to suffer fools.

At a fraternity party, the legend had it, Rocco was in his car in the house parking lot with a date. The testimony from Elmer Post, Rocco's only accuser, was that he saw them in the car and "as far as I'm concerned he was screwing her."

Since I was only a pledge and not admitted to this "court" it is difficult for me to understand how this resulted in the booting of Rocco, but it did.

I now wonder if there wasn't some mechanism in place that would have enabled the brotherhood to incise this demon from the ranks. Did no one think of it? He had aggravated *every*body and yet we suffered this transfer fool until he left of his own volition the end of my sophomore or beginning of my junior year. I never retrieved my yearbook. I hope he enjoyed it—though I expect the real pleasure he got was throwing it in the dumpster.

It just occurs to me I should use him in one of my mysteries.

One of his parting shots was at John Hvasta. An older guy—war vet we pledged when I was pledge chairman. To carry the flag for our frat pledge a bunch of us went to hear him speak at a large Congregational Church downtown. It was a freedom series or some such laudable term.

Hvasta was introduced as a guy who had fled the communists who were bent on killing him—he escaped prison where he was politically incarcerated and he told a vivid and wild tale of his escape over the countryside until he got to Italy or somewhere where he caught a boat to freedom.

The story was so-so, John was a so-so speaker, but apparently he was a celebrity of sorts and we should have been proud of him—even without our desperation. Until Elmer opened his mail, or simply swiped it from John's drawer.

The letters revealed John Hvasta was a con and that didn't seem to set well with whoever was writing to him—his mother perhaps. The trouble was he was in jail for being a thief, not for being an anti-communist activist.

I can still see our meeting where this was revealed by none other than Elmer Post. Of course, we voted to let him explain before we unceremoniously dumped him. After all, there could have been a mistake.

There was a knock on the clear glass door to our room.

John Hvasta was there to resign.

I was in charge of the meeting and rather than do the honorable thing and say thank you very much—and perhaps we wish you well and we'll miss you—I said, "We just voted you out."

My brothers were taken with my stance and complimented me on my quick (if fraudulent) thinking.

I must just touch on our cook, a delightful Black woman, heavy as can be. If you could cook like that you'd be heavy too. She came five or six days a week—half the membership did not live in the house so weekends were, as they say down at the mortuary, dead. She must have left home in Watts before six a.m. to get the bus or buses required to deliver her at the frat house before seven a.m.

In the morning all the guys who even made it to breakfast were dragging, morose and barely communicado. So I took it as my responsibility to lend some cheer to the proceedings and it wasn't that taxing to get her to laugh.

What a life and burden she had. I expect she was at the house a minimum of twelve hours a day working for a pittance with nary a complaint—it made me feel good whenever I got a hint that I had helped lighten her burden.

She was a wonderful, memorable woman. I was fortunate to know her in my young years.

The state of our fraternity membership, peaking in those years at about twenty-five, somewhere below subsistence level. This caused the interested alumni some alarm as I expect they were expected to pony up the difference between our reality and sought after solvency.

Lou Fetterly was a lawyer and our alumni advisor. Perhaps one of the poniers. What he could have gotten out of that I don't know, unless he got pleasure from looking at young boys, a state at this remove would not surprise me.

I was elected pledge chairman, in charge of getting new pledges. He said we should have a goal of ten pledges. No easy task in the postwar frat glut when we were further from the campus than the other fraternities.

I suggested we needed a draw. We had a perfect place for a

pool in front of the house—already walled. (I forgot to mention the early silent film star, Fatty Arbuckle, lived in the house in his day. Rumor was some hanky-panky went on, but he was acquitted.)

I said, "If I get you ten pledges (I had no idea how I would bring that off—my class had three), would you get us a swimming pool?"

He said he would.

I got the ten—obviously *he* didn't believe I could do it, so he simply reneged. He said all he said was he would consider it.

I was young, but not that stupid. I would not have killed myself for a maybe.

Some years after I graduated they got a pool.

Then the university took the house and the frat was obliged to move closer to campus and the membership shot up.

DATES — WITH PERHAPS A FEW FIGS

Free love is too expensive.

—Bernadette Devlin

There may have been some unwritten rule about the girl not being ready when the boy came to pick her up. It was an opportunity for a parent to give you the once over.

It was Barbara Kuss's mother who did the honors before Emmaus High School Junior Prom. I remember being seated alone with her in their living room. She was an attractive woman herself. She asked me if the girls in my own class and school wouldn't be jealous of Barbara who went to a different school district.

"Gosh, no," I might have said. "I don't think so." Had I been more with it I might have considered strategy in my answer. "Heck, yeah!" I could have said, "but there were just so many girls who wanted to go to the formal dance with me, I couldn't bear to select just one among them. Too many hurt feelings."

The other side of that pose was they were all taken and *no-body* wanted to go with me. It must be acknowledged that I was neither quick nor effective at securing the interest of girls. I thought of all those answers later, of course — sixty years later. Barbara Kuss was beautiful and soft spoken with an understated, engaging smile. As I recall she too had a boyfriend. I seemed to gravitate to girls who had boyfriends. Why? Well, perhaps because the most desirable girls were taken. Perhaps in spite of that I thought one of them might throw her boyfriend over for me.

Never happened.

My brush with celebrity was Barbara Young. It was just a simple evening out at the college hangout, but her father, Robert Young—TV's Father Knows Best, and later Marcus Welby, MD— vetted me before she appeared. He was a most pleasant, down-to-earth guy.

When we got to Julie's, the campus hangout, we squeezed into a small table amid the hubbub. When the waiter came Barbara ordered a beer, I ginger ale. Barbara was startled and quickly changed her order to soda and stood firm against my protestations. I think she was relieved. I found her very amenable. My recollection was she had a boyfriend and perhaps went out with me to see if I might not be a better bet. Apparently I wasn't. On the other hand, she might have been so polite she couldn't say no.

In my celebrity quest, I called another fellow student, the daughter of Danny Thomas, Marlo's sister, I believe. She wasn't in show biz if I recall correctly.

Also very pleasant and down to earth. Also, I recall, pleaded a prior boyfriend. Why didn't I just persist and muscle out the competition? Perhaps because if I *had* that kind of muscle, I didn't know it. Or how to use it.

Joyce Farris, an actress in the summer stock Guthsville play-house.

I saw her in some ingénue role and my heart had an out of body experience.

Why do we get crushes on performers? Perhaps that is why so many aspire to the stage. She was a bit older than I was (okay, six or seven years) but I thought staggeringly beautiful. I left a note with the bartender of the Guthsville Hotel where the acting company was housed. The theater was behind the hotel. I really expected to be snubbed—I'd had my share of it—but was delightfully surprised when she responded she would love to go to lunch with me.

Her father was Editor in Chief of the International News Service, a pedigree that couldn't fail to appeal to Momma Baby and Judgie.

At the country club we swam and rode the seesaw, a some-what compromising situation for a girl in a bathing suit.

To my chagrin, while we were frolicking in the swimming

pool I looked up and saw my mother making a formidable and purposeful descent of the wide and imposing brick stairs that connected the pool to the main clubhouse patio and dining room; a descent of ten feet or so. A guy who is trying to appear five or six years older than he is has no interest in showcasing his mother. Sporting perhaps seventy-five to eighty-five pounds more than was strictly necessary, you might think her simply overweight. But to see her on those steps coming toward you, painfully apparent she was up to no good, she was absolutely Wagnerian.

Brunhilda to the rescue.

I did what any self-respecting young Lochinvar would be forced to do: I immediately set out to hide from her. But where do you hide in a swimming pool? I ducked under the water, but she wasn't fooled. How long could I hold my breath? She could easily wait it out without breaking into a sweat.

When I surfaced for air, there she was leaning over the edge of the pool addressing me as only a mother could.

"I talked to Katherine," she said referring to the club manager, "and she said it's all right for you to sign for a drink for Joyce." I glared my 'get lost' glare at her in vain. She turned to Joyce and said the immortal words that have stuck with me (in my craw to be accurate) for a year or two shy of sixty years. Not only will I never forget them, if I lived another sixty years they would ring in my ears as resoundingly as though I'd heard them yesterday.

"Teddy isn't twenty-one, you know."

The damage done, Momma Baby took her leave. Not only did she put me in my place, she gave fair warning to that cradle-robbing actress that if she proceeded to sinister seduction with her young and innocent first born, she did so at her peril. Momma Baby would not roll over and play dead.

Joyce was sensitive to my feelings in the matter. How could she *not* have known how I felt about that display of maternal suffocation? I hadn't the slightest talent for hiding the stinging outrage I felt. I had gone to considerable trouble to expand and exaggerate my accomplishments so that one year since high school would seem like four — making summer jobs and school jobs appear to be a year or more each. I'd still have been younger, but not so embarrassingly much younger.

At lunch on the terrace — the originating point of Momma Baby's regal descent — Joyce told me how she could have fun with anyone from six to sixty.

It was no secret into which of those extremes I fit.

Janet Picard's real last name was Lowenstein. I discovered that when I visited her modest, furnished apartment in one of Allentown's seedier sections. The lot of a summer stock dancer was not up market. Yes, yet another thespian. There were perhaps four mailboxes. One said Janet Lowenstein. The others weren't even close. When I knocked on the door she answered it.

The relationship fizzled due largely to my inability to connect with Ms. Lowenstein on a practical level. Sometimes visual excitement does not transcend verbal realities.

She had given me an 8 x 10 publicity photo. I was enamored of it. Somehow my father saw it. Did I show it to him to impress him? He made a face at the glamor showbiz full-body, leotard pose of a dancer and pronounced her cheap looking. In retrospect not a wildly inaccurate observation — to which on inspecting the photo Uncle Carl replied, "Are you kidding? You couldn't get anyone this good when you were good yet."

You can see why I loved Uncle Carl.

How do you explain physical and emotional attraction? Do opposites attract? Or similars? Why should girls I was attracted to not be attracted to me? And vice versa.

Years after I remember being gaga over some damsel, I am hard pressed to explain it rationally. What did I see in her? When you subtract the physical, what is left? This conundrum may help explain divorce. Why two people who were madly in love wind up hating each other. Madly.

Chemistry? This is a handy explanation but what does it mean? We are *all* made of the same chemical elements. You don't both have to like basketball or ballet to feel the pull. Nor do you have to *dis*like the same things.

Of course, this pull, whatever it is, is necessary for the prolongation of the species. Whether or not that is desirable is another argument. The earth is scheduled to implode or explode in an unfathomable number of years. In the meantime do we want people traipsing all over, killing each other with ever more sophisticated weapons? Do we want man's inhumanity to man honed to an even finer art?

I think the gods of boys and girls know what they are doing throwing monkey wrenches into these relationships. For I have no idea what I would have done, how I would have survived long-term relationships with many of these girls—or women if you prefer. Perhaps given some encouragement I might have come to those conclusions on my own. But perhaps not. I put the brakes on some of them without realizing why at the time. Perhaps I had some sense of reality after all.

Lee Green:

A Midwestern barrel of bubbly good nature, as though to distract one from her firm, corseted, less than perfect body.

As though her good nature was not enough, she had the most charming mid-western (Missouri or Mizur-ah) twang. And she could sing like an angel.

I took her to a fraternity dance, but when it came time to invite someone to her sorority dance, did she invite me?

'Course not. She invited the *director* of the varsity show, where I had only been the music director/conductor. This is the guy who propositioned me during rehearsals, who I thought was kidding until the out of town rehearsal when the chips were down wasn't kidding. I couldn't imagine doing what he was describing but he took the rejection in good grace.

Dave Worth, said director, asked me if I wanted to take a bow after the overture.

I said I didn't care.

He said it's more professional if you don't. So I didn't.

What baloney. Did he think that would put him in a momentary shadow?

Dave Worth joined a fraternity with good-looking guys and was rumored to have set his sights on a guy who was a dancer in our varsity show. A mutual acquaintance told me he felt some for the prey because the predator, Dave, would ruin him. I never learned the denouement.

Somehow I spoke to Lee about her asking Dave instead of me to her dance. She said she just wanted to know Dave better, etc. All a lot of baloney, I thought. I'd like to say I had been a large spirited person who didn't mention to the smitten Lee Dave's sexual orientation, but that would be wishful thinking. She seemed to take the news with blasé disinterest which just now makes me wonder about her.

For his part, Dave gloried in the situation. He said, "You like Lee, Lee likes me and I like you. Now if we could each only back up a step…"

SC was a large school—tens of thousands of students—and I don't remember ever seeing either of them again. Never found out how the date turned out.

Skipper (Margaret) Spelman (as was the lamented Lee Green) was from Missoura. We had a telecommunications class together. Notice it wasn't called television—not pretentious enough, no academic ring. Lee was big boned and perky, Skipper was small and perky. Some unhappiness with a boyfriend had driven her from her first year at Tulsa, Oklahoma, to USC.

While I had just begun to date Skipper Spelman, I went to the beach with a friend of hers, Jodi Carter.

Jodi had exceptionally fine body proportions. While we were lying on the beach in our swimsuits, she ran her foot up my leg. This should have been the cause of terminal excitement, but I was so shocked I was helpless. This was unprecedented in my sheltered life, but I was in Southern California now and I should have been able to adjust.

When I think back on these relationships, I frequently cannot understand on an intellectual level, the attraction. If it is all Sigmund Freud, how does it get there?

Skipper, too, saw fit to invite someone else to one of her parties/dances. Was it a Missouri syndrome? But with fifty states in the union and ninety percent of the students at USC from Southern California, how did I wind up with two girls from Missou back to back?

I remember the telephone call with Skipper after her other date. I was trying to keep the conversation from my roommate, Bob Chase, a fool's errand, a large guy with a bigger brain who could speed-read like a demon. What I took from the conversation was her date was a guy who liked to party and by implication, I wasn't. Perhaps because I didn't drink.

In her goodbye Charlie swan song she replayed this theme. She said how I was the finest person she ever knew (which I had heard before in similar circumstances) but in essence the market for fine persons was severely limited.

But we had some good times before the breakup. The summer before our senior year we accompanied each to our families and ended in New York where she was catching a plane for a European jaunt.

Before we left we drew house floor plans. I expect it was *her* idea since she was so inordinately proud of her house.

When I got there I was surprised at how modest it seemed, and when she pressured me for my reaction I said, "You drew it well."

Her father was a doctor and I duly addressed him as Doctor. I told her my father dearly loved to be called "Judge." When we got to my house she said, unsolicited, "You drew it well." The statement had a certain bite to it, but nothing like the bite when on being introduced she shook old Dad's hand and said pointedly, "How do you do, *Mister* Gardner."

At least she didn't call him "Ted."

After she left, the grand old judge passed this judgment: "She is a nice girl, but she isn't very bright, is she?"

Well, there are all kinds of intelligence.

Skipper married a Marine. A patriot who no doubt, knew how to party.

* * * *

Diane Disney:

I always thought I'd make an ideal son-in-law. One Old Dad would be happy—even overjoyed—to take into the business—Robert Young, Danny Thomas, Bob Hope, Bill Paley all had daughters within striking age of me. But the big fish was Diane Disney, daughter of the estimable Walt. She was a classmate at USC. It wouldn't be long before I ran Disneyland, which had just opened my senior year in college.

I had a fraternity brother who had been "pinned" to her. An amusing ritual where the frat brothers gather on the front lawn of the sorority and the fella pledges his troth to the girl in sort of a quasi-engagement ceremony that announced to one and all they were "going steady." She wears his fraternity pin on her chest in lieu of an engagement ring. Cheaper too.

The frat brother in question had shared his pin with a number of lovelies before I met him, none of which could hold a candle to Diane Disney celebritywise.

The union was fragile and prevailed no longer than his other dalliances. The wonderful girl he married didn't need his frat pin; she got a ring *and* him. They were married more than fifty years before he died. But I think Diane Disney married a football hero named Ron Miller. So weren't the chances good that she would have preferred me, had we ever met? I *was* in the band after all. Less chance of brain injury.

My fraternity brother in question, Jerry Virnig, had a number of special old cars. If he worked, I saw no evidence of it. He was, rather, I suspected, indulged by his parents, he being an only child. Mom and dad, according to Jerry, had been married and divorced to each other at least three times. There comes a time in relationships where so many unusual things happen that you have to ask yourself how much of what he says is true. Perhaps he was never pinned to Diane Disney.

At any rate, he told me, "Don't touch her with a ten foot pole."

He began to regale me with a story to give me an insight to her character. He was passing out free cigarettes in these little packages of five or so sample cigs whereupon she is reported to have remarked, "I have some."

If I understand the thrust of Jerry's deprecation, it was that she was such a spoiled rich kid she could turn her back on five free cigarettes. This from the guy with a stable of antique cars.

I never found anything in this remark terminally offensive, but he did not seem disposed to introduce me, so I never met her. The cigarette caper didn't dissuade me. I didn't smoke. Maybe she didn't either.

No doubt Disneyland's loss.

It was made up by the guy who preceded me in Skipper Spelman's affections, Bob Matheson, a roommate who became a frat brother. At graduation he was offered a job with AT&T at the then lordly sum of six thousand dollars a year. I myself was already working for CBS at less than half that. My father earned that as District Attorney ten years before. Bob took instead a job at Disneyland being in charge of their sound systems. With a slightly altered turn of events, I could have been his boss, running the entire Disneyland operation. It's a small world, after all.

It could have been smaller.

Around this time I connived to pledge one Gus Antonini to our fraternity. His father was Alfredo Antonini, Music Director for NBC. Surely this would be my entrée to musical stardom as an arranger/conductor. It was at that age my fondest hope.

After I had successfully snagged Gus, he told me his father didn't speak to him. It was a general lifestyle thing. To hear Gus tell it, he had more sensual experiences in his eighteen year old little finger than many of us would have in our lives.

In retrospect I certainly seemed to have a zest for getting some celebrity connection that would magically solve my employment future.

I don't know how long it took me to realize that no one was going to hand me anything. Nepotism was out the question—I didn't want to be a lawyer. If anything was to be gotten career wise, I was left with the option of doing it myself.

I always was a slow learner.

UNCLE SAM'S NAVY

It is upon the navy under the
good providence of God
that the safety, honor, and welfare
of this realm do chiefly depend.

—Articles of War Preamble
Geoffrey Callender
The Naval Side of British History

A QUESTION
OF ATTITUDE

In the era post World War II, and the Korean "conflict" and pre-serious Vietnam "intervention," my number came up at the draft board. You couldn't buy your way out of the service like you could in the Civil War, but you could put it off, famously by going to college.

And while you were in college you could join the Reserve Officers Training Corps (R.O.T.C.), attend a "drill" once a week (which I was able to finesse by being in the marching band) and a class, and the real good news was your junior and senior year they actually PAID you.

Imagine my surprise when I returned to Los Angeles for my junior year at USC to discover my name was not on the list of those favored to advance to the junior year ROTC and beyond, pasted outside the Air Force ROTC Quonset hut.

Realizing there must be some mistake, I alighted on the office of Lieutenant What's-his-name who ran the whole show single handedly. He liked to muse he was the longest first lieutenant on record.

I remember his famous put down of a football player in our class. The burly but young lad posited that Hitler was still alive. When the lieutenant challenged the source of his information, Mr. Pucci (a left guard in a day before wimps when he played offense *and* defense) stoutly maintained he read it in a reliable source.

It took some further cajoling by the lieutenant to squeeze out the name of the reliable source. Finally, the footballer parted with the intelligence: "The Police Gazette."

"Oh, Mr. Pucci," the lieutenant said miserably stricken, "every time you think it hurts the ball club."

I made my pitch to the lieutenant suggesting there was surely some mistake in my name not appearing on the roster of the lucky fellas who were set to start receiving government checks for their loyal service to their country, as well as thanks for the two years we put in harness gratis.

The lieutenant whisked a file out of his drawer. "No mistake," he clucked. "You flunked the attitude test."

"Attitude test?" I said, flabbergasted. "When did I take an *attitude* test?"

"It was part of the aptitude test we gave in the spring. You flunked it."

Herein there ensued a dialog on the tenuousness of such sneaky testing with me more or less ridiculing the notion of an assemblage of words in questions that could predict what kind of success you would have flying an airplane; and the lieutenant was stalwart in his maintaining that you could indeed tell—it had been proven—who would pass and who would fail in pilot training (it was very expensive) and after that who would succeed as a pilot and not plunge his million dollar plane into the earth. By implication putting a strain on the defense budget, as well as the national association of morticians.

Unfortunately I got no credit for trying and at graduation was compelled to weigh my remaining options. They seemed to be the ubiquitous foxhole, or the U.S. Navy. They also had a flight program which offered the handsome additional 'hazard pay' of $100 the month, "with a recruiting office near you." This time I would be armed with the foreknowledge of a hidden attitude test, which I surely would be able to ace with my instant recognition of such tricky questions as: Do you get a thrill out of speed? Does your father own a motorcycle? Would you rather be a fighter pilot or a transport pilot? Are you a snob or a slob? Do you like to take cold showers in the wintertime?

I did gain one thing from the experience. Knowing what to say and saying it were two different things. Pesky doubts crept in. Remember, I was essentially still wet behind the ears, not yet twenty-two at the time of the test. What if I said my father owned a motorcycle and they checked with him? Yes, a preposterous notion now, but I'm older. If Navy pilots had to take cold showers in the wintertime, did I really want to be one of them? Speed *doesn't* thrill me, it *scares* me. Fighter pilot? Landing on an aircraft carrier? Let someone else risk their life. I'd probably have a better chance of survival in a foxhole. So I did my best, which I now realized was none too good, handed in my answer sheet to the petty officer who was manning the recruiting center, and asked when I would find out if I snowed them or not.

"I'll correct it now," he said, and held a key up next to my answers and quickly marked a bunch of them. I suspected doom.

"Well, you passed," he said.

"*Really?*" I pressed. "Did I pass the attitude part?"

He checked the answer sheet. "No," he said, "you flunked the attitude section, but you had enough in spatial relations to pass."

I would be notified in due course when I could begin packing for Pensacola, Florida and the Navy flight school.

COAST TO COAST IN A STUDEBAKER

The trip from Los Angeles to Pensacola, Florida was my sixth car trip across the country. There would be one more.

The trip was made in a late 1940s Studebaker convertible. I was on my third engine in as many years. While my father was Lehigh County district attorney, his friend Ollie Peter was the county sheriff. He was also the local Studebaker dealer. So all our cars were Studebakers while they continued to make them. Mine was one of the last for good reason.

The Studebaker I drove to Florida had somehow developed a vapor lock. This was explained to me, as someone with zero mechanical aptitude, by mechanics and others in the know, as air getting into the line that delivered the gasoline to the engine block where it was burned to spontaneously combust in the cylinder chambers causing the pistons to move up and down which somehow made the car move. If this didn't happen, the car didn't move, or more to the immediate point, the engine would stall. In that year, 1956, there were many opportunities to stop the car on cross-country routes. A lot of stoplights and stop signs, not to mention food and bathroom stops. The method of restarting the engine after one of these vapor lock stalls was chancy, intermittently successful, and annoying.

The Studebaker had a stick shift and clutch. The method of avoiding this vapor lock at a stop was to throw the gears into neutral and keep feeding gas with the pedal. If you had to stop and get out of the car, it behooved you to park on a hill. Restarting was best if you could push the car down an incline where it could gain momentum. You could then put the car in gear and when it was going, take your foot off the clutch and sometimes the engine would jerk to life.

The car was sold to me in exchange for the five hundred, perhaps eight or ten thousand in today's money, I earned by not drinking or smoking until I was twenty-one.

Somehow I made it to Pensacola U.S. Naval flight school nursing the gas line every step of the way. The vapor lock condition was exacerbated by heat so I drove at night and slept in the daytime.

En route I tried to stop at my Lambda Chi Alpha fraternity houses for cheap (free) lodging. The only memory I have is of a frat house in Baton Rouge, Louisiana. The brothers were engaged in a roaring hell week that seemed to go all day long. Though they had given me a bed reasonably removed from the storm center, if I got any sleep, I don't remember it.

1948 convertible Studabaker

PRE-FLIGHT, PENSACOLA

Don't let the Marines kid you with all that rah-rah stuff about being a fast striking, highly mobile force, as a major connected to Pensacola Naval Air Station never tired of saying.

The reason for the Marines' being was to harass the new Navy kids, most of whom had grown up with more advantages (enough by itself for major disdain) and all of which had more education. Their livelihood was one of taunt and ridicule. "You guys look like a Chinese fire drill," or a "monkey trying to f____ a football."

It was my fortune to meet one of these redoubtable chaps early on as I drove onto the base.

I thought I would unload my meager stuff then go into town for a touch of sightseeing.

Alas, after getting my assignment to a room of perhaps five to ten bunk beds, and choosing a bottom bunk—the upside of checking in early—I made my way to the duty officer to check out for my sightseeing in Pensacola.

He quickly disabused me of my ambition. No, I couldn't leave the base. I had checked in and I stayed in until leave was granted to the entire troop, not just one punk who apparently thought he still had the freedom of a civilian. My freedom was restricted to the base. Ignorance led me to check in early as though I was in a resort hotel.

My natural bent to antisocial, I feigned sleep as the new troops arrived. I heard one of them say, "Some don't sweat the program." Oddly, I was complimented. It soon became apparent that many among us were program sweaters. Afraid they might be thrown out of the program if the back of their belt buckle was not polished or the blankets and sheets on their beds were not tight as a drum. To this end a number of the cadets made their bed only once, then slept on top of it.

Our names were posted in the vestibule — mine as Gardner, Theodore Roosevelt 2nd. There was one Black in the class. A cheerful bright-eyed, amenable kid. Everyone thought he was Theodore Roosevelt Gardner.

His last name began with H so I stood next to him in formation. One morning the marine drill sergeant was running off at the mouth as he was wont to do — I don't remember if it was the Chinese fire drill, the awkwardness of the monkey *vis à vis* the football — whatever it was it apparently made me smile.

"You there," the sergeant barked in my direction, "do you see something funny here?" I looked to both sides of me to see to whom he was addressing the *bon mot*. No one was smiling. Eyes forward, the sarge was unmistakably making eye contact with little ole me.

"*You!* Take a lap around the track. Work out that amusement." Natch, I did what I was told.

After I trotted around the track and took my place in the formation, I heard the sarge say, "Still think it's funny? Take another lap," during which I rehearsed, strenuously, putting a frown on my face: which practice I utilized on rejoining the troops.

At the break I asked Mr. H, who had been next to me, if I had been smiling, still being loath to believe I could be guilty of such a breach of military discipline.

He got his patented twinkle in his eye and responded, "Well, I'd say you had a mighty pleasant expression on your face."

My fellow aviation officer cadets were a congenial bunch, a couple cuts above your garden variety college students. They came from all over the country and ranged from the painfully shy (from Washington state) to the boisterous hale fellow from New York. Another notable classmate was Bob Haberstock who was, at twenty-six, with a balding pate, the senior member of the corps. Bob was positioned on the bunk above me. Early one Sunday around perhaps three a.m., I felt a rumble and before I had adjusted to it, Haberstock, Robert's head appeared and he sprayed vomit over my bed and coincidentally, me. I remember the cleanup operation being not pleasant and his apology, the sincerity of which I question to this day. What are the chances a guy could will vomit, and given that, direct it on the guy in the bunk below? Conversely, if you had to vomit, wouldn't you try to get it as far from your own person as possible? But then, wouldn't it be more natural to spray it on the floor rather than on the person below?

Haberstock gave me another cause for doubting his veracity. He asked me to ask my lawyer father what his legal status was in connection to a girl he had "dated" who claimed he had made her pregnant. His opinion was that if she really were preggers, there was a passel of guys who might be responsible. "No kidding," he said, "I'd really appreciate it if you could write to your father."

I did—having an empathetic compassion for my fellow man—though I'd never found myself in a similar fix.

My father wrote back some reassuring words, but I still wonder, did Haberstock set me up so my father would suspect this "I have a friend who…" was me?

As I recall it turned out the damsel in question was not with child—fanning my flames of suspicion. But I suppose one can't be too careful—though an argument can be made that the time for care was *before* the act in question.

After four months and who knows how many unpolished belt buckles later, we appeared in the auditorium for our ceremony granting our diplomas.

A mistake was made between calling of the names and the passing of diplomas. Instead of starting with the A's, they reversed and A got Z's so everyone got someone else's diploma, except the person who happened to be in the dead center of the alphabetical distribution.

Me.

I so hoped that would be a good omen and a guy predicted to have no aptitude for flying would rise above it.

Alas, it was not to be.

I was—see alas above—a terrible pilot. Never again will I ridicule attitude tests. Mine were right on the money. I have come, by experience, to realize there isn't an attitude test written that I could pass.

One of the AOC's (Aviation Officer Candidates) was a painfully shy young looking guy, even for this young bunch of mostly recent college graduates. I don't remember his name or ever speaking to him, but his physical characteristics are as plain to me now as they were then, almost sixty years ago.

But what was most memorable about him is he was our class's first and I think only fatality. This shy boy froze on the stick while landing. It was a psychological/physiological reaction to perhaps his first flight. He crashed, killing not only himself, but also the young father in the back seat who had been his instructor. This instructor was unable to break the hold on the landing stick or to talk his student out of his death grip. If that were not sad enough, the boy's parents were en route in their car trip for a visit across the country from the state of Washington. It was a leisurely pleasure trip, but no one was able to contact them until they arrived in Pensacola.

Another cadet was a devout Catholic who every night before he crawled into his bed made an elaborate show of working his rosary beads, genuflecting and generally carrying on like the most devout of Catholics. He may have been a seminary student for a time.

Those of us with less attachment to religion considered him a fanatic.

This fanatic, doubtless celibate young gentleman, fell in love with a married woman and spent a goodly number of nights off base in the bed of this self-same woman.

It takes, it is said, all types…

Then there was Marty, or something like that. I've forgotten her name but not her person.

Marty was a hostess at a downtown watering hole. She was faux sophisticated. Impeccably dressed and expertly coiffed, she made her living spewing inanities to give the pilots and would-be pilots a touch of the feminine—without touching the feminine.

If she had some other *raison d'être* I don't know what it was. But I adore the opportunity to throw in a little French, it makes me appear so sophisticated.

We baited her mercilessly. I was the worst offender.

She was not unattractive and was within striking distance of our age demographic. (I would guess comfortably in her thirties.) Her hair color was one of our subjects, a reddish hue and could hardly have been natural, though she insisted it was.

"There's one way I can prove the color is natural, but I'm not going to show you."

I wondered, had someone the desire just what it would have taken for her to show…

On our last day, after our graduation from Preflight School, we were invited to pass by the worst of our training sergeants and allow him to congratulate us, and salute us as his new superior officer.

What the parade of graddies really was, was an opportunity to tip the marine who had abused you for four months. It was an honor I declined. I accepted, but I never forgot, the glare I got from him when he realized there was nothing in his hand I shook but my hand itself.

What could he do? I outranked him.

THE ACE OF THE BASE

Lord guard and guide the men who fly
Through the great spaces in the sky.

—Navy Air Hymn

Kneeling down in front of an SNJ airplane, used in our training, with my flight helmet perched on my bent knee, resplendent in my leather flight jacket, I had my picture taken.

It was in celebration of completing my first solo flight. Yes, I *did* complete that without compromising life or limb.

I had every reason to ridicule that ridiculous attitude/aptitude test I had so ignominiously flunked. I *soloed*, flew *alone*. No instructor who knew what he was doing in back. I'd shown them! My picture appeared in our local paper to prove it. Didn't I say all along those aptitude/attitude things were ridiculous? They certainly didn't apply to me. My mother, after all, had always said I could do anything I put my mind to.

I'd proven that flying a plane was no big deal. After all, look at all the people who are doing it. True, it was a little trickier than driving a car, but not that much.

Then several things seemed to conspire against me.

1. In an emergency landing with an instructor in back, I landed perfectly in a field. (The Navy wasn't about to risk life and plane by picking a tough spot for the emergency practice.) There was plenty of room and I acquitted myself handsomely.

Until I took off. Then, unaccountably, the left wing dipped and hit the ground. I certainly didn't do anything to cause the glitch. The instructor said as much, positive it was some atmospheric abnormality, an air pocket perhaps, that caused the dip of the wing which immediately righted itself.

The instructor flew the plane back to the base—just in case—without incident.

Safely on the ground he told me he was obliged to give me a 'down' for the session. Accidents demanded downs. He would explain in his opinion it was not my fault, but the down was mandatory.

Furthermore, accidents were sufficient cause to drop one from the program—if you were still alive to be dropped. He said he would go to bat for me, though in perusing previous assessments of my flying ability, it was short of a sure thing.

2. Formation flying proved dubious, though I passed the requirement I nearly passed out. While flying virtually wing tip to wing tip in the middle of this formation (the value of which was doubtful at best unless you coveted a spot in the famous flying Angels, I looked out at the plane next to me to discover my wing tip was perilously close to his wing tip—what seemed inches from sending us both down in flames. Of course in the shadow of the emergency landing "accident" I had no illusions about surviving the program if I had hit his wing tip as I was poised to do. If anyone else saw it, no one mentioned it.

3. Instrument flying. This is the stage where a hood is placed over the cockpit and you fly solely on the use of your instruments. Mercifully there is an instructor in the back seat who can see out of his window. I expect that simple expediency saved my life—again.

You were obliged to memorize patterns of speed, altitude, the wing angles and distance all the while fixating on the germane gauges. If you have ever engaged in a mental exercise that was beyond your capabilities, you will have an idea of how I felt. I could concentrate on one gauge. I could memorize the patterns because there were at least four more gauges and if I looked at one and it held steady while I repeated the process with the other three, I might have been all right. But that was not to be. Needless to say, I got another down for the performance. Now I am over the limit of downs and I am thinking this career cannot be saved. Even with the argument that my accident was not my fault. Who was I going to blame these failures on? I had visions of finishing my two year commitment in an airless submarine off the coast of Korea.

Then something happened that I continue to list as one of the best things that happened to me in my life. I devoted thirteen months to unsuccessfully disproving the attitude test instead of three years, had I succeeded. I was about to be mercilessly thrown out of the program when miracle of miracles, the government had decreed it was costing too much to train and maintain all these pilots. The conflicts were on hiatus so we were given the opportunity to extend our time to five years after getting our wings, or getting out *scot free*. Note: this did not happen to the classes before us, nor was it necessary after the classes on board. The Navy simply turned off the spigot.

All of us, save two, got out…one was a lad named O'Neill who seemed to most of us the dullest tack in the box academically, but he sure knew how to fly. Though I feel a little sorry for him if he didn't want to remain on board.

The other was a big Texan named Foster Teague who wanted to make a career of it.

Apropos of my aptitude, I like many of my fellows opted to take a private license which was available to those of us who had sufficient hours in the saddle with the simple expedient of a cross country flight, which was one gas tank each way. Perhaps a couple hundred miles each way—I don't remember.

All went well until I tried to land at the designated airport—somewhere in the sticks of the deep south.

I checked the windsock on the ground which indicated the direction the wind was coming from but the plane didn't seem to want to land. I just kept floating, but not touching the ground, which was of course my destination.

As I recall, I landed with a few inches of runway to spare.

This was in a tiny plane that didn't require a lot of runway.

I taxied to the modest terminal building and began the gassing process. Inside a young gentleman had a mysterious smile on his face.

"Did you want to land with the wind?" he asked. It didn't dawn on me what he was talking about for a few moments.

Aha! That was it! The floating, the endless landing, the increasing scarcity of runway. I looked at the windsock as I was taught to do, but my decision based on what I saw was 180 degrees off. One is supposed to take off and land into the wind.

He signed my form without adding any gratuitous comment about how I landed bass/ackwards as my mother used to say.

I qualified for my private pilot's license, got it in the mail, and never used it.

Of course, it's only been fifty-five years. There's still time.

ARE THOSE TEETH HERS?

On an Eastern Airlines flight to Pensacola, Florida, I met the working stewardess, Joyce Chelf. She was attractive to me after a dry spell, had a nice way about her, and was very nicely put together.

She had a heart-wrenching history. Her mother was a wheelchair-ridden invalid by the time Joyce was six, polio perhaps, when her father died. Being the senior child she was tasked with preparing the meals, buying the food and went out to work and earn bread at twelve or fourteen, whatever seems more dramatic.

Is that a story that could evade any heartstrings? Not mine.

Joyce managed a flight that weekend to Pensacola. Sometime later I took her home to meet the folks. There was a family history of the Grand Old Judge coming down hard and negative on my girlfriends, but Momma Baby stalwartly defending them and my judgment in making the choice.

After Joyce was safely gone from the house, mother inquired if she had false teeth. She was five or so years older than I was, but hardly in false teeth territory.

Well, I must have been outraged at the suggestion. "Why do you think that?" I asked.

"She chews her food in the back of her mouth."

"Don't we all?"

"No, you watch her. She pushes the food back right away without starting at her front teeth."

"Geez, you were *watching* that?"

"I saw it," she said.

The Judge, usually the fault-finder sat by smugly, without a peep leaving me to fend for myself with Momma Baby.

"So you are saying you didn't like her?" I asked Momma Baby.

She denied it. After all, hadn't she prided herself in liking all my girlfriends? And that was true. She *had* in the past. But perhaps that was because she thought I was hopeless at the boy/girl stuff, and no reasonable argument could be made against that. Maybe she even bought into the homosexual fear. As a naval officer I eased closer to marriageable age and inclination, and Momma Baby thought it behooved her to get her two cents in.

"All right," she finally 'fessed up, "I don't like her. So what?" Through it all the judge maintained a bemused calm, his only contribution to the drama was to say, "I haven't heard any engagement announcements."

We drifted as boys and girls do. I can't credit Momma Baby's wrath. Joyce had two stewardess roommates and on one overnighter there the two roommates had flights in the early morning and must have cleared the home by five a.m. One made a huge show of placing her uniform and underwear on a chair in the living room, where I was billeted on a hide-a-bed. The conceit was she was going to dress in the living room so as not to disturb her roommate and coincidentally give me an exciting diversion at 4:00 a.m. I expect there was some subplot with Joyce, her sister stewardess, though they all laughed about it. Of course, if she did turn on a light in the living room to give me a skin show, I didn't wake up. I suspect all the thrilling stuff went on in the bathroom.

After I shrugged free of the U.S. Navy, I went to New York to visit my friend from music camp, John Shroyer, a Manhattan attorney. The plan may have been to visit Joyce also, but the time flew and visiting her would have taken two hours round trip, so I begged off.

She was not happy. She said, "I cleaned up so no one would know." Which I thought must have been a colloquialism in her neck of the Kentucky woods. I didn't ask her to explain what that meant precisely. I assumed she meant she had made the place spotless which, with two roommates, was no walk in the park.

I must have continued a correspondence with her, because the three of them showed up in California to visit me. I may have picked them up at the airport in my Volkswagen beetle.

I took them sightseeing to be a good sport, though the bloom was off the rose. I expect we went to dinner. I wonder if I paid or they insisted on "Dutch."

My last memory of them was sitting in my VW in front of my bachelor apartment on Hollywood Boulevard — 7740 — a small apartment building that was razed to put a street through. I proffered a half-hearted invitation for them to come up to my one room digs hoping they would beg off. I wish that had gone a little smoother. I gathered the plan was for Joyce to come up and the others go to their hotel. This lit no fires in my heart, the bloom being, as heretofore mentioned, off the flower.

I'm sure at the roomies prodding my encouragement did not even rise to half-hearted. "Sure...do you...want to?"

"I don't think I should."

"Why not?"

From the Greek chorus, "Go ahead. We'll be okay."

"Do you want me to?" The damsel had looked like she might benefit from an antacid tablet.

"Well, it's up to you. You're the guest."

"I better...not..."

"Well, okay. I guess it's pretty late."

No argument. All three of them seemed to be disappointed — my duty being to make believe I didn't realize it. But there is verily no place to hide in a bachelor apartment.

Somehow we settled it and I breathed a sigh of gratitude as I dropped them at their motel, never to see Joyce again. I have thought of her from time to time, but there was definitely no cigar.

I remember a line she repeated from her stewardess training:

If the pilot tells you his wife doesn't understand him...tell him you don't either.

WITLESS WISDOM TEETH

I have it on good authority that there is no relationship between wisdom teeth and wisdom.

If I have one wisdom tooth left in my face, shouldn't I be twenty-five percent wiser than someone with none, or seventy-five percent less with than someone with four?

But it ain't necessarily so.

Perhaps we should change the name.

I had three extracted in two different circumstances. Both, as is my wont, on the cheap.

The first two in the confines of the USC Dental School where the anesthetic put me out and the procedure was painless — though I bled all night in my fraternity house bed.

The third was under the auspices of the United States government while serving my time in that patron's navy. This was a more rudimentary operation. The dental surgeon on the base of the U.S. Naval Flight School didn't seem to have available the fairy dust that puts you to sleep and out of pain's harm's way. I got a needle instead which numbed the gum, but as it turned out, sleep would have been better. It took three and a half hours and two hackers. First the dentist, then with the assist of the captain, the chief dental guru with hammers and chisels.

Of course in all that time I was awake to share not only the jarring hacking of the hammer and chisel, but the banter that traveled from the hammer man to his chief. It was not an easy task, for any of the three of us. But I got it *free*.

I am assuming that they pounded out every last morsel of the offending tooth — but how would *I* know?

During the other dental work I had done at USC on my

mandatory health charge (was it one hundred the year?) I paid the difference with a check where I left the payee blank. The school had a rubber stamp with their name on it for checks and I saved ever so much effort in not having to write USC Dental School in the payee line.

On one occasion I gave the dental student who did the job the check with the payee line blank and jokingly said, "Write your own name in there." I don't recall if he smiled or not, but sure enough when I got the check back it was made out to him in an obviously different handwriting than my own.

My first big ethical dilemma since I stole candy bars from my aunt's gas station, and since I'd peeked at the winning number in a punch out card I took door to door, selling a chance on the grand prize — which of course I won. I don't remember what it was, because the fascination with it was short lived, not to say that lessened the larceny or absolved me from the evil of misplacing the trust of strangers.

Did I turn him in to the dental school administration? I thought they would throw him out of the dental school and ruin his life because all the time and effort building to the point where he was doing the actual dental work would have been wasted. What he did seemed wrong, but *how* wrong? Was it thirty-five bucks? Fifty-five? I was the judge and jury. Was it worth ruining him?

On the other hand, it seemed clearly dishonest and did we want dishonest dentists preying on society?

And what of *my* integrity? Did I have a *duty* to society to right this wrong? But how exactly would I go about it? I could rat on him and he could riposte in his defense that I *told* him to write his name on the check and he was simply obeying the order of this patient, which could certainly be found in some code of dental conduct.

After some time agonizing I took the easy way out and let it drop.

CBS
THE STARS' ADDRESS

We're not going to pay you more.
If you don't like it you should leave.

—West Coast Comptroller
My big boss at CBS

CBS—ENROUTE TO THE PRESIDENCY

Man is a clever animal
who behaves like an
imbecile.

—Albert Schweitzer

During my senior year at USC I began pursuing a job in the entertainment industry. Television seemed to have the most reliable entry level opportunities. To wit:

Ushers who herded visitors to the audience for shows, keeping them in well-behaved lines while they waited. Perhaps they also led tours of the facilities for those who qualified for that rarefied activity.

My recollection is that it paid about fifty dollars per week or $1.25 per hour for full time work—and I'm not sure all the ushers were on hand forty hours per week. This job required little skill— I'd say zero, but I don't want to be a snob about it. It seemed to be a repository for those fellas (all college graddies I believe) who had connections. I had none. The other option for us orphans was the typing pool. $52.50 per week but you had to be able to type. Fast. I filled the first requirement, but not the second.

Sixty words per minute was required. That's one word per second. Try it sometime. Remember errors are subtracted—so that's sixty *correct* words the minute.

I made the rounds of the TV networks and was treated as a piece of meat by NBC and ABC with half-hearted assurances they would call me (unspoken was "in the unlikely event we'd ever need you").

CBS was different. The employment department director was a nice, eager-to-put-you-at-ease man who smiled and stammered. But I had to get past his secretary before I could be considered.

She was so blessedly cheerful and friendly, and made me feel so much better than the other two networks—though she hadn't really given me much more encouragement. I went home and wrote a letter to the unseen personnel head praising his secretary to the sky for the above-mentioned qualities and adding because of her I would rather be rejected by CBS than hired by the other two networks.

The letter did the trick. I was immediately called back for an interview with the boss and a typing test.

I practiced. I got close. I went to the personnel office where I met the man himself who was demonstrably pleased by my letter (I was there, wasn't I?). My impression was if I passed the typing test I would get the first opening. Typists were from time to time promoted to better sounding and better paying jobs.

I took the test. Close, but no cigar. He let me take it again.

He gave me the good news. Either I passed it with sixty words per minute, or he fudged the results. After all, how different is it if you type sixty words per minute or fifty-six? Chances are when you are typing radio scripts your speed will get up to speed in no time. At any rate, I had the sense I passed it and before I knew it I was hired to work at KNX Radio typing scripts for radio programs that originated in Hollywood at the CBS station on Sunset and Gower, I believe. Somewhere around there.

When I got the job, I think I sent the secretary flowers and a thank-you note. If I didn't, I should have. $52.50 a week was better than zero.

I arranged the schedule for the second semester of my senior year so I had all my classes in the morning so I could make my shift of noon to eight.

I had two bosses which makes me think the department might have been a little top-heavy. One was a thin older gentleman (to a twenty-one year old he was probably an "old" fifty) and a younger guy (thirties or forties?) who was so incredibly polite as though every time he made a request I would be doing him an important personal favor by complying—but only, he made clear, if I agreed with his request. This initiation into the world of big business was needless to say never repeated. I suspected the two male bosses were oriented to favor the male gender. That, I was given to understand, was show biz.

What did I type? Radio soap operas and an extracurricular pitch for investing in cantaloupes at the behest of a minor executive in the radio division.

From time to time job promotions were posted and the typists could compete with the ushers for the spots.

My job description was clerk/typist connoting the lowest of the low.

When I was about to graduate and be available for a full time day job, nine to five-thirty, I saw a posting for an administrative assistant in the Film Production cost control department in the network offices at the glamorous new CBS Television City on Beverly and Fairfax. From Dingy City of the typing pool to the glamorous TV City was an exciting prospect.

In college I rushed fraternities. As noted, it was a buyer's market with a glut of frats courtesy of the GI bill. But most of those soldiers and sailors (marines and airmen) had passed through the system. The university boasted some thirty-five thousand students, of whom only two thousand were full time day students. The music school where I matriculated was even smaller. Could there have been thirty to forty fraternities and sororities on campus?

My father and Uncle Carl had been members of ΦΚΤ. Though he told me all chapters were different and I should not feel any obligation to join just because he had, I went to lunch. A tall, big shouldered guy named Jack Foreman displayed an attractive *joie de vivre*. I remember someone teasing him about a relationship and he said it was all sixes and nines. This guy, I thought must be very sophisticated, far in advance of poor me. ΦΚΤ didn't light any fires in my heart, though I did think Jack Foreman a pretty neat guy. It was the same Jack Foreman who interviewed me for and offered me the job in his fledgling new department. I don't know if the USC connection helped, but I doubt it hurt.

The week I graduated from USC I settled into my new job. There were five of us administrative assistants in Film Production Cost Control whose job it was to track and verify the legitimacy of the costs charged to CBS by the independent movie studios who made the films. The shows assigned to me were *The Twilight Zone*, *Rawhide* and *Gunsmoke* which was winding down after a superhuman run. Matt Dillon, Kitty, Doc Holliday, and was Dennis Weaver Chester? Imagine wanting a career as an actor and winding up in one of those roles for years. The money and security were probably appealing but the artistic challenge I suspect was wanting.

Other shows in the department were *I Love Lucy*, *Perry Mason*, *The Lineup*, *Dragnet* and some pilot films for shows that didn't catch on.

After my stint in Naval Aviation CBS was required by law to give me my job back with all the raises I would have gotten while I was gone, so I'd be making about double the $52.50 per week that I started at.

But I wanted to live in New York. I applied to networks and ad agencies but was only offered a similar job at CBS in its imposing granite skyscraper they call the The Rock for something like eighty-five dollars a week. They were not obligated to match my salary since it was a different location—so I followed the money.

Mercenary qualms aside, I'm not sorry I did.

I have recently been to New York City and concluded it's a nice (frenetic) place to visit, but I wouldn't want to live there.

Back in Television City with the same cast of characters I left, I dug in to prove my worth working longer and harder than anyone else, attributes which were sure to be noticed by the bosses whenever a promotion was a possibility.

In time a job came up in the Standards and Practices department. Censorship. You got to hobnob with producers, vet their films for prohibited practices which seems almost laughable today when almost anything goes.

Charles Marquis Warren, the Rawhide producer, recommended me to Bill Tankersley the head of the department.

I didn't get the job. Mr. Warren called to find out why. He was told I didn't dress very well.

Astonishing. I bought all my suits at bargain prices from the fashion plate in the office, Bill Shelly, who wore them once or twice, then sold them to me for a fraction of his cost. He fancied *new* clothes.

The night before the interview I attended a concert at USC's Bovard auditorium. Outside at intermission a little bird apparently successfully targeted my shoulder.

The Standards and Practices troops were fastidious. I didn't see the bird dropping on my shoulder telegraphing that I was not so fastidious.

In Film Production Cost Control I found myself completing my shows before my fellows completed theirs. Ergo I'd help them out. I had no doubt this carrying of the load would be noticed in my favor.

Wrong.

The world-class schmooze, Jim Allen, got a promotion and an office of his own. I'm still not clear what it meant and what he was going to do in his new job.

A new man was hired for our department. I was delegated to teach him the job. I had two or three years in the saddle, but they paid him more than they paid me. I sought an audience with the company comptroller to plead my case.

"We had to pay him that to get him. Perhaps if you don't like that you should leave the company. We aren't going to pay you any more."

I can't say he didn't make himself clear. I left.

I had been contemplating alternatives. The boss (Jack Foreman) asked me what my goals were in the company. I said that I'd like to be a director of shows.

He said most of them came from writers. I should try to write something.

I wrote a *Rawhide* story and they bought it. The first thing I wrote! I thought I was a genius. They got the story editor's wife to do the screenplay. I didn't mind—though I thought the special expertise that took was exaggerated.

Then I sold them a second story and they let me do the screenplay. I was sure I was a genius.

With the push from the comptroller I left CBS and rapidly discovered I wasn't a genius. I didn't sell another TV script though I had several encouraging agents.

I decided to write books instead. It offered me some integrity.

I wrote ten books before a publisher offered to buy the tenth. It was the thirty-fifth publisher I sent the book to.

After I had left CBS I went to see Jack Foreman who had also left to run Goldwyn Studios. I asked him why Jim Allen got the promotion when I was not only doing my shows on time, but finishing Jim's as well.

Foreman seemed genuinely astonished. No, he said, Jim was a good worker. That can't be. I assured him it was, but I don't think he believed it.

HARRY AND KIPP

The hurriedier I go, the behinder I get.

—*Pennsylvania Dutch Proverb*

Before I leave CBS entirely, I should mention another memorable incident during my stint auditing *Rawhide*.

My main reason for being at MGM was to audit their charges. They had a cost plus contract and I was to make sure they didn't cheat us.

They didn't—but our own person did.

Coincidentally with my job at CBS I was taking night courses at USC in telecommunications. I did a paper on auditing Rawhide and noted some discrepancies in our Production Manager's records.

When the company went on location he was responsible for hiring cattle and paying for catering, transportation and other costs incurred in the production. My job was not complex. It involved checking receipts for expenditures which was simple when a supplier billed us for goods or services. The rental of lights perhaps, or the purchase of film raw stock.

What was less clear was the petty cash account controlled by the Production Manager. There would be tens of thousands of dollars for rental of cattle without any signed receipts.

I was tactfully deferential when I questioned Harry Templeton, the production manager, about these and other large amounts which were undocumented. He was low key and understanding of my inquiries. He told me among other things the ranchers who owned the cattle wouldn't rent them to us if we required receipts because they didn't want to pay taxes. He further told me the cattle cost so much to rent because we ran them hard and they lost a lot of weight and on the market the animals were worth what they weighed and feeding them to get them back to their regular weight was expensive.

It might be noted that Mr. Templeton earned four hundred dollars per week as a production manager (I was making one hundred-sixty by then). He had a Rolls Royce automobile and joined the Los Angeles Country Club (initiation fee $100,000). He also had a brother who worked as an assistant director on the show. Said brother displayed none of these signs of wealth, which could rule out inheritance as the source.

I mentioned the undocumented charges to my boss who directed me to write a report, which I did, and copied it for my Telecomm class toward a masters degree.

The report was sent to the VP—my boss's boss. He called me. That was a thrill of a lifetime for a kid in a room full of desks. He complimented me in a conversation noted for being studded with long pauses from the VP with me wondering if I should be volunteering something, opting instead for only speaking when spoken to. Perhaps this was simply a brush with multi-tasking.

I was assured heads would roll.

Nothing happened. I went back to my mundane auditing. Suspicious excesses continued from the same quarter while MGM treated us impeccably.

About a year later I got a call from my boss Bob O'Neil. "You remember that report you did on Templeton?"

"Yeah."

"Do it again. They want to get him this time."

"It's a waste of time," I said. "Nobody's going to do anything. They didn't before."

"No, no. This time the vice president wants to get him."

It was a new vice president, a delightful, down to earth man from my scant knowledge. I did as I was told.

Now, for the first time I am wondering if they didn't question him and he didn't simply con them as he did me. Though I didn't believe it, perhaps they did. Perhaps he would work his out-door smile on the VP and tell how I was a nice enough kid, likeable and polite and all, but just a kid who never did any of this heavy lifting himself. Gosh, he might say, I understand why you've got to have someone like him snooping around—keeps the studio honest if nothing else—but, between us—he doesn't know TV production costs from shinola.

Not only was Mr. Templeton not relieved of his job, nor even given a tap on his wrists, but he outlasted every other em-ployee on *Rawhide*.

One Friday afternoon the office made a retreat to a saloon across Fairfax Avenue. Since I didn't drink strong spirits I was at best ambivalent about these soirees. Not wishing to stand out for my ab-normalities, I blended into the pack.

There were perhaps six or eight of us, most looking for an excuse to forestall returning to their wives and kids (I had neither, the only one in that condition).

When we were seated at our long table and the waiter came toward us Jim Allen rose to intercept him. He seemed to be having an unsubtle whispered conversation with him and I thought I saw four eyes darting in my direction.

I expect I ordered something clear like 7Up, or water, and something clear came. It didn't take a super perception to notice eyes on me as surreptitious as the lookers could muster. Which is to say not very surreptitious at all. The clear drink smelled funny. A flick of the tongue verified it was booze and I noted a mistake had been made. Instead of my 7Up I got booze. At some point it registered with me that *it was* no mistake.

Jim Allen sputtered how I couldn't possibly tell—vodka had no odor or taste. I couldn't argue that from my lack of experience but whatever this was in front of me had both odor and taste. Per-haps if you had imbibed sufficient strong spirits it deadened your taste and sense of smell so we both could have been right.

The episode put me in mind of Willie Stark, the hero of Robert Penn Warren's *All the King's Men*, perhaps my favorite book.

Early in his political career some of his bosses took him to a bar room and being a teetotaler he ordered a soda pop. One of his elders scoffed and told the proprietor to bring him whiskey. Willie said, "No thanks, a soda pop please." The boss reiterated he should have something stronger. The proprietor said, "I only serve liquor to them that wants it," and Willie got his soda pop.

Jim Allen's aunt was Barbara Hale who played Della Street on Perry Mason, one of CBS's shows. It could have been his entrée to the job and/or his promotion. He left the network not long after I did for, I believe, related work, though I don't remember what it was.

When I was still in college I took an acting class (hope, verily, springs eternal in the human breast). I was, I believe, a sophomore and frustrated at my inability to attract women, or girls as they were known in those days before they became uppity.

In said class was an Irish beauty named then Rita Hamilton. Unless I was mistaken she made an unmistakable and unprecedented play for me. She had sparkling eyes and a pixie sense of humor though she was more voluptuous than pixie of stature.

Rather quickly she took me home to meet her mom and dad. They lived in an apartment building somewhere in the vast city—and it seemed a commodious apartment but it has been my experience since that places often seemed larger than they were. This was perhaps on the order of what we would call a condominium today, with it's own entry from outside, perhaps even their own patch of daisies outside.

Dad was a serious, unremarkable-seeming fellow who had some job with the railroad where he wore a white shirt, jacket and tie. He didn't say much. The volubility in the family belonged to mom. She was a dietician in a schoolhouse. Might have been a hospital. She was a firecracker. Super sense of humor, the perfect antidote to her husband's rather dour demeanor.

Rita, displaying her own humor told her parents I was there to ask her hand in marriage—my immediate thought (fear) was they might take her seriously. But her mother fielded it like a pro, "I don't know," she said, "an arm or a foot maybe."

The Hamiltons were Irish Catholics, but they managed to keep the "be fruitful and multiply" edict in check, foaling to my recollection only three kiddies. An older brother whose biblical name escapes me. I don't think I ever met him. The middle child would have been Joseph who did his duty as a Catholic by managing to crank out eight additions to the population pool in not many more years. A one-man population explosion you might say. That was before he threw it over to marry Carol Burnett, and popped three more bringing the total progeny from that stallion to eleven.

He was a singer/arranger for Burnett's TV backup vocal group and something must have clicked.

I remember loaning him my Rimsky Korsakov orchestration book, which took forever to get back. Said he couldn't find it. It was out of print and irreplaceable at the time. But after some years passed he found it and I got it back to savor until my house burned down some fifty years later.

I visited Joe Hamilton in his basic office at CBS. He told me he had been made head arranger for Carol and that put him five years or so ahead of what he could expect on his career path.

The next thing I knew he had left his wife and eight kids to marry Carol Burnett. So I imagine his Catholicism went out the window with his wife and eight.

I met his first wife once, she seemed nice and quiet—how could she not having eight kids in perhaps ten or twelve years?

Rita cast me in the role of stage door Johnny which was okay for awhile—a *short* while—then it got old before its time.

It seems to me I went to see her perform at Loyola College in Los Angeles. Perhaps she had matriculated there, and perhaps she was making the rounds of Los Angeles theater departments. There seemed to be precious little physical romance. As any actress worth her salt, she was self-centered in the extreme. I remember taking her home from some performance or post performance gathering where the conversation centered on parts-I-have-played, replete with dialogue, which effectively shut me out of the conversation. My last part was in *Harvey* and if I remembered the dialogue, I didn't see any opening or necessity in the nonstop conversation to insert it.

We were seated in the front seat of my car and we may have even kissed a little and exhausted the rehash of her play and performance when she fell asleep. That is I *think* she fell asleep for even at the time I wasn't sure it wasn't an act. She was wearing a low cut gown, something you might wear to a prom, perhaps I had taken her to a frat dance, and I thought she might have been giving me the opportunity to do something daring—which was beyond my maturity at the time—though I can't deny it crossed my mind.

It couldn't have been too long before she "woke up" and begged my reassurance that I didn't do anything untoward. Her eyes were sparkling, her lashes flashing. "No," I said, but I expect she knew that.

At Christmas time I went back to Pennsylvania for the holiday, when I returned Rita thrust a gavel in my hand that was engraved

Ted Gardner
President
ΛΧΑ Fraternity

and informed me I was elected in absentia. She expected me to be pleased.

I took the presidency—I can't think why except there just didn't seem a viable alternative. That is, a brother with blood in his veins who might have taken it instead.

Rita Hamilton faded from my life shortly thereafter when I met another girl in a telecomm class. Then Rita reappeared when I was working at CBS after the navy. She had become a *real* actress with a real agent and landed a part on *Rawhide* as a young gypsy. Not a big part, perhaps, but there she was. It happened to be the only location I was on, in Tucumcari, New Mexico, lot of cattle in those parts (unreceipted cattle). She had a new first name: Kipp—she didn't want to be mistaken for Rita Hayworth who I suspect might have been relieved.

We renewed and reviewed old times and it was amazing to realize how little there was to replay.

We had breakfast together on her first day of work. Picture the scene, Tucumcari, New Mexico is not Los Angeles. It isn't even Sheboygan. It is a dinky little town, we were perhaps at the *only* restaurant in town and the waitress had seen all there was to see in

Tucumcari which I imagine could be seen in less than five minutes. She stood over hungry patrons, her pad and pencil at the ready for could it have been thirty years in harness while a vast slice of humanity passed before her? Yet I would venture the opinion she had never experienced the likes of Kipp née Rita Hamilton.

The starlet agonized over the menu which had the standard breakfast fare as befitting a motel dining room in the sticks, some eggs, meats, probably canned, potatoes.

I made my simple order, Kipp was still dithering. She finally came to terms with the offering and it was obvious the waitress was not suffering gladly this young snip who thought her status somewhat above a top box office star, when in reality she was an unrecognizable ingénue with a bit part in a TV horse opera.

Well, she would take the number two special but didn't want hash browns potatoes or the bacon that came with it leaving I can't remember what, but not much. The long suffering waitress gave a tight lipped nod, vastly relieved to be free of the temperamental bit player, and retreated to the kitchen.

When she returned it was with the number two special intact. She had ignored Kipp's orders, perhaps deliberately. Kipp threw a tantrum for the benefit of the room, "I told you I didn't want the potatoes and bacon."

"Don't eat them," the waitress dug in.

"*I don't want them on the plate,*" the ingénue declaimed in her Lady Macbeth mutation. "Take them back and give me what I ordered."

I wanted to crawl under the table and I'm not easily embarrassed. Perhaps if Rita (Kipp now) had mentioned her brother would someday be Mr. Carol Burnett things would have been different. There was someone this timeworn waitress could relate to, but not this young, pretty snip.

The denouement of this scene has faded to oblivion. I could write several:

1. The waitress took the plate back to the kitchen but never returned.

2. The waitress left the plate and Kipp removed the offending food to her coffee saucer or

3.to my plate or
4. scraped it onto the floor and left.

That afternoon Kipp had her scene in the *Rawhide* episode. She played a gypsy fortuneteller and was to throw a knife at the ground and where it landed would solve the riddle, whatever it was. I was on the outdoor set for it.

The director wanted to substitute a rubber knife to prevent a nasty accident. Kipp wouldn't hear of it. She was an actress of integrity after all. Nothing but the real knife would suffice.

"Roll 'em," the assistant director called. Kipp raised the knife over her head and intoned the words she had been given in the script and threw the knife at the ground.

It landed perfectly in one of her feet and she fainted.

Someone rushed her to the nearest hospital and that was the last I ever saw of Ms. Hamilton.

If she ever got another part I never saw or heard of it.

The legendary, omniscient internet insists that Kipp died in her mid-forties. The cause of her death is not mentioned.

PURSUIT OF LA FEMME

I have never, ever been pursued by anyone I wanted to be pursued by. I know how some girls must feel.

In Santa Barbara—a homeless, youngish thirties, not unattractive, woman whose family lived not far from me said she wanted to hug me. It scared me—sure I was bigger—she lived outdoors on the Cold Springs Trail and probably didn't eat too much.

She rang the bell all dressed and perfumed one day, but I didn't open my gate for her.

Sometime later she appeared at the rear of my property. I don't know how long she had to have been waiting until I appeared at the greenhouse, but now (the woman scorned?) berated me for planting thorny agaves on the park side of my fence. Of course I was trying to discourage people from coming too close to our property—and jumping the fence. "*It's illegal!*" she said.

She must have walked more than a mile through untamed parkland to get there, so I tried to be civil. She was a fellow human after all. She seemed inconsolable so after I devoted too much time to placating her, I threw up my hands and walked away. I half feared she would climb the fence and come after me. Not as remote as it seems—in the early days of our occupancy some chap managed to get his motorcycle over or around (or under?) the fence and his tire marks were everywhere, not the least on the steps in the cactus garden.

I have not seen this woman since she berated me for my distance-keeping plants, but when I think of her I think of the sadness of unrequited love. Somerset Maugham did a super novel on the theme—Mildred was her name, *Of Human Bondage* was the title. It was a crushingly sad opus. Philip pursued her like there was no tomorrow, but she kept treating him in a fashion not conducive to encouragement. Some years later someone told me, "You know, Mildred was a guy," letting me in on the author's proclivities, of which I was uninformed.

God knows I have experienced rejection numerous times. The hurt is directly proportional to the investment. On the low side is a few-day build up to asking a girl for a date and having her struggle to reject me without being overly nasty.

Two experiences come to mind. The first was when I arrived at USC and got a job in the university bookstore. A girl came in who took my breath away. Carol Couts was her name. After I sold her her books, I made a note of her name. After work I repaired to the great table in the entry hall which contained the individual schedules of the some thirty thousand plus students registered. I found her and copied down her schedule with the locations and times of each of her classes.

I found some school event I could take her to. Then I stationed myself outside her classroom in Founders' Hall. I'm only sure of three things about the set-up: 1) I'd had a difficult time with the approach. I settled on simple and direct. Indeed, I didn't have the wit to do otherwise. 2) It was a huge class and it seemed I stood there forever—perhaps she was sick or skipping. At the very last moment she sashayed in, an armful of books shielding her bosom. I made my inadequately phrased but over-rehearsed pitch. She paused only briefly in her resolute march into the auditorium, and said in a tone she might have used on a serial rapist: "Do I *know* you?"

"No, but I'd like you to." Now that was a decent riposte. Apparently she didn't agree for she quickened her step to get free of me and find a seat.

At this remove, sixty years, I am ashamed of myself for being demoralized. She may have looked appealing—not glamorous perhaps, but wholesome, but what was under the skin? I can see someone with more character saying, "How nice of you to ask." Or perhaps offering a low key meeting instead. "Do I know you?" and an escape seemed wanting in tact, not to mention human warmth.

Our family had friends in Pasadena, who were kind enough

to invite this vagabond to spend the day with them culminating in dinner. Zwahlen was their name and they had a son a touch younger than I was. Wonderful people. Mom and pop had a house trailer business, sales, remodeling I believe. In her formative years Hazel toured the country putting on plays with local talent. She stayed at my grandfather's Broad Street Hotel in Emmaus, Pennsylvania when she hit that neck of the woods.

Jack, the man of the house, was an easygoing friendly sort who was ten or fifteen years younger than his wife—so we all expected she would die first. Not to be. She outlived him by, could it have been fifteen years? I went to his funeral, probably after I had moved back to southern California after my charmed Navy stint.

I remember Jack telling me while he was growing up he had to get out of bed early for work and school, so he vowed when he grew up he would never get out of bed before eight o'clock, and he brought it off.

Carol Couts was a Pasadena girl. Pasadena for some reason experienced a housing bust. So the Zwahlens were able to pick up a two story mansion for $35,000, about a third of what it had sold for prior, before people the race of our 44th president moved to Pasadena from Watts scaring the local gentry into visions of bottomless property values. They sold and skedaddled. The Zwahlens not only stayed put, they traded up never experiencing a moment's remorse.

Hazel Zwahlen must have asked if I had any girlfriends—a frequent question for young fellows. I must have regaled her with the saga of Carol Couts (I wonder if anyone ever called her Couties or a cutie Coutie? I hoped so).

Hazel confided in my mother via long distance telephone circuit—a fairly expensive proposition in those days—that the Couts family owned a gas station in town, the implication to me on rehearing it, that they were not socially up to snuff and I didn't miss much.

Gas in those days was a lot cheaper, twenty-five cents a gallon.

SC was so large, I don't think I saw Carol Couts again.

The second unrequited love was a CBS receptionist who

sat at a lone counter at the inside entry to the inner sanctum. I thought she was knock-out gorgeous. Of course I didn't have the sophistication at the time to realize that a woman that gorgeous in a piddly job like that was not hired from the general public for her brains. She was moderately pleasant as we passed her going to work and leaving, but again, hardly a recommendation for a relationship. Once I got a grip on my fear, after a number of dry runs, I asked her out.

No, she said. Marginally more pleasant than Carol Couts. Marginally.

I didn't require a lot of encouragement in those days so I didn't give up after the rejection for a specific lunch. I inquired about other possibilities. No, she said with her languid voice. No.

I don't know what in the world I would have found redeeming besides her beauty, but when you are young, beauty seems everything. There were more interesting girls, but physically they were not enticing. And perhaps they felt the same about me.

LITTLE
WEDDING BELLS

Ring in my heart.

—*That's for Sure*

PAY DIRT—
THE REAL THING

Virginia and I go way back—back further than two people can go. It began with our fathers in law school at the University of Pennsylvania. They were both members of the James Wilson Law Club; they played poker together and my father lost. So before I realized—before I was born—the marriage was arranged to satisfy the debt.

If I had been the girl and Ginny the boy, the result would have been similar, if not precisely the same—the marriage was foreordained before either poker player was even married.

My parents, being six years older, married first. They attended the marriage of Eugene Kennedy Twining to Martha Colley, Virginia's parents, in a picaresque church in suburban Philadelphia.

Martha had no middle name. Her father, Robert House Colley, captain of industry, thought it was superfluous to give a girl a middle name since she was destined to marry a fellow which would give her three names—and ensure that the Colley would endure and not be dropped in favor of Ann or Jane or just such a frivolity.

Little did he know his only child would have string of names to choke a horse before she was finished marrying. Four fellows in all—making her Martha Colley Twining Fernading Curts Hilton. Whenever the opportunity arose—and sometimes when it didn't—I used 'em all.

I'm still not certain which accrued to her credit more, the fact she could get four proposals of marriage, marry four times, or get free of four, by decree (two), or death (two).

Martha's father, Robert Colley, rose to be president of Atlantic Refining Company (East Coast), an oil company that merged with Richfield (West Coast) to become the Atlantic Richfield Company. The fever of acronyms took over in the modern age, rendering the company ARCO.

Martha's mother, Mabel, died in the flu epidemic when Martha was young, eight or ten. Mabel was the love of Robert's life. He used to drive her to dances in a horse and buggy, then wait patiently outside for her to have her fun, then took her home.

He was a serious man who told Pat and Mike Irish jokes. He was born in Connecticut and the Irish were their Blacks.

Before she died Mabel made Robert promise to marry her friend, Louise Smith. He promised.

And he went through with it. Robert H. Colley was a man of his word. His new wife was solid, no-nonsense matronly. Mabel knew what she was doing: forestalling her own husband from making a fool of himself chasing young, sensuous women.

The only fly in this ointment was at that very time Robert H. Colley acquired a new secretary who rather quickly stole his heart. She *was* young and pretty—down to earth and while his second wife filled the bill strictly speaking, she wasn't very amorous. Woods were filled with girls like that she said. But Robert with his still burgeoning red blood cells wanted to visit the woods.

And for many years no one was the wiser. Robert got Franklin Roosevelt to appoint him to some petroleum advisory board. It gave him opportunities to cavort with his secretary in Kentucky—where she stayed when he got promoted to president and moved to the home office in Philly.

They must have agonized about taking her with him, but decided it would be just too suspicious. It wasn't done. Perhaps had he asked, she would have gone, but her home was Kentucky and she liked it there.

Years later it came to a head.

Meanwhile, both the Eugene Twinings and the Ted Gardners sturdily married and living in the same Pennsylvania county, Lehigh, it was inevitable there would be social interaction. The women both joined the Allentown Woman's Club, the men, the Lehigh Valley Bar Association. By virtue of their livelihoods the men were bound to run into each other in court.

They were both fortunate in the depth of this thirties depression to be appointed to sinecures: Eugene K. Twining to the Wage and Price Stabilization board and Theodore Roosevelt Gardner I the U.S. Commissioner (Federal Court's public defender). Both men had some in-law help. Eugene K. Twining had what passed for a wealthy father in-law who wasn't averse to lending financial help when called for. Theodore R. Gardner I's father-in-law was an operative of the Republican Party, had a successful, if small, hotel, and was able to throw work his way. Both our fathers weathered the storm.

Virginia's mother liked to tell about seeing me in my crib—knowing me before she knew her own daughter. She also claims I hid when she came to call...so my attitudes go way back.

Mother says I was born on the hottest day of the year, July 20th, 1934. I can't dispute it. It was apparently a long, arduous birthing process which led me to later say I was a thirteen-month baby.

Later, when I was perhaps four or five (Virginia would have been one year, nine months to two years, nine months) I had my first stage experience. I was a goat in a Christmas pageant at the Allentown Woman's Club. Was Martha Twining in charge of it? I have a memory of her having some connection.

My costume was made out of gray cardboard, fashioned to

suggest a goat. I suppose I was one of the animals that paid court to the baby Jesus.

If I saw Virginia at that juncture I couldn't have been less interested. At the time she was just a baby. I was a sophisticated actor of four or five.

Sometime later she had grown into a real person with braces on her teeth and a book under her arm while I was traversing the country club swimming pool.

Since I spent most of my time in the water, rather than out, I recall her pausing poolside to lean over and introduce herself. She was attending the private George School, a Quaker concoction down Philadelphia way and allowed, in answer to my question, that she liked it. The only drawback was she didn't have time for outside reading. If I'm not mistaken the book under her arm—okay, probably in her hand—was *Gone With the Wind*. You might have heard of it. I wonder if I had. As noted, I was not much of a book reader, having read my first book in the fourth grade—a condition not much improved by this time, perhaps five years after that. But I might have seen the movie, though I saw very few in those years. Later at USC I met Cammie King who played the five year-old Bonnie Butler in the movie. Cammie wrote a lovely autobiography which I read after she died too young in her seventies.

I have another dim memory of Virginia at our house with her mother. They spoke of her horse, Reds, and I was dying to ride it while she was away at school, but it never happened—probably because I was too shy to ask.

Then my senior year in high school, Virginia's sophomore year at the George School, I wrote and directed the smash-hit musical *That's for Sure*, and performed it two consecutive nights in the school auditorium. Sitting room only.

My mother, who wrote the libretto and the song lyrics beat the bushes for an audience—and as with most of her endeavors, was successful at it. Two of the audience snagged in her net were Twinings—mother and daughter—as well as a strapping lad named Bob Phillipson, who was squiring the daughter at that juncture.

They offered some kind words at the performance conclusion and that Christmas I received a card from Ginny Twining as it was de rigeur to call her then. It was a brief but welcome note to remind me how much she enjoyed the musical.

Fast forward to California six years later. I was working for CBS at the MGM studios. Ginny's mother called up and asked for a tour for herself and Maynard Campbell—an interior decorator from Pennsylvania. I'm sure the gratitude expressed was adequate, but Maynard asked, "How's Virginia's vagina?"

I thought I must have misunderstood him. But then I couldn't imagine what sounded like that that might get him off—hook-wise.

The Twinings had a floppy eared beagle, built low to the ground—or was it a dachshund? They named it Maynard—though I was told in no uncertain terms the reference was to Mayard G. Krebs, a character on a TV show—could it have been Dobie Gillis?

Not long thereafter I got a call from Ginny—who chatted easily and amiably.

I finally offered the possibility of a dinner. For lo and behold, she had obtained a job at the Architects and Engineers Service *across the street* from CBS Television City. The small world became even smaller. She said, "I was thinking we could go somewhere Dutch."

A nice thought.

We went to a steak house that I favored, perhaps on Sunset Boulevard. It was a congenial evening and when the bill came I didn't have to arm-wrestle her for it. By that time I was probably making one hundred fifty dollars or so a week, while she was getting half that and she had to throw her car into the mix.

She was interested and interesting and *bright*, I always liked bright. She was so well read she could converse intelligently on any subject. By now she had graduated from Smith College as one of two botany majors. She was delightfully modest about her achievement. When someone asked her where she went to school she replied, "A small college in Northhampton, Massachusetts...called Smith." The initials of her alma mater were SC. Ditto mine. Another bond to go hand in hand with Pennsylvania, Lehigh County—our fathers' law school camaraderie, the country club, our mothers' women's club and what have you.

The Architects and Engineers Service was—I wouldn't want to call it a scam—but I'm searching for a kinder word. Illusion? Ephemera? Built on hope taking precedence over experience.

Young, attractive, well spoken, preferably Ivy League women were hired by two older women, sisters, unattractive in body and soul, to huckster building materials to, well, architects and engineers. The pay was low and required a car for them to hop from one office to another, laden with material samples and specification literature. The conceit was the girls would sit with the architect (and/or engineer) and extol the virtues of the products they were representing—hence the young, attractive requirement.

In practice the architects who had enough work to profit from their service were usually too busy to listen to the pitch so they just left the materials organized in a drawer or on a shelf where it was probably never looked at again.

Lonely, idle architects (and engineers) were often happy to schmooze with the girls, but since they had time that wasn't otherwise put to use in the service of their profession, scant benefit of the service accrued to the patrons.

But, it was a living, more or less.

Meanwhile, I was whiling away the hours across the street—and across town at MGM making conscientious preparations for the day I was in the first rank of television writers.

Didn't happen.

My unrequited genius in this line is covered on other, gloomier pages.

PAY DIRT—PART TWO

In the section titled CBS—The Stars' Address, I relieved myself of the rationale for relieving myself of the company. This was during my assiduous courtship of Virginia Louise Twining. Notice how her mother broke with her family tradition of not blessing the daughters with middle names. Virginia landed Louise from her childless step grandmother whom the kids called Nana. Virginia's ten year younger sister, Patty, was actually Martha Alice for Patty's Aunt Alice and Martha—get this—not for her own mother but for some distant great aunt or something.

Aside: I also had a sister ten years younger than me, Audrey Ann was her name, but we didn't have a tradition of depriving the girls of middle names.

During the courtship I went to see Virginia's father in his law office in Allentown, Pennsylvania. He seemed laid back, perhaps less than enchanted to spend these few minutes with this awkward kid who very well could wind up married to his daughter Virginia—who was named for the woman who became the lawyer's second wife. The gal who had been the maid of honor at his wedding to Virginia's mother.

He had sired four kiddies from the first union—the *bride* in his first wedding—but none with the maid of honor—his second nuptial stop. (There was a third.) This seemed fitting for a guy who engineered the first divorce in the Lehigh Valley among our acquaintances.

After my interview with Virginia's father Eugene, he passed the word that I was nervous. I had no sense of this at the time, but I suppose it would not have been unusual.

Back on the West Coast I proposed marriage with a self-conscious—dare I say pretentious—prose poem. I hope I had it memorized but I fear I read it. As I recall I ended the reading with, "I love you dear Ginny," or some such unoriginal twaddle. But it was good enough for her and we moved to the preparation phase where, both being first-borns, we agreed to please our mothers with big shows in the homeland.

Muhlenberg College where our fathers had met was the scene of the crime. The chapel was an imposing structure giving full-blown gothic cathedrals a run for their money.

Cousin Mervin—Judgie's oldest sister's oldest son—was the first choice to run the show. He was a Moravian minister who at the time was posted somewhere in Florida. Later he was to run the whole Moravian shebang.

He decided he couldn't make the trip so the dubious honor of officiating fell to my fraternity brother Lloyd Saatjian who I later introduced to Martha Elliott whom he married.

John Callos, another fraternity brother and early school chum of Lloyd's, was also in the wedding party. Neither asked me to be in his wedding.

My groomsmen were rounded out with John Shroyer, a New York City attorney (wills and trusts) with the firm old Tom Dewey headed after his ignominious surprise defeat at the hand of Harry S. Truman; Doc Graul, my revered "Uncle Carl" and my brother as best man.

I asked my childhood friend Jeb Backenstoe, a local attorney in the throes of a race for state assembly, but the wedding ceremony conflicted with a local parade for Richard Nixon's failed race for president against JFK, a political necessity he didn't feel he could shun.

He later wistfully asked who the best man would be and I wondered if I had selected him instead of my brother Jim, if he would have shunned the parade.

When he married a year or so before I did, having no brothers he had selected Carter Buller, a local attorney/socialite to be his best man.

As I may have noted, my father and mother attended Virginia's father and mother's wedding, but the Gardners' own nuptials were in front of a justice of the peace with one witness, comprising the entire party.

Which may beg the question—had there been a proper ceremony attended by a churchful of pals, would the resulting marriage have been happier?

I doubt it. From my vantage point—long in tooth—it seems that less than happy marriages are the rule, not the exception. I don't mean to suggest all marriages are dreadful, though enough of them are—to wit the divorce rate for starters—but too many of them are something less than joyous. My own, despite some mundane bumps in the road was, I venture, good. Virginia may have a different slant, but I credit her with her first class temperament for seeing us over the waves.

There is a saying about marriage that it begins in the same bed, then in time reverts to single beds, then separate bedrooms— to which I added if you could afford, separate houses. After forty-three years or so we got separate houses.

About which, more later.

THE WEDDING MARCH

Virginia and I got hitched at the Muhlenberg chapel without a hitch. The hitch came at the reception.

The magnificent organist played a piece I wrote titled "Virginia" to astonishing effect— it sounded far better than I ever imagined it. He had a connection to Albert Schweitzer, however tenuous and played for him or studied with him?

It opened with a plaintive love theme that some years later Andrew Lloyd Weber copied note for note in his hit song, "Memory" from *Cats*.

Eat your heart out Alfredo Antonini and the NBC orchestra. But really, I had no idea Weber was even at the wedding. He would have been twelve years old and was living thousands of miles from Muhlenberg in Allentown, Pennsylvania, but stranger things have happened. With zillions of combinations of the twelve-tone musical scale, combined with infinite rhythms for that many notes, you could begin to believe that it couldn't be a coincidence. After the soothing melody my piece segued into a melody reminiscent of the martial arts built on a pedal point of the doxology. Weber's piece drifted to some saccharine sentimentality.

Symbolism abounded, whether or not the composer grasped its significance.

There was a glitch with this fabulous organist. Somehow I got the news he had not been paid. I checked with him—this is weeks after the honeymoon—and he, with gracious understatement, said nothing was left for him.

I verified this with my mother-in-law and that was the case. I don't know if she thought that was someone else's responsibility— she and her father did foot the considerable bill for the country club reception. She showed no signs of wishing to rectify the slight.

So heroically, I did it myself, though I imagine the fifty dollars involved (some five hundred dollars in today's bucks) was no easy matter at the time. The things we remember fifty-three years later.

The little organ ditty was reprised at the wedding of Reverend Lloyd and Martha Saatjian which I found flattering. Then, as though that weren't enough, on the couple's thirty-fifth or fortieth anniversary, I snuck a copy of it to the organist at his Santa Barbara Methodist church where someone tipped him off at the last minute so he could ooh and ah appropriately. As I recall he had me *stand* in the congregation—never one of my favorite activities.

The Allentown Cadillac dealer had loaned us getaway cars for the trip from the church to the country club. There were telltale indications on the cars of where they came from, fairly blatant advertisements. I trust license plate frames were to be expected, but not the stickers on the windshields setting out the price, the extras, tax and license. Did we take them off or live with it? There are verily no golden apples.

Eugene K. Twining was given his due at the church—he walked his daughter down the aisle and dutifully answered the minister's question: who giveth this woman, etc. "Her mother and I do." Whereupon he slinked into the pew behind his former wife and next to Virginia's namesake.

His comeuppance had to be postponed to the reception. My memory is the Lehigh Country Club could seat and serve around one hundred fifty wedding guests, but this maximum number required two rooms, and though the opening between the rooms was generous, it still left a feeling however subtle of eating either with the wedding party or with the servants.

Do you have to guess who graced the servants' venue? None other than the father of the bride and the maid of honor at his first wedding.

A scene was made—a bid to get him and his admitted to the inner sanctum—and you don't have to speculate—rebuffed by the man's former wife and one could expect her father and main support and footer of this considerable bill—even without anything left for the organist.

What was not generally known by the assembled guests of the Twinings' was that Martha herself had snagged a second husband—no mean feat for a woman of fifty some winters. He was a handsome devil with an easy way about him. But less generally known was the man had psychological problems. Not known at all was the shiner she sported in one eye and valiantly covered with partial success with makeup was given to her the night before the wedding ceremony by the very man she had married a few weeks before so she might have a *husband!* for the show.

Her story was not a very convincing one in hindsight—she said she was putting her suitcase on an upper shelf in her hotel room when lo and behold it slipped and fell on her, the corner hitting her eye. And this companionship/showmanship cost her twenty-five thousand dollars ($400,000 today) from her divorce settlement. Through it all she would never complain that the financial loss was not worth it—so vital were appearances.

Of course, appearances being what they are, the sponsor of the wedding reception Robert H. Colley sat in upright dignity—he was a short man, rendered shorter with age, in excellent shape and he had exemplary posture, with a closely held smile.

He was angry at Eugene K. Twining for leaving his wife for her maid of honor whom he had entertained in his home for godssakes. He himself was loyal to his second wife Louise Smith Colley whom he had married at the behest of his first wife as she was fading from the landscape in the flu epidemic.

Louise was older and matronly, but perfectly presentable so I expect his mind was on his pretty girlfriend in Kentucky while he was harshly judging his former son-in-law for leaving his daughter. Robert himself may have preferred his Kentucky gal, but he kept up appearances with Louise, or beloved Nana. Why couldn't his son-in-law (ex) have done the same for his daughter? Robert took a vow till death do us part, and he stuck to it—in his fashion. He *did* stay married until Louise died. The hanky-panky with Miss Kentucky notwithstanding. So those were the warring factions at the reception. It is amusing to think of John Fernading the assault and battery affectionado being Robert H. Colley's (somber captain of industry) son-in-law. Colley was so much better off with attorney Eugene K. Twining—though he may not have realized at the time. Fernading, to put it gently, was unemployed. I have no knowledge of his ever holding a job. He was the adopted son of someone deep in the Cudahy family—the Chicago meat packers.

I neglected to mention Ginny's brothers Michael and Stephen were also ushers, and so seated at the head table. The boys were as different as they could be with Steven the younger earning a master's degree in finance from the Wharton School in Philadelphia, while his brother, Michael, I believe, had to be bribed with a sports car to get a high school diploma from his second or third private school.

Robert H. Colley did not approve of Michael's lifestyle. He was child-free in his first marriage to a photographer perhaps ten years older. Her first husband had minor celebrity status. It was a short marriage. Nicole was next. Her mantra was, "Someday I have got to get myself organized." She never did, but bore him a son and daughter. The daughter was killed in Mexico in an auto accident with Nicole's father. She was four or five years old. The son, Tiki (Nadir really, which seems an unfortunate choice for a young man) who in the event seemed to try to live up to his moniker—he dropped out—worked off and on as a telemarketer to earn his bread and drugs and when they looked for him to lay on his great grandfather's bequest, he could not be found. He did at least one stint in jail. He is, as they say, incommunicado.

Nicole had a number of subsequent children—one or two of them she graced with the last name Twining. It was at that juncture still her legal name.

Michael's third wife—a Santo Domingo Indian squaw, hefty as all get out, who had in her checkered career, given life to a half-dozen or so children—a few of them apparently with known fathers. Marriage for the most part was not troubled with. We were led to believe *he* married Delores, as she was called. They produced a delightful daughter named Barbara who was set back traumatically when her son hung himself. At some point she married the boy's father. She later, thanks to a bequest from Robert H. Colley, became a nurse. I expect she is a good one.

Mike's fourth wife, Barbara, is his longest relationship—more than thirty years. She had a son who OD'ed. She was the former mayor of Corrales, New Mexico.

As is the custom at weddings, speeches were offered by sundry members of the party to the captive audience. Ginny's brother Michael made a toast to "all you good Democrats," to the frozen silence from the rooms full of Republicans (with the exception of him and his father and stepmother). Mike was such a maverick.

Grandpa Bobby said aloud to Ginny, "I didn't think he would do that to you." To which I, the sniveling, attention seeking malcontent, interjected to my lingering discredit and shame, "What about me?"

"You too," he came through.

Was I trying to make sure he and they realized *I* was a Republican?

The night before the wedding I was obliged to share a basement room with this maverick—as all the good rooms were occupied by important people.

While Michael had four wives Stephen had only one—a conventional French woman whose mother and father (a retired French government servant) gave them financial aid, and she—Marie France—worked for the French Embassy in Los Angeles—a press attachée at a good, untaxable salary and benefits that can only be bestowed by a benevolent socialist government.

Monsieur Biet, Marie's father, worked in customs in Marseille for the Vichy government. When I visited him in his country apartment in France he showed me his copious collection of Nazi helmets. My first trembling thought was that he picked them up on the battlefield after a bloody skirmish. I asked him, I suspect awkwardly, where he got them. Without showing any discernible shame he said, "From the German officers." I don't have a real sense of how palsy the Vichies were with the Nazis. Perhaps they thought it necessary for survival and it is no stretch to believe that might be right. I have read that the number of Frenchmen in the French Resistance during World War II was miniscule.

Before we leave the country club and the main players, let's glance at the marital histories of those *dramatis personae*:

> Maid of Honor: Patty Twining Pitt—divorced
> Best Man: The Honorable James Knoll Gardner—divorced, remarried for more than thirty years
> Mother of the Bride: Martha Colley Twining Fernading Curts Hilton—thrice divorced, widowed, remarried
> Father of the Bride: Eugene Twining—twice divorced, widowered
> Handmaidens:
>> Joan Miller—twice divorced, remarried
>> Alice Miller—divorced
>> Audrey Gardner Racines—married fifty-plus years
>> Ann Van Vleck Webb—separated
>> Suzanne Spector—divorced
> Ushers:
>> Michael Twining—thrice divorced, married to fourth thirty-plus years
>> Stephen Twining—married forty-plus years
>> John Shroyer—never married
>> John Callos—divorced
>> Carl Graul—married fifty-plus years

So among the fourteen participants in our wedding fifty-three years ago, ten divorced: three three times, one twice, or a total of seventeen divorces out of fourteen principals.

To put divorce in perspective, the Twinings were the first divorce in Lehigh Valley, Pennsylvania of anyone I knew. In our town of Emmaus, there were zero divorces—though my mother considered it, only to be talked out of it by a lawyer who said her husband could hide his assets and she would get nothing. Though in my judgment that was not in his nature. He was too jealous of his reputation to muddy the waters with a divorce, or to stiff his would be ex.

Before leaving the wedding reception, a few fleeting memories—Johnny Callos making a spectacle of himself dancing with the bride, tilting her back, kissing her. She was a better sport than

I was.

He and Rev. Saatjian had plans to travel to New York state and perhaps elsewhere, but John was seized with homesickness for his girlfriend, Linda Lathrop, so he cut his and the Reverend's trips short and flew home.

He married the girl, had three children, one a successful moneyman, one a schizophrenic man, one a well-adjusted woman. He divorced Linda.

Someone loaned us a car to travel to New York City where we stayed overnight in a lovely apartment which belonged to Ginny's stepmother, I believe.

Michael, the card, Ginny's brother who far surpassed me in the number of his relationships with women, left suggestive notes all over the apartment. I expect he thought they were funny.

We flew to Miami the next day where we climbed aboard a ship arranged for us by my parents, the selection seemingly based on price. It was my first cruise and its only saving grace was it only lasted two days.

Perhaps surprisingly in spite of the experience, I became a fan of cruising culminating in a fifty-three day hop from Australia to Egypt. So far glancing every continent except Antarctica.

HONEYMOON—OR LOOK AT THE MOON, HONEY

Our first honeymoon stop was in Port-au-Prince, Haiti, where we stayed at a hotel run by a relative of Theodore Roosevelt's. He regaled us with stories of his beating the president in tennis. If true, he couldn't have been much older than a teenager playing the former president who was on his last legs. It was 1960 and Theodore Roosevelt died in January of 1919, so his latest tennis gigs could not have been after 1918, or forty-two years before we showed up at this Roosevelt's hotel. So if he was thirty years old in 1918, he was playing a frail older gentleman. Perhaps I shouldn't be so skeptical because this Roosevelt was a most entertaining man.

We loved Haiti except I may not have grasped the seriousness of the situation when I wandered up on the lawn of the presidential palace, home of the redoubtable Papa Doc—who got out of there with his skin and a zillion Swiss bank bucks.

I was met with a bevy of rifles pointed by some nervous kids in uniform. Ginny was frightened. I was oblivious. Would it do for them to kill honeymoon tourists?

I decided not to ask.

The kids in Haiti were the most charming beggars I ever encountered. No hard sell, no pitch to save little sis from prostitution, just good-natured cajoling. Always with an engaging smile. In Jamaica the beggars were older and grumpier—all business, almost resentful.

I asked one of the Haitian beggar kids, perhaps a small six or seven year old, to give *me* money. He reached in his pocket and offered me a handful of change which probably on the money exchange market amounted to two or three cents. I hope you will be pleased to know I didn't take it.

But it's the thought that counts.

In Haiti we went to some voodoo ceremony—something to do with chickens, I recall. I expect the audience was largely tourist.

We went on some trek into the hinterlands and as was my wont, I questioned the guide about life in Haiti. He said he couldn't answer my questions because he was not free.

Through it all Haiti was my favorite stop of the three: Kingston, Jamaica; Mexico City, and Port-au-Prince—with Mexico being a close enough second, though the wretched dysentery I must have picked up in Jamaica kicked in to commandeer the first couple of days there. I was scrupulous about drinking only bottled water on the trip, but I always wondered who put the water in those bottles and where they got it.

On one of our plane rides, perhaps to or from Mexico City, the pilot had tuned in election results Kennedy/Nixon 1960. It was inconclusive but a memorable venue. Nixon seemed to be losing. This may have been the presidential election with the starkest personality contrast between the candidates. Kennedy, personable, philandering, matinee idol who had no pressing need to work for a living, vs. the brilliant but bland, tightly wound poor-boy-made-good Nixon who would lose by a hair, then foolishly run for governor of California two years later and suffer an ignominious defeat.

Famously he lamented and blasted the press blaming them for unfair reporting, then compounding his erroneous judgment by announcing the end of his public life with the statement, "You won't have Nixon to kick around anymore." Wrong again. Six years to the day later, Nixon is elected president, four years after that reelected while mired in the two-bit, high school-ish burglary called Watergate, named for the residential-commercial complex where the festivities took place.

I'm sure Nixon had not heretofore had the slightest notion how he or any other president could be kicked not only around, but out of office to boot.

ROLL CALL OF MARTHA'S HUSBANDS

There were the four husbands—official unions blessed by the imprimatur of church and state, and there were, it must be confessed, a number of other fellas—perhaps a testament to the free spirit capabilities of mankind in general and Martha in particular.

My mother-in-law's last known paramour was in the nursing home—a religion based facility where some of the staff who took the dogmas seriously objected to Martha and whatever his name was, sharing her bed in broad daylight and beyond. Privacy was nonexistent—you could close the door but that was about it. Sometimes they neglected to close it.

Some felt there was no harm in it, and even grudgingly admitted that these two souls in their eighties (she was the older) were entitled to this amusement and if they could still get some pleasure from it, more power to them. I was in this camp.

The Christers won the battle. The gentleman's (though some might consider that a mite too flattering) daughters thought the behavior unbecoming for a stallion of his age and station, and yanked him unceremoniously from the premises, where one can imagine him dying shortly thereafter of a broken heart, his daughters being relieved of another burden.

Martha, meanwhile, can be imagined prowling the halls of the home for a replacement of what she liked to call "an admirer."

Martha was a widow by the time she landed in the "retirement" home. Four times a widow—all of her husbands had gone to glory before she.

In reverse order there was the retired dry cleaner whose shop was near the marine base at Camp Pendleton, San Diego County way. Those military uniforms were made of a fabric that seemed designed to stimulate the dry cleaning economy. He was a good guy so his name escapes me—but he claimed to make a pot of money in that line of work. I don't know how he stood the chemicals, but he seemed to have enjoyed a reasonably long life span.

Ed—that was his name. Ed Something.

Ed Something was a kind soul who told me he was legally blind. This I couldn't fathom as he seemed to be able to maneuver okay. He told me things were a blur—as though in a dense fog.

That could help explain the dark, black hairs that protruded from his nostrils and ears. The hair on his head was white—but the facial hairs were those of a teenager.

Virginia commented on them to her mother—who as far as we knew had reasonable vision.

The next time we saw Ed, the hairs were gone. Hilton! That was his name. I felt rather sad that a man his age (eighties) should be subject to the judgment of someone who could be his granddaughter and feel moved to remedy it.

Before Ed Hilton there was Admiral Curts. Could that goon played by Brando in *Apocalypse Now* have been named after him? He, Admiral, was touted for something to do with radar on ships. I don't think he invented it, but perhaps he was the first to use it in battle or something. By the time Martha met him he was deaf as a stone.

By some accident of circumstance I was alone at Martha's Rancho Santa Fe home when he called. I said hello—not an exceptionally creative greeting. The Admiral started in as though he were talking to Martha. *Sweet* talking, if you please. If you've never heard a ninety year-old man flirt on the telephone with an absent eighty year old woman, you haven't missed much. For my part I tried to explain I was not Martha, but her son-in-law, but the dear man couldn't hear me.

"Well, you know," he said, his deep sandpapery voice glided over the telephone lines that we used in those days, "I'm going to the party with the widow, but I'd much rather be with you. I can't wait to see you again."

"I'M NOT MARTHA," I finally shouted into the phone.

He paused. "What?" he said.

I repeated myself, capital letters and all, then added, "I'M HER SON-IN-LAW."

"Oh," he couldn't help but be disappointed.

"I'LL TELL HER YOU CALLED."

I *think*, I satisfied him.

THE SLOG

What is the end of Fame? Tis but to fill
A certain portion of uncertain paper.
.   .   .
To have, when the original is dust,
A name, a wretched picture, and worse bust.

—*George Gordon, Lord Byron,*
Don Juan

THE CHRISTIANS

After I discovered what a writing genius I was and quit my day job, reality encroached—big time. It occurred that a little income, not forthcoming from the TV producers, would not be amiss.

My college buddy, Lloyd Saatjian began his ministerial career as an assistant minister at North Long Beach Methodist Church. His delightful sister Gloria married one great fella—how often can you pair married couples with such superlatives?—George Deukmejian "Duke" on the political paraphernalia. Duke was that rare human being in politics who paid his dues through the California Assembly and made an improbable run for governor and surprisingly won. Perhaps more surprisingly he held his ambition in check and rejected all overtures to take a fling at the presidency. He could have been a contender—the Republicans had been in ascendancy at the time. Today

Republican office holders have virtually disappeared from the California landscape. Perhaps the thing that discouraged him about the presidency was not only the killing campaign necessary to run—from pre-primaries, primaries, then general elections—but if he had been successful he would have had to transfer his household across the country to Washington, D.C., a hot and humid hell hole of a town, not a fair trade for coastal southern California.

Enough stargazing, back to just plain Lloyd who was a do-gooder of major dimensions who decided to devote his life to the ministry of Jesus Christ. The decision in itself was not that remarkable. After all, some twelve would-be do-gooders graduated from the seminary when he did. What was remarkable was he stayed with it. Of the twelve who got their divinity degrees, the do-gooders dwindled to three active ministers in short order, then two and before you knew it the Reverend Lloyd was the last man standing. And for fifty some years he tended his flock, visited the sick, the lame and the halt—loved them, doted on them, gave inspirational vignettes of a Sunday morning that charmed and moved his congregation. He did hospital duty for strangers whenever someone needed bucking up, perhaps had no church of their own—the Reverend Lloyd was there for them.

I once asked him how he got into this life of altruism. "Oh no," he said, "I *enjoy* it. I was on a trip with a Bible group (or some such) when I was a student and I saw so many people in need and nothing makes you feel better than helping those in need."

Money was no concern; he expressed surprise that some of the good erstwhile members of his seminary class lamented the piddly income that the trade bestowed on their servants of the Lord. You'd have thought if money was an ambition they might have made inquiries in the nascent days of their pursuit of becoming foot soldiers for the Lord and Savior Jesus, the Christ.

Lloyd had no illusions himself. He recognized being a servant of the Lord was never intended to be a big bucks calling, unless you happened to be Jimmy Swaggert or Jim Bakker with their pants up.

This digression is to give you an idea of how I wound up in the choir directing racket. It was, if you will forgive the expression, a Godsend while I was weaning myself of pipe dreams and on the road to real employment.

You may well feel this build up was a waste of your time — but what would you rather have been doing? There's nothing on television — hundreds of channels with nothing on.

The Reverend Lloyd's North Long Beach Methodist Church consisted of upper class people, somewhat lower economically. They were in want of a choir director. Lloyd called me and began with the sales pitch that he didn't think I'd be interested. The church had less than a thousand members, the choir usually fielded ten or twelve. But he remembered what a great job I did directing the frat boys at SC in the tryouts for songfest. I hope I mentioned our bid to be among the worthies in songfest did not succeed — no matter. If I wanted the job I could have it on his recommendation. It paid two thousand dollars the year. No benefits, no nothing, just good hard dollars backed by the full faith and credit of the United States government.

If I cared to, I might prepare a resume though he could practically guarantee the job. Just a formality — so the minister and the board (all these churches seemed to have "boards," like General Motors) could see what they were getting.

Goodness, how easily impressed they were.

For my debut rehearsal I counted perhaps fifteen stalwarts, wonderful people to the woman. Sure there were men, just not very many of them. They were good sports, appreciative of my efforts and they worked hard.

As near as I could tell, none of the members of this church suffered a surfeit of this world's goods. But they were good souls. These were the people for whom was coined the phrase, "the salt of the earth."

There was a good feeling among us. I expect they had never had a director who cared so much about making them sound good. And it didn't take that long to achieve a fine sounding group. It began to grow and attract people with voices who learned how to use them. We were one happy group...

Except for Grace Marchant, an alto who was rather disgruntled. Nothing seemed to be to her liking: not the music selected, not the way I directed. She was not a happy camper but she was faithful. Of course with acolytes like that, enemies are superfluous. But in a way the negative members of a group serve a positive purpose—to wit: it doubles the efforts and devotion of the overwhelming positive souls—in this case, all but one. And the good guys grew from fifteen to fifty, with only the lone naysayer.

Grace finally left the choir. Perhaps some other members might have whispered in her ear, "Grace, if you are so unhappy, why don't you leave?" At any rate, she left. So we should have been one big, happy, upbeat positive band of singers. And we were—*except* a faithful, positive, overtly complimentary member heretofore stepped in and took Grace's place. Her name was Carol something. It has been fifty years and I still remember the first Mrs. Negative's name. The second naysayer is less certain.

We put on a pops concert in the social hall. The minister put his fine voice, heart and soul into "The Angel Rolled the Stone Away" with choir back up. Don Cooke was his name. It was an egalitarian outfit and everyone was on a first name basis—except I called Lloyd the Parson and he called me Maestro.

I was able to prevail on him to play his violin at the choir concert. He was shy about this ability and I got the impression he didn't want to do it, but he thought he owed it to me for taking the job. I don't believe he ever played again. He rebuffed all my efforts to play violin/piano duets.

Lloyd left the church after a few years to take a congregation where he was the big cheese. It was in high number streets—perhaps 115th? Northeast of Watts, but not by much. But he was his own boss.

He arranged a musical performance getting together the small churches in his neighborhood and perhaps Inglewood—I was the guest conductor. To help strengthen the men (always in need of a boost) Lloyd, the Parson, sang in the group.

Back at a North Long Beach Methodist Church choir rehearsal, a handsome young woman came to sing. Martha was a good doer and she taught deaf children. Of course a light went immediately on—it was time for the Parson to take a wife. He had come to dinner at our humble abode (four hundred square feet atop

Sunset Plaza Drive) with another young woman whom we may very well have arranged. I couldn't divine her reaction, but the Parson was definitely not smitten. *Au contraire,* he even uncharacteristically, certainly unchristianly, made some comments that would have warmed the heart of the devil. I guess I atoned for the slip by producing Martha for he married her—or she married him—or both as the case may be.

I suppose I had delusions of grandeur and lusted for a large choir of super singers somewhat akin to the magnificent sixty-voice choir of the Hollywood Presbyterian church whose services I attended while at USC. There was a choir directors' clearing house sort of operation which kept me apprised of openings. I went on two interviews.

The first was a large church in Santa Monica. I don't remember the specific denomination. It wasn't of any great moment to a choir director—you used the same twelve tones and the words were interchangeable.

I gathered from the first interview they were not only looking for a choir director, but also a pal who would hang around the place and be a social butterfly. Like a fool I told them I was jealous of my time, but I expected something could be worked out. The making of music was paramount to me, and in that regard I wouldn't stint. All I needed was an audience—a chance to show them what I could do.

Didn't happen. I did have the nerve to call the interview committee chair and ask him, "What happened?" Naturally, he didn't want to tell me anything. Confidentiality and all that. But I pleaded I really wanted to know for future reference. That was when he imparted the intelligence about their interest in the buddy system.

Later I had a similar experience with a group in Palos Verdes called Los Carncioneros. They favored PhD candidates—but at a minimum master degree holders. I recited a list of people they would have had to reject on that basis: Arturo Toscanini, Robert Shaw, Roger Wagner, Giulini, just about every symphony conductor. Ice wise it didn't cut it. People believe what they want to believe—don't confuse them with facts.

The next opportunity I deemed worth pursuing was at the
Westchester Christian Church. It was in the flight path for the Los
Angeles International Airport which intelligence escaped me at the
time. But it wouldn't have mattered. The job paid twenty percent
more than North Long Beach. A jump from two gees the annum
to $2,400.

Their interview committee was copasetic and they offered
me the job. I jumped ship in North Long Beach. I never learned if
Grace Marchant returned to the choir, but on my last Sunday we
had forty-some singers. I was a little sad to leave them, though nobody begrudged me the "advancement."

Between my hiring at Westchester and my leaving North
Long Beach the minister at the former asked if I could drop in to
chat about a few things.

The things he wanted to chat about were the salary. They
were in the middle of their fiscal year and somewhat strapped for
cash. He could almost promise the promised salary would be available in September (this was perhaps March) but in the meantime
he would like to meet my current salary of two gees the year.

It struck me as a rather unchristian bait and switch. I put
on my long face and said, "Gosh I wish you would have told me
that in the first place. I would not have quit North Long Beach. I
am very happy there, they treated me very well. I didn't shop your
salary to them but they might have met it. The *only* reason I have
for leaving there is the extra money you offered, and now you are
telling me you want to renege on the offer."

"Well," he said, "it's only for a few months."

"Perhaps I should stay in Long Beach until you can pay the
offered salary."

"But we need a choir director now."

I must have shrugged my shoulders. I hope I did. "If the
offer has changed, I must change my mind. I'll stay where I am."

He came around. Somehow he must have found the two
hundred or so bucks it would take to make good on their promise.

CHRISTIANITY HITS THE SPOT
TWELVE APOSTLES, THAT'S A LOT
HOLY GHOST AND A VIRGIN TOO
CHRISTIANITY IS THE THING FOR YOU

And so it was in my memory of my choir members. It's been fifty years and more, and it's the names of the heavies that stick in my bankrupt memory bank. Lollie Briscoe and her husband Bob were in the forefront of the contrary faction. There were complaints a plenty. For all I remember they could have been well founded, I just don't remember what they were. But you could always count on the Briscoes to suffer the rehearsals and services with long, off-their-feed faces.

But I do remember some of the sweetheart supporters: Blanche Powers who had a shower at her home to celebrate the birth of our second born, Julia.

Mrs. Gibbs, the minister's wife seemed a good sort in the world of Christendom. You might say he done her wrong.

The organist, Rebecca Thompson was a superb, peachy instrumentalist, a youngish unmarried woman who didn't seem a happy camper. We gave a performance of the Brahms German Requiem as a Sunday morning service. May I modestly say it was a triumph? Compliments abounded, the troops came through with flying colors.

The only one who seemed inexplicably unhappy was Rebecca Thompson, our organist. She had performed splendidly, as she always had, but had in the aftermath of our modest triumph seemed a bit grumpy.

When I mentioned that feeling to the Reverend Gibbs, he opined it was understandable because I had gotten so much praise and attention, she felt left out. Correct or not, that seemed to me a perceptive notion.

The funk passed in good time, as funks usually do. It wouldn't surprise me to learn that at the next rehearsal I ladled the praise on our shining organist.

Is there a danger in us taking ourselves too seriously? But, what if we didn't? What would become of us? A world of bonobos who live for pleasure? And what would be the downside of that? No Beethoven or Abe Lincoln, no Shakespeare or Siggie Freud?

The Westchester Christian Church baptized by immersion, a new experience for me. A curtain behind the altar was parted (like the Red Sea) to reveal a glass front water tank—ostensibly so the congregation could see the baptismee actually under the water, every square inch of her body, holding her nose, her head cupped in the parson's hand (he was in the tank with her).

This was reputedly like John the Baptist dunked Jesus in the River Jordan. It has not been definitively reported whether Jesus held his nose or not.

A white garment was supplied to maintain a modicum of privacy, though it couldn't help but reveal the contours of the body when sopping wet.

I'm so happy I was baptized as an infant with a few dabs of cold water on my head.

In the choir at the Westchester Christian Church was another couple, polar opposites of the Briscoes. In keeping with the good oft interred in their bones dicta, I can't remember either of their names. He was a good guy, more or less taciturn, she was his opposite, upbeat, unfailingly pleasant and outgoing. They were in their late twenties or early thirties (around my age at the time) and I can't remember them ever missing a rehearsal or performance.

At North Long Beach I began a routine of writing an insert to the Sunday program highlighting something about the anthem—a musical commentary.

When I moved to Westchester Church I continued the tradition with the minister's blessing. Sometime later, perhaps a year, Reverend Gibbs who seemed a bit grumpy and out of sorts, told me to stop the tradition. He called my insert a lot of garbage, which I trusted was not a comment on the quality of my writing. But then, we believe what we want to believe. In hindsight I should have realized my days were numbered at that sacred enterprise.

I had initially signed on to direct the youth choir in addition to the adults. That effort did not go well. As pleased as I was with the adult result, I was disappointed with the kids. It was difficult to field a team. The minister's daughter showed up and a handful of others erratically, but making quality music eluded me.

I suppose this was obvious to the powers, and a young, eager man named Byron something (was it Hanson?) was brought on board to inspire the kids. He was closer to their age, was a junior college student, I believe, and he worked cheap. I was an old man by comparison—thirty something, not much at first glance, perhaps, but I was fifty percent older than Byron. He was an affable chap and I recall he did a credible job, though it never seems to be easy to get honey from lemons.

One day, perhaps before a rehearsal, the Reverend Gibbs confided in me that he was counseling a couple. He then went on to explain they were just so different and it was a real challenge to find common ground. One of the couple grew up in the church— the parents were long-time members. They were a happy cohesive family. The other partner in the marriage came from the opposite environment—perhaps a broken home—mom worked—it was just a struggle to get by.

I had no idea why he was telling me this, but I listened politely. He had a bit of a swagger to him—not egregious, but one could imagine him in some other line of work, tuning up his swashbuckling charms.

My distaff said she imagined the Reverend and Mary Ellen (which might very well have been his wife's name) were the most handsome couple on their college campus. Sometime in our musical acquaintance Mrs. Gibbs was riffing on mysterious persons wanting her to be something she was decidedly not. "You are what you are Josephine," she said, "and nobody can change it."

Now I wonder with hindsight of the forthcoming intelligence if she wasn't referring to her husband, the Reverend Gibbs, and his desire for her to be something she was not, nor was she about to be—nor *could* be.

The other shock of my directing career dropped soon thereafter. The heart to heart with the preacher who let me know my services were being dispensed with. He blamed it on the austerity straits the congregation found themselves in. Membership was down, not that unusual in the Jesus business perhaps, but the Westchester Christian was hit especially hard because with the advent of the noisy jet airplane and the church being smack dab in the center of the flight path to Los Angeles International, he too often had to stop his sermon until the heavens quieted down. The choir just sang through it, it being more difficult to pause twenty to thirty singers and start again in unison.

The youth choir director Byron, Reverend Gibbs informed me, would take up the responsibilities of the adult choir. It was an economy move—the finances being so precarious and all, that it really couldn't be helped.

I had managed my income by taking up real estate part time—and in the first six months after getting my license to sell I made three times what the choir paid for the year—so being out in the cold, choir wise, wasn't a catastrophe. It is perhaps telling that an offer for me to reduce my pay was not forthcoming.

The big news came shortly thereafter. It turned out the couple the Reverend Gibbs was counseling—the polar opposites—was the aforementioned couple in my choir and while the Reverend was searching for a solution to their dilemma (irreconcilable differences, if you please) he (and my alto) decided it would be just the ticket for him to leave his wife "Josephine" and children (I think the girl had a younger brother).

It is well known church hierarchies do not suffer these shenanigans gladly. The offender would be summarily dismissed out of hand. Reality in the Christian Church forced the hand in a different direction.

Verily ministers of the gospel of Jesus Christ are not in abundant supply, so Reverend Gibbs and his new love interest were unceremoniously transferred to a tiny congregation in the least desirable neighborhood in Boyle Heights, East Los Angeles.

I was told a year or so later by Blanche Powers the new couple were "happy as clams."

SANTA CLAUS

At our house we were fortunate to have Santa Claus take care of our Christmases. Saved us a lot of trouble.

I still feel sorry for those who didn't believe in Santa and had to do all that work themselves.

Most people who celebrated Christmas put their tree up a week or so before the big day. Santa brought ours Christmas Eve— after the children were in bed.

Santa also obliged with stockings for each of our three girls (of course we had sons too, but we drowned them).

Piles of gifts under the tree courtesy of Father Christmas. If that wasn't enough there were wrapped gifts for each of the seven days after Christmas. We had many memorable Christmases which began for us the minute the kids went to bed. Of course they were probably so excited about the big day as I was as a child that sleep was not easy to come by.

The year of the jungle gym will not be forgotten while memory endures. It was purchased in good time in West Los Angeles somewhere, and delivered in pieces to a kindly neighbor's garage. We could have had the builders assemble the pieces, but it seemed so expensive at the time. And how could I hide such a mammoth structure? Besides, how much can there be to screwing some pieces of wood together? A lot of people do it.

I found out.

I, who had never assembled anything that I didn't have to redo because I did something wrong along the way.

As I recall, Ginny, the distaff who worked her heart out at Christmas, mainly to humor what she considered my brainless excesses, drew the line at decorating the tree on Christmas Eve. No one else we knew did the Santa default with the tree. She let it be known she would gladly help with the tree if it were done within the scope of minimal reason.

It goes without saying she was not going to help with the jungle gym. Why would I even consider it? It was a man thing. And I was perfectly capable.

So after the tree was installed and decorated, our neighbors Arvin O. Basnight and son delivered the pieces to our backyard: sliding board, swing, seesaw, ladder to a little house on top and climbing bars. How hard could it be?

Arvin was the retired head of the Federal Aviation Administration. His college age son had assembled an automobile from scratch.

So when these two mechanical geniuses asked if I would like any help putting it together it pains me to tell you what you already know.

"Oh, I can do it, thanks."

"You sure?"

There, they gave me a second chance to come to reason, and I let it go.

That was perhaps ten o'clock on Christmas Eve.

"Sure," I said. Now if I am asked if I am sure, I respond, "I'm not sure of anything."

I watched them retreat. Sure he put together a car, but this was no car. How hard could it be?

Hard.

It was about three a.m. when I was reading the directions for the final steps when I realized I had done something wrong and to right it I would have to disassemble it and virtually begin afresh. But I was anything but fresh. I had developed a rather wicked cold and the great adrenaline rush about the spectacular nature of this gift from Santa and the joy it would bring the girls was beginning to fade. I could have left it unfinished with a note from Santa saying he ran out of time, then assemble it in the luxury of daylight. Could have – but didn't.

I got it back together sometime after four a.m. and was in bed before five. Virginia was asleep, being a much more rational soul.

I have never forgotten that forty year ago Christmas Eve, nor have I forgotten the excited girls waking me up at perhaps seven with the news that Santa brought them a jungle gym. The memory doesn't fail to set me blubbering and there are tears in my eyes now while writing it.

TECHNICAL ANALYSIS OF STOCK TRENDS
AND OTHER ECONOMIC MIRACLES

I've learned so much from my mistakes,
I think I'll make a few more.

— T-shirt slogan

John Magee wrote a book, *Technical Analysis of Stock Trends*. I read it and became an acolyte.

The gist was you charted any listed stock you wanted to—daily—with high at the top of the vertical line you drew on the logarithm paper you bought from Magee and Co. The bottom of the line was the low for the day and the small horizontal line signified the closing price.

At the bottom of the page you charted the volume for the day. Formations appeared on these charts like the musical symbols for crescendo and diminuendo and when the price broke out of these formulas it signaled the direction the stock headed. This movement was tied to the volume number of shares traded for the day.

Head and shoulders was another recognizable formation—say a stock began at ten and climbed to fifteen where it turned around and sank to the vicinity of ten again. Then it climbed to twenty or so. Then back to ten again, and another surge to fifteen before it retreated and this time sank below ten. That indicated a strong sell signal as it was likely to go lower. At least as low as the shoulder was high. In this example, that would be five.

It sounds like hokum, but in a surprising majority of cases

it worked. So I charted seventy some stocks to get the feel of it—
and to test the hypothesis.

This was in the early days of the marriage to VLT aka Ginny
who often read the quotes to me from *The Wall Street Journal* or
The New York Times. I plotted the prices and volumes on the loga-
rithmic chart (so designed so you could see at a glance the percentage movement of the prices so you got a handle on what kind of
relative gains and losses we were experiencing). This was in the
early 1960s.

After I'd seen a number of these predictions pay off, I
thought it was time for me to make my killing. Magee offered an
advisory service where he sent you, by special delivery mail, his predictions for the week. It arrived on Sunday—the stock analysts having worked all Friday evening to be able to get their
recommendations in the mail on Saturday. It cost $500 a year.
Lordly sum in those years for a young realtor. I observed Magee's
recommendations for a while before I made my plunge.

I must have had *some* success.

Must have!

I must concede the conceit was that there would always be
losses, but you put stop orders when you bought (or sold short) to
minimize the losses. You might have multiple losses, but the
amount you lost would be minimized—a lot less than your handsome gains when one of them worked out.

I remember a lot of losses, but the gains were few and not
startling. I expect I struggled for a while until the big bust with CertainTeed. It broke through a wide crescendo format—dramati-
cally—losing perhaps twenty-plus percent in one day. I put a short
sale offer with a comfortable stop—or buy back order to prevent
wipeouts. When you buy you can only lose what you paid. When
you sell short, the sky for your losses is the limit—it never stops. But
it must not be overlooked—the glitch in this short selling instituted
in the market crash of '29. You are only allowed to sell short on an
uptick. So in order to make the sale, the price must *rise* however
minimally. CertainTeed crashed. There was no uptick until it
reached bottom—so my sell order activated *after* a fifty percent loss
in the stock—but the price rose after that meaning every one dollar

the stock share gained, was one dollar I lost.

Wipeout. That wasn't supposed to happen. But why wouldn't it? Markets overreact—all the selling was done, there was nowhere to go but up and I paid for it. Had it been a buy instead of a short sale, the system would have worked. *C'est la vie.*

I took a trip to Springfield, Massachusetts, the home of Magee's stock shop, the second floor of some commercial building where he sealed the windows so no one in the shop would be influenced by the weather. I assume they counted on everyone forgetting what that weather was when they came to work.

Mr. Magee took me to lunch. A gracious erudite gentleman who repeated the lot of small losses in exchange for fewer large gains mantra.

CertainTeed was an anomaly he allowed.

I had by this time come to the conclusion that you could indeed predict the directions stocks would take by the movements of prices plotted on his charts. What I didn't believe was it was possible to make money doing so. Little freak movements would trigger your sell or buy orders, then the stock would move contrary to your predictions. I suspect the poor man had come to some kind of conclusion like this over the years, but he could only fall back on the mantra of small losses (many) in exchange for large gains (few). What else could he say?

My exit from this get rich quick scheme was cold turkey, decisive. I held onto three stocks for old times sake, I suppose, as well as an inability to countenance the obvious. U.S. Steel, IT&T (International Telephone and Telegraph—now absorbed by some other entity), and Ampex—ditto for some electronic outfit. I sold all three at the *peak* of the market...

...and lost money.

It seems to me I had $6,600 worth of stock at my peak and in 1966 I saw it slump to the neighborhood of $600.

I started putting my loose change in the government insured savings accounts. My father-in-law dubbed this "stupid." After taxes it didn't keep pace with inflation.

Theoretically true until it bought some income property and benefited from the depreciation which sheltered the income from the tax man.

My father-in-law sunk the bulk of his wealth acquired in his second marriage, to his wife's best (and richer) friend, into an insurance company of his own devising. He got additional investors: by this time from his third wife; and his decades long secretary gave him all she had saved in her life. He asked me, and I must say his presentation was a wonder. He wanted, he said, to make me and his daughter this gift. All I had to do was (this had to be dragged out of him) to pony up some thousands of dollars. By this time we had two or three daughters and my thirst for quick and easy wealth had been slaked by my investment failures. So I declined with thanks for his wanting to make this *gift* to us. It was at this time I believe he ridiculed my savings accounts as stupid.

Of course, the insurance company met one obstacle after another and Grampa Gene lost it all. His, his third wife's, his secretary's nest eggs.

I came upon said third wife's son at my brother's inauguration to federal judge ceremony. Something Rapaport, by name. He was inconsolably bitter about my father-in-law, now his stepfather, having decimated his inheritance. He was working at the job my father had early in his career—called U.S. Commissioner then (the 1930s) now with a new title (U.S. Attorney?). It was, at any rate, the public defender for federal court.

I listened patiently. It could fairly be said Mr. Rapaport did not think highly of Grampa Gene and was at some pains to be sure I grasped his sentiments.

I trust I thought at some point, as I do now, that when I lost money, it was my own and not someone else's.

But I did get rich—fairly easily I would say—but only when that fanciful notion was cleared from my consciousness and piling money on money was no longer the goal. I was motivated rather by:

The need to make a living.

To do so as efficiently as possible allowing me time to write my books.

The genesis of this thinking was:

I wanted to earn a living doing what I loved—at the time

writing books and arranging music. This I achieved on a subsistence level directing and composing for church choirs.

Marriage and the family elevated my financial responsibilities but I was not ready to give up my creative dreams now centered on the writing of television shows (I *did* sell two after all — deluding me that I was a genius) and books.

With the second child, Julia, reality encroached. Two hundred bucks a month from choir directing would no longer cut the mustard.

Success I had getting three precincts, heavily Democratic by registration to vote for archconservative Barry Goldwater (carrying all three) convinced me I could sell. Goldwater didn't put a lot of faith in government. His idea was don't expect the government to solve your problems, do it yourself. That appealed to me as I set out to solve my problems.

THE MASTERLESS BUILDER

In my time I have built a number of houses. That number is only five — it just seems like a lot more.

The first was in Palos Verdes Peninsula, which became by popular vote Rancho Palos Verdes during our tenure. Someone commented the new name made it sound like a trailer park, but no matter. Pretension is revered across the board. It did send some of the mail to Rancho Cucamonga, but see above. In my first six months as a part time real estate salesman I earned six thousand dollars which was laudable for 1968. Gas was 25 cents a gallon. Rent on our two-bedroom house in Manhattan Beach was one hundred twenty-five dollars a month.

The next year I earned eighteen thousand for the year. This in a fourteen to fifteen person office where no one else made any sales. So I thought there was nothing for it but to build a house for our new family — mom, pop and two daughters.

I bought the cheapest lot in the new subdivision called Monte Verde (speaking of pretension?). It was a flag lot (looked like a flag on a plot map — narrow 'pole' to the street with the building pad being the flag. $16,500 — one third of an acre including the pole ($16,000 after my generous commission). It was the least expensive lot in the subdivision. (Golf course, ocean view lots climbed to the $30,000's if I remember correctly. This meant you didn't have to be rich to have rich neighbors.)

In some print media I saw a house which struck my fancy. It was designed by an architect below the radar known as Ron Grunt. One of my friends had a riotous time with that name.

Some of us are saddled with awkward names — I know a Fugitt, a Fatzinger and a Sterling A. Fake.

But imagine being on the receiving end of "Hello Mr. Grunt" and hope to see a straight face after that escapes someone's lips.

The house in question turned out to be his personal residence with his wife and possibly some children. It was definitely one of a kind—in more than one way. It was unique and it was the only commission he'd had in his architectural career. I expect he was in his late twenties at this time—I was just past thirty.

Ron Grunt had a physiological aptitude for impeccable posture. His chin always seemed drawn back as far on his neck as possible without disconnecting from his spine.

He didn't joke around much. I understood this when I met his father, a thin, taciturn sort with light, thinning hair, who always had a comb at the ready and seemed to run it through the diminishing hair every few minutes.

I loved the design Ron Grunt came up with: an open ceiling and roof floating over the central core of the living room/dining room and library, with clerestory windows all around under the eaves.

I remember our first meeting with the Palos Verdes Peninsula Art Jury, the body of men (sorry, no women then—1965) with bona fides in the architecture/construction trade. I was so high on the plans I thought the jurors would love it.

Ron Grunt made his serious pitch for the high ceilinged redwood house and I was optimistic—with some of the pastiche ponderous overhang houses being built, how could these jurors not glory in this refreshing contemporary home?

So I was shocked—*shocked* to hear the head guy criticize it. "It looks like Hermosa Beach after the war." Hermosa Beach was a funky beach town. I never saw one house that looked anything like this in Hermosa Beach. But ours was damned for all time.

For our redux with the design review board, or art jury as it very well may have been called, architect Ron Grunt was shrouded in mystery. He sat in the jury waiting room with the plans cylindered in his lap and an inscrutable cast to his lips which didn't alter an iota when I asked if he might share with me his redrawing of the plans. Did I have to buy him a hearing aid? He passed off my repeated requests to see his "corrections" in a manner that suggested for me to see them I would have to wrestle him to the floor and snatch them from his semi-erotic embrace and doubtless kill him in the process. I decided to be surprised.

And I was. More accurately shocked when we sat before the jury and he opened the plans and spread them before the august jurors.

What do we say now? I went "ballistic." Then I'd just say I blew up.

"He didn't show this to me. It's not what I want." If any of my tirade affected my stoic architect, I saw no evidence of it. He was speaking to the jurors as though I didn't exist. And the jurors spoke to him as though I wasn't there. Professional courtesy—like lawyers and sharks?

Of course they passed it in spite of my tirade—or perhaps because of—and why not? The new design the roof and ridge skylight was just like the model house designed by the head of the architecture review board.

And you know what the sincerest form of flattery is.

* * * *

I got through the early conflicts of the building approval process and in order to do it on the cheap, as my economic circumstances fairly demanded, I decided to act as my general contractor.

I got bids and took the lowest ones, a practice I have continued through the four houses I have subsequently built—not always, I will admit, to my advantage. But I *was* consistent. Someone told me you get enough bids until someone makes a mistake. Later that seemed unduly harsh. I got rarely more than three. It's a hassle.

On the other side of bidding I think one is duty bound to take the low one or else why bid? I've heard many variations—get three but eliminate the high *and* the low—take the middle.

Use the low bid to get the person you like to lower his bid.

All this seems to me sleazy ethics. To start you shouldn't ask anyone to bid if you wouldn't use him. These are fellow human beings and bidding takes time and trouble and it is important to treat everyone fairly.

By the time of my final two building projects, we took the low bid and sent checks of appreciation to those who lost the bidding.

In our early apartment days we had a painter, Ray Simikich, who could paint an apartment quicker and better and hence cheaper than anyone else. He told me he bid a great number of jobs and never got any of them. His bid was used, he thought, to get a favored painter cheaper.

The window and door man on our first house in Palos Verdes said he made a mistake. He had been the low bidder and I had signed him up.

Mistakes will happen. The window and door man had inadvertently left something out of his bid. When he discovered it, perhaps half way into his contract, he asked me to pay for it.

I considered it very briefly. As I recall had I granted his request, he would no longer have been the low bidder. Ergo it would not have been fair to the other bidders.

So I said no, we had an agreement which I was honoring, I hoped he would too. And he did. I have often thought of this man whenever I get competitive bids. I expect that he thought I was rich since I was building the house and he was working for me, but on the contrary, I had just squeaked by to qualify for the necessary construction loan, and I didn't really have a nickel to spare.

On my next house I wanted to make sure no one got hurt in this way. What I didn't realize in my naiveté was the other part of the equation—the contractors would not share that feeling and I opened myself to get hurt instead.

I got three plumbing bids on the Palos Verdes house. The low one was C.E. Hutton. Admiral Plumbers was second lowest as I recall. When I told him Hutton got the prize, he asked if I would tell him what his bid was. When I told him he said "I couldn't buy the material for that." I watched the men work and I never saw anybody work so fast. Their speed was almost dizzying. I wondered if Hutton was paying piecework. That might explain his labor savings, but how could he buy material so cheaply?

I became friends with C.E. Hutton—who had a nickname—Pete. His wife's name was Ora Ann which I thought a special name, but she dropped the Ora. Ann was okay, but it didn't
have that zing. The Huttons retired soon after my house was complete and he virtually gave me a five-unit apartment in the Walteria
section of Torrance. They had lived in the largest unit and on retiring moved to the northwest, Boise, Idaho at first, then Washington.
After a handful of moves in the Northwest, Pete died. Ann keeps in
touch—she returned to Boise, a spry eighty years old.

We wrote a land sales contract where I would not get title
to the property until I had made perhaps forty thousand dollars in
payments. I didn't have to make any down payment.

The property mushroomed in value and I refinanced it for
a nice multiple of what I paid. As a thank you to the Huttons for
giving me such a "sweet deal," I sent them a check for ten thousand
dollars when I got the proceeds from the new loan.

Perhaps the most memorable aspect of the construction on
this Ron Grunt redwood house was the concrete foundation. I got
the itemized low bid and it had an item for $110 for stripping forms.
I asked what that entailed and the contractor told me it was remov-
ing the wood forms from the concrete, some reasonable interval
after it was poured. I asked if I could do that. "Sure," he said. "Just
be sure you get them off quickly. The longer they are on the concrete, the harder they are to get off."

No problem, I said. I'll get right to it. And I did. In three
twelve-hour days. And I didn't get them all. I left some food for the
termites. About three bucks an hour and backbreaking brute force
with a crowbar.

When we moved in, Melora, our eldest daughter informed
us in her very own brand spanking new bedroom, "I miss the house
in a Hat-man-hat-ten Beach." She was four years old. Her sister Julia
was fifteen months old, not yet articulate with her opinions.

Mercifully.

JESUS SAVES AND SO DO I

Two young guys did the custom tile installation in the master bath, a sunken tub/shower thing. The tiles were large, daisy-like flowers, orange center, yellow leaves as I remember.

After agreeing to a price they presented me with a schedule of payments which seemed reasonable. I always wanted everyone to be paid for their work in a timely fashion. But I was just as conscientious about not paying in advance. This lesson hit home when I paid a painter in advance, ostensibly for paint, which he never put on our walls.

So as the master bath was nearing completion the tile boys asked for the final payment. I allowed as how the agreement was that payment would be made on completion.

Well, they said, the weekend was coming up and they needed the money.

I stuck to the contract. It seemed so much simpler, not to mention safer.

I left the construction site and when I returned there was an eight-foot cross facing the street outside the bathroom. Emblazoned across these construction site remnants were the words:

TEDDY SAVES

THE WORST

If there is a worse experience in life than buying a car, I have been mercifully spared it. As a result I am prone to hang onto my cars: fifteen years the recent model. I now realize I would be spared this unpleasantness if I simply paid full asking price. But that is not my nature.

I was obliged to take the driving test in 1950 two (possibly three) times until I passed it. Another precursor of a wanting aptitude. The remaining high school years (two) saw me enabled to drive a car, which I famously did to New York City and Carnegie Hall where I inconvenienced a fine gentleman named Paul Sterret whilst suffering him to give me musical composition lessons in the Schillinger System: a system that married music and mathematics (not a particularly new idea) by ascribing values of music—pitch and duration of tones—from random sources—like the serial numbers on currency.

George Gershwin and Duke Ellington reportedly used this system. I guess I thought it was kind of neat but in retrospect might have taken the fun out of it. I mean if the serial number on a dollar bill was writing the piece, what connection did one have with it, really?

As many if not all young fellas get their first taste in the saddle of an internal combustion machine, I drove like a hellion. In my case I don't think it was a macho getting-a-thrill-out-of-the-speed thing, it was rather a lust to reach my destination in the least, most efficient amount of time. I had a few close calls, but no calamities accident-wise. In these years—1950 and beyond—there were no freeways in that neck of the woods and all automotive travel went through towns with beaucoup stoplights. I remember when sixty some years ago stretches of highway were added enabling even faster travel.

Some of my first trips to Carnegie Hall were via the train from Allentown. Then the train service was disbanded and a bus was impressed into service. Then as I was legally sanctioned to drive a car, that mode of transportation filled the need.

The use of a family castoff convertible Studebaker did the trick until I returned to Pennsylvania in the hope, after my fortuitously short Navy flight stint, of finding gainful employment in the Big Apple. When that failed I was obliged to return across the country, and what better mode than automobile? Everyone knew if you lived in Los Angeles you had to have an automobile.

There was nothing for it, but to buy a car with money I made in the Navy—almost all gravy because expenses were nil. Toothpaste and a little soap were about it. Studebaker had taken the hint and closed its doors, driving me elsewhere. I was hardly swimming in money, so my lack of interest in the knowledge of cars drove me to seek out the least expensive new car I could find in the area. That turned out to be a Fiat which must have been manufactured with the thought of taking you from the curb to your garage and back again as cheaply as possible. Anything farther was a calculated risk.

This Fiat, a postwar product of an Italy that had been quickly brought to its knees by our war machine, was certifiably the least expensive car in the U.S. known to man.

For good reason.

But at least driving that toy across the country afforded me the luxury to take my foot off the gas pedal without the car stalling.

You know, those Italians, we joke about them having no stomach for war, were able to string their leader, Mussolini and his mistress, up by their heels—no fuss, no muss.

Where were the tough and efficient Germans when we needed them?

I recall I got about 13,000 miles out of that car before it gave up the ghost climbing one of those Hollywood Hills—Sunset Plaza Drive, I recall.

Now I looked to join reliability with economy. Gas was

twenty-five cents the gallon so the economy aforementioned was in the price of the car. Could it have been $2,500 for a 1961 Volkswagen? At any rate their ads were priceless. The sales manager seemed to have a desk in the basement of the dealership—dark and sinister.

I wanted, of course, the stripped down model—absolutely as basic as it came. And white. I had read studies that showed white was the color easiest seen on the road. My sister argued that was not so in snow country, but it didn't snow in Southern California.

That seemed to pose an insurmountable problem for the sales manager. They were all coming with radios. Everyone wanted a radio. I may have posited that was now everyone minus one.

He made extravagant gestures looking at what seemed like an early computer print out which purported to be a list of Volkswagens sailing the high seas for the port of Los Angeles. There was indeed a white car on the load and he would be pleased to let me have it, but gosh darn it, it had a *radio*, and that would be one or two hundred dollars extra.

"No thanks."

He shrugged.

"Take the radio out. I'll buy the car."

That seemed to stymie him. What would he do with a radio?

"Put it in another car."

Oh, no, he couldn't mess with a car from the factory. It would nullify the warranty. He would knock something off the price of the radio.

I didn't *want* a radio, I told him. And I am just now wondering if that wasn't some point of pride with me? An intellectual pretension? I remember listening to the radio in the fiat (how did I get that? It must have been standard equipment) going to work from CBS to MGM—Unity Viewpoint was an inspirational five or ten minute clip that aired on the classical station while en route. So I suppose my stand against a radio was based solely on the cost. It was perhaps a week's pay.

This was probably an unwitting test of my early salesmanship. He wanted to sell the car. I wanted to buy it but without the radio. You'd think it had been a matter of life and death. Yes, he could order one, but it would be six months till we got it. When I remained adamant—why, is now a question—I can easily afford a two hundred dollar radio, but I didn't think I could then. I was a married man, newly, with a lust for making ends meet.

I think it was solved by his discovery that another dealer had one to my specifications. Why he didn't come up with that earlier I can only imagine was the potential sacrifice of his commission on the radio which must have been twenty-five to fifty dollars. When he finally realized I was hopeless, he threw in the towel. I was perhaps twenty-five years old by now and fought being intimidated into submission by this perhaps fifty year-old bully. Could I have gone to another, more accommodating dealer? I don't remember. Probably not convenient.

A gas gauge was also an extra as I recall—if it was available at all. My car did not have a gas gauge so I was a slave to the odometer—every two-hundred fifty miles rain or shine, whether I felt like it or not, I gassed up the old jalopy.

I kept the car as our only form of transportation for thirteen years and I like to say the biggest mistake of my life was selling it.

Howsoever, I did manage to blow out the engine at around 70,000 miles. It was cheaper to rebuild the engine than to buy a new car, so you don't have to guess what I did.

This was the car that I famously used to sell real estate when the veterans of real estate trenches said you needed a large car to impress clients you were successful. In retrospect the dozen or so salesmen at Crest Realty where I was selling all had large cars. None of them sold anything, so I suppose it might have been something other than the car.

In a way my fellow salesmen were admirable in that they kept at it in the face of continued failure.

It was not until our third daughter was growing beyond the infant seat that I bestirred myself to buy a normal sized car—an Audi—was it 100LS? 400LS? Some numbers, some letters—all immaterial. It was a lemon. I don't remember anything about the buying/negotiating experience—I'm sure I tried to get a better price for that was my nature. But now I can't remember why I even considered an Audi. What did I know about them? Made by Germans? Cheaper than Mercedes and BMW? I do remember it fit the family and we had *mucho problemas* with it. So this was not to be a thirteen-year hold.

In the subsequent twenty-five years, before I purchased the Lexus I have now had for fifteen or sixteen years, I owned three automobiles: a Mercedes diesel, a larger Mercedes diesel, and another Lexus.

On my first visit to the Mercedes showroom I encountered a salesman who may have sized me up as a deadbeat. He seemed disinterested in me and my business. It is an easy psychological pit to fall into for a salesman. I may have broken the ice by asking, "Could you answer a question?"

"What is it?"

"Can you tell me what makes this car worth six thousand dollars?"

He blew up—waved a hand at the car and said, "There it is, that's the price, take it or leave it," and he walked away.

At that time cars were selling at perhaps three to five thousand dollars—this was a thousand or so more and, I wondered (not being a car buff) why? He couldn't or wouldn't tell me. Probably thought I was just some wise guy who couldn't afford it anyway.

I left to think it over. I think I got the Mercedes idea from a fellow real estate salesperson at Crest Realty. When I mentioned shopping for a car she said, "Why don't you get a Mercedes?"

Cost was the first thing that came to mind, hence my visit and gauche question above.

I arranged with the sales manager at Mercedes to get a different salesman. I explained the plight to the new guy and told him I was not used to buying cars in that bracket so I simply asked why it was worth more than the average car.

"Oh," he said, "that's simple—it's excellence."

He let it fall there—not what specifically was excellent—or even above average. So I had to take it on faith and reputation and the car magazines which seemed enamored of Mercedes Benz.

Sold, I called the Audi dealers to see what I could eke out of my lemon. I got low figures that astonished me—but were uniform. Until I got Mr. Candid who told me the pitiful figure, then patiently waited for my inevitable reaction before responding, "You are talking about the worst car ever made," he said. "And you're getting that from an Audi dealer." The candor was unique for his trade—only exceeded by his follow up trying to get me to buy another Audi—which he reassured me was miles better than the lemon I had on my hands.

How could it not have been?

It seems to me the family picked up that new Mercedes in Europe after a tour of the factory in Stuttgart.

The five of us drove it around Europe to a fare-thee-well. In planning our itinerary Bernice Anfuso, shouldering the travel agent chores, opined I had planned too many places—the distances were far.

Knowing it all, I riposted, "Far? Europe is far."

But she was right. We overdid it. There was some shared opinion among my coworkers that the diesel smelled bad. I countered that it didn't pollute because the particles fell to the ground rather than floating in the air.

That may have been, but it still smelled.

The second Mercedes diesel didn't smell as bad. It was more of a deluxe luxury market thing—still with the amazing mileage to be sure, and gasoline had begun to climb in price, increasing the gap between diesel and gasoline. Our first trip in it was Palos Verdes to Santa Barbara and I remember six year-old Julia's vocal astonishment in how quiet the turn signal was. Its predecessor had more of the characteristics of a truck.

Julia herself is now the owner of a Mercedes SUV.

When it was time for yet another new car, I test drove a gas Mercedes—the commodious family number and a sporty thing priced in the stratosphere.

Then, I suppose at someone's suggestion, I tried the Lexus. The sales manager sported a Mercedes ring on his finger. "I used to be the sales manager for Mercedes. Lexus is twice the car for half the money." It seems to me I foisted the first Lexus off on Virginia and went to the dealer to buy a new one.

The salesman let me drive it myself. It was astonishing.

When I returned he asked what I thought.

I said, "I think we're damn lucky we won the war."

For fifty-three years we have owned cars made exclusively by the Germans (VW, Audi, Mercedes) and Japanese (Lexus). My rationale is if we buy their cars they won't start another war. So far it's worked. There have been two exceptions: an EV1 (General Motors), and Jaguar—both Virginia's choices. She being the more sophisticated about cars. The Jaguar was a Christmas surprise parked in the garage and she was led to it by a treasure hunt which had been a family tradition for the girls. Her stepmother had had one and Virginia thought it was the cat's pajamas. Clate green was a Pennsylvania Dutchism for the Jaguar racing green—called glade green in English.

Somewhere in this mix Virginia got a General Motors electric car called the EV1 (Electric Vehicle 1, get it?). In addition to the promised mileage being wildly exaggerated, not a small matter when you consider recharging it took a special charger available at few places—and a long process—the cars could only be leased. After purchasing our own charger for two grand or so, GM yanked the lease, recalled all the cars and pounded them into disposable cubes.

The conspiracy theorists had a field day with this claiming it was a conspiracy of big GM to defeat the huge demand for electric cars. We attended a motion picture given to the proposition that the electric car's demise was a collusion between big oil and big motors. There was one—only one voice in the wilderness in the entire movie that countered its premise. It was a journalist for the *Los Angeles Times* who famously said baloney. "If General Motors could sell a car that ran on pig shit, they would." I find it kind of amazing the many conspiracy theories about so many things. Setting up these wild schemes that conspire to undermine our fellow man seem to me would take superhuman effort, cooperation, secrecy.

Why did GM make the electric car that had a range of eighty miles or so? To help the company qualify for mileage requirements which, with the best of intentions, were promulgated by the benevolent U.S. government. The ploy resulted in a zillion dollar loss for GM. They cut their losses by cutting the car. Remember the ads? A tiny car on the bottom corner of a page dominated by blank space. One could legitimately wonder if they really *wanted* to sell the little car. It was only feasible to operate it in sunny states. The cost of it was less than GM's cost of the batteries needed to operate it. So GM was subsidizing the car to get their company mileage numbers up. And out of this another conspiracy theory is born. Big oil wanted to kill the electric car—it was a threat to their selling their product—gasoline.

Hybrids are catching on. New electric cars are proliferating—albeit expensive. You have to be a real green devotee to buy one. They *are* selling, but the niche in the car market is minuscule. One or two percent. Standard oil and those rapacious Rockefellers need not run for cover.

So when Virginia had to give up her electric toy—and it *was* a cute thing, and soon thereafter gave her Jaguar to her sister and nephew—she took the old Lexus, then a smaller Lexus, then the sporty convertible Lexus. She has done her bit for the automotive economy while I am slogging along for fifteen or sixteen years on my Lexus which has just passed fifty thousand miles or about 3,300 the year. But buying cars is just no fun.

And still no war.

Of course, there are those who will say, not without logic, if buying a car is the worst experience in your life, it is good you were never in a strong wind.

CUSTOMERBURGERS

Old and young, we are all on our last cruise.

—*Robert Louis Stevenson*

Customerburgers is what our four year-old firstborn daughter, Melora, called the clientele.

The gentleman who printed my business cards was my first sale.

Then there was the fellow, a builder, who was looking for bargain lots. I found him one with an ocean view. He was enchanted. He said he'd make an offer, "See if he will take a lot in Big Bear in exchange." I thought, no chance. I was wrong again.

Fortunately the seller was suspicious. "Are you sure you're looking at the right lot?"

Of course we weren't. There were two: one for sale, one not. There may have been a house between them, but reading maps was never my forte—an unfortunate handicap in residential real estate. The lot that was for sale was straight up and down. The lot he thought he bought had a manageable slope to it. Had I been at it longer and had more sense of reality, I should have realized that. This unhappy proclivity was somewhat assuaged when I began selling—and buying—apartment buildings. They were a lot larger and easier to differentiate.

I made a similar *faux pas* with the Readys. Fortunately it was not fatal.

My acquaintance with the delightful Readys began while I

was "on the floor" as they say in the trade. Meaning I was manning the office. This was considered a dead assignment and laborers in those vineyards could say at the end of the day, it was dead. Our Crest Realty office was on a side street. The good spots on the modest commercial center with parking were all taken—and the rent was a lot more. In essence, no one came into our office unless they were lost. Palos Verdes Estates was not a cheap place to live, so the clients were usually at least middle aged.

So when I saw this handsome young woman about my age entering our shop, I thought she was perhaps lost. So I said, "Hi, you want to buy a house?"

"As a matter of fact," she said, "I do."

Like the good sport I aspired to be, I showed her a bunch. There was a tract overlooking the ocean, but the houses were pushing the limits of their financial comfort zone. As I recall, they had three kids—they belonged to a religious organization that shunned birth control—the reliability of which was on a dramatic ascendance.

In my defense, the houses in that tract looked an awful lot alike, so when her husband Tom came along for her second look, I showed them the house and Margaret—the client mind you, not the professional realtor—said, "I don't think this is the right house."

"It isn't?" I said looking around. Hm, the insides looked even more alike to me than the outsides. This one was apparently a flip of the floor plan we saw previously. But I'm left-handed. We (she?) found the right house and they bought it. Tom was starting work at the giant law firm of international repute, O'Melveny and Meyers in downtown Los Angeles—a bit of a schlep from Palos Verdes, but Tom would make the sacrifice so the residual of the clan had a nice place to live—good schools and the whole enchilada.

I began the custom of taking the buyers out to dinner upon the close of escrow. We didn't earn our commissions until escrow actually closed, title passed and the money to pay the commission was there. Any time before that and you risked paying for the dinner

out of your own pocket. Not a happy prospect for a fledgling realtor.

At the dinner at Papa DiCarlo's nonpareil Italian restaurant
in Los Angeles, I teased them about having so many kids, three I
said, Margaret corrected me.

"Four," she said. She was in the early stages of a pregnancy
which would coincide more or less with our second born, Julia.
They became best friends in school. Annie was a bit of a tomboy.
She was the third girl in the clan. Tom IV was the lone male—he
was a Marine fighter pilot in Vietnam who had the misfortune to
see one of his buddies shot out of the sky.

Now, the necessity for this personalized killing is on the
wane. It will soon all be done by guys playing video games in the
Arizona desert. Hatred, wars and killing never abate, but the technology makes it more humane. Marginally okay, but less dangerous.

Tragically, after a career in the theater in the Northwest,
Annie was cut down with some insidious cancer, leaving two small
children.

Her father Tom died years later of another form of the same
killer.

Christian Drake, the stage name for the male lead in
Shena, Queen of the Jungle, an early TV series was the owner/broker
of Crest Realty where my early real estate shenanigans took place.
His real name was Ludvig Christian von Droste. He claimed some
remote relationship to the chocolate von Drostes. Distant enough
so none of the largesse from the cacao beans flowed his way.

Mr. D treated me handsomely. First he agreed to take me
on working part time so the international citizenry would have the
blessings of my written word. I could write in the abundant down-
time that went with residential real estate—sitting in the office and
open houses trying to snare live prospects.

Then the percentage he paid on sales and listings were
somewhat more than some other offices. I suppose he quickly recognized I was making sales when his veterans were not.

I recall you had to work for two years as a salesman under the thumb of an honest-to-God broker before you could become a broker yourself and go into business by yourself and hire salesmen if you desired. I didn't.

At some point after my sales grew exponentially, Ludvig Christian von Droste offered me eighty percent of the office share.

One day while putting in "up time" in the office, I got a call from an ophthalmologist on a residential lot we had listed. I offered to show him the lot. We met and he bought it. Albeit not before some serious price slashing negotiations. As I recall he didn't fuss about my commission on the property, he told me he'd like to buy apartments, what did I know about them?

Nothing, but I was willing to learn, which I did by taking courses offered by the National Association of Realtors. We began small—twenty some units in Watts—soon after the Watts riots and a passel of foreclosures were for sale. Most of them boarded up and devoid of human habitation. But this one property was in the real estate owned bucket of Lytton Savings and Loan—spearheaded by the inimitable Bart Lytton—a flamboyant character who was not shy of publicity. I once heard him proclaim on some TV program that most of the Savings and Loan companies were named after dead presidents: Washington, Lincoln, but his was named after *him*. He was a generous lender and didn't fear poor neighborhoods like Watts and he may have done passably until the riots when people moved—scared out of their homes. Properties were damaged, abandoned and great Bart Lytton was left holding the bag.

The doc thought this would be a good test of my abilities, a good learning experience—so we got the place for next to nothing down. As I recall we agreed on five percent or ten percent down payment and my commission was thrown into the pot in exchange for a note that was to be paid as long as there was income from the tragedy to cover it. Incentive real estate you might call it.

There was a wonderful elderly black woman who managed the property. She walked haltingly with a cane and was, as many in her station, overweight. She had two daughters who had reached their limits of foaling welfare-worthy children, so she took the excess. Between the three of them they were reaping benefits from the U.S. treasury in conjunction with the taxpayers of nine, or was it twelve? children from I don't know how many fathers. Grandma, as Mrs. Williams our manager was called, was a disciplinarian. The kids in her charge were perhaps three to six, she having inherited the younger of the litter. They were taught to be unfailingly polite. If a little guy would walk in front of me and not say "scuse me' she reprimanded him and he said 'scuse me.

We considered the project a sociological experiment. If we treated people right, would they respond by treating us right? The two bedroom apartments rented for sixty-five dollars per month. The one bedrooms fifty. We never raised them. Comparable apartments else where in Los Angeles rented for three to four times that. When the mail carrier showed up Mrs. Williams met her residents with her cane at the mailboxes to get her hands on their welfare check to guarantee their rent was paid.

In our two-year stint, nobody held her up. Perhaps they knew they would have her cane to contend with.

The sociological experiment was, I would say, a qualified success. They paid their rent and we kept the property clean and in working order, making all repairs in a timely fashion. The owner had to add only a few hundred dollars to the pot in two years and enjoyed a handsome tax write-off relative to his investment. I got paid my monthly installments on my note and a reasonable management fee—my first.

Mrs. Williams was, I believe, in her late sixties, and a simply delightful woman who never failed to laugh at my jokes. She is one of the few old employees that stand out in my memory. Alas, she, like the rest of us will, wore out and went to glory. I went to the super emotional funeral, her daughters bereaved perhaps because they had misgivings about taking advantage of her, perhaps not.

I wanted to give them some money to help with their funeral expenses. They apparently had not gone the cheap route. But when I asked how to make out the check, the girls (women) couldn't agree. I was a little put out and let them know if we couldn't pay the expenses or divide the amount between them, I'd withdraw the offer.

We settled.

Before Mrs. Williams died (I always called her Mrs. Williams and she called me Mr. Gardner) someone bombed the building. It was a mistaken gang revenge — they got the wrong guy, they thought he was his brother. The bomb was set under their bed to go off after the bombers thought he would be in bed with his girlfriend. But he wasn't. They were still in the living room on the couch, but their baby was in her crib in the bedroom. The explosion blew a hole in the wall and sent the baby through it. *But she survived* and no one was killed.

But most of the windows in the twenty units were blown out and everyone moved out. Can you blame them?

A footnote to the Watts experience:

A young man who worked on and off, somewhat more unique to the property than elsewhere, couldn't pay his rent. He moved and promised to pay all he owed. It was a promise we heard before and would hear again, so we didn't take it too seriously.

But he surprised us — making small payments on his debt until he was gunned down in the streets by someone who wanted to steal his radio — who met resistance.

It was a tough existence in that part of the country.

MORE CUSTOMERBURGERS
(MEDIUM RARE)

The Alberts, Beryl and Bob, were delightful people. She was one of those women who had beloved grandmother written all over her though she never had children. She carried some extra pounds as women her age were prone to do. Her husband Bob was younger (five to ten years?), thin and fit. Naturally it was he who should suffer the stroke—suddenly while opening the overhead garage door in the house they had bought from me.

After that he lost the power of speech. It was heartbreaking to see him struggle to connect two or more words to form a sentence. The concentrated therapy to restore his speech made no discernible difference.

Beryl was a rather good artist. She'd done a small Mexican scene—a girl in indigenous dress—which I admired and she gave it to me.

She was a school teacher in the lower grades. Such a pleasant, gentle way she had about her.

Bob worked in the aerospace game. Some kind of engineering beyond my ken.

I recall after they made an offer on a charming house atop a hill in the Westfield section of Palos Verdes (it was a new house built by a fellow realtor but the times were such that it had remained unoccupied for many months) I presented a counter offer from the realtor/owner/builder. I thought it was fair, and when Bob Albert signed it he said, "we're probably being flim flammed" (before he lost his speech lifting the garage door).

The sentiment saddened me. Usually in this kind of sales the buyer thought they paid too much and the seller thought they got too little, and who better to blame for this sorry state of affairs than the broker.

This was a mild—I thought self-preserving—protest while agreeing to the offered terms.

There was only one truly unsatisfied client in my career. All I remember is him dressing me down on the phone for attempting to misrepresent something. I don't remember what—I don't remember the property in question—I don't even remember what he or his wife looked like—but I remember the accusation which I found baseless and startling. Where did they get the idea? Did another broker badmouth the deal in order to lasso his business? I never learned.

The Alberts had us to their house for dinner (sauerkraut and knockwurst) after we took them to our obligatory thank you dinner after the sale closed.

We kept in touch through the passing (merciful?) of Bob. Then their end of our correspondence ceased without warning and I never found out what happened to her. She was in the pipeline to the great beyond and I expect she made it there where her delightful nature will stand her in good stead.

Dr. Rosso looked ten to fifteen years younger than he was. His wife *was* twenty years younger than he. He liked to tease her—she suffered it, but not gladly.

Their home had plastic covers on the chairs and carpets. This I suppose is a step up from the old days when no one was allowed in the parlor.

They had a son named "Ronnie" who gave the mom fits. He was just a little fellow in those days with a body type favoring his mother. His father was thin and spare. The last I heard of them Ronnie was on his way to being a doctor.

The doc was an accomplished violinist, his brother Nino was principal cellist for the Los Angeles Philharmonic. This expertise might have been attributed to a super strong willed, doting mother. I met this paragon once at the Rossos' home. She had made a lemon meringue pie for which she was erroneously revered by her son. I was given a piece in spite of my lament that I didn't think I could eat anything. The pie was placed before me as, I thought, a challenge to my manhood. Was I a wimp? How could a slice of Momma's lemon meringue hurt you? Verily the skinny doc wolfed down two slices while his wife Ellen wisely passed.

I did my duty. I tasted it. Worst pie of any description, *bar none*, I ever had in my life. It seemed to be solid cornstarch and sugar. And I am not a guy known for any particular restraint when sugar was nigh, but I was on the spot. I couldn't see how I could *not* eat it and insult them when the doc thought it was the best pie in the world—but nor could I see how I could get down the entire slice of *the worst pie I had ever tasted.*

My feeling now is the doc could not let down his mother, so he had seconds. He couldn't possibly have liked that bilge. But just now I can't recall how I extricated myself from the embarrassment. The Rossos were not only super clients, he treated our whole family with nary a hint of a bill. Since I was on the receiving end of his largesse, I couldn't see that he owed me anything—so the next commission I waived (or half of it?). He said he didn't want to do that, but he couldn't stop it either. I just instructed the escrow on the divvying of the commission which was paid from the buyers' funds.

It seems we had several transactions together, but I only remember specifically the glorious coastline view of around an acre in Palos Verdes Estates. The woman who sold it was a piece of work. As any chauvinist pig worth his salt would do, I asked when she could present the offer to her husband. She said he couldn't be bothered (he was a professor of transportation at UCLA). If she liked the offer, she would get him to sign it. She encouraged me to just mail it (no fax machines in those days) but I said I would have to bring it—she said they would have to consider it and wouldn't respond on the spot. I remember what she looked like (skinny) so I must have gotten inside her house—which was down a long driveway from PCH on the ocean in Malibu. I got at least as far as an open front door. That glamorous community is a far piece up the coast from Palos Verdes, *and* it is twenty-seven miles long *and* these people lived at the northernmost distance from Palos Verdes.

Somehow we completed the transaction and the Rossos built a glorious house with beaucoup windows on the coastline side.

It was on our first visit I spied the plastic covers on the living room furniture and carpets.

Dr. Rosso asked me to find an apartment building for him—but I demurred. The other doctor's hunger for buildings was insatiable and I thought of him as my first loyalty. I put myself second because I was buying buildings of my own. Plus, I didn't consider any investment risk-free and I couldn't see putting Dr. Rosso's money at risk. He had a small office in a small strip mall and I couldn't see that he had a lot of cash to blow. When I asked him how much he wanted to invest he was cagey and I never got a good feeling that his resources were generous.

Besides, it was (and has more or less remained) a seller's market—there were more buyers than sellers and suitable apartments were not plentiful.

The doc had a nurse/receptionist/assistant—I'm never sure what to call those women (usually) who man or woman the area where you present yourself for your appointment. She was a woman of commanding charm and good looks—delightfully personable. I was very fond of her.

We were all shocked to hear that she called the doctor at home urging (demanding?) that he return to the office where he reluctantly went to find her with slashed wrists. The opinion from the medical expert was the cuts healed by themselves. If you seriously wanted to end it, you had to do the cutting in the bath where the warm water would draw the blood from the body.

Ellen—you will recall, the doctor's wife—told me there was no romance. Her husband certainly didn't do anything to provoke such a dire reaction, to which the doctor replied in our presence, "How do you know?" Which had been my impression heretofore.

Naturally she had to be replaced, and Ellen did the hiring for that round.

Instead of retiring when the time came, Dr. Rosso lent himself out as a hired gun for insurance companies.

Mrs. Coe, who worked for us, more or less running the office show for twenty-five years, told me a tale of a friend who had a trial for some injury she sustained in a parking lot through no fault of her own. Dr. Rosso had apparently appeared for the other side to say the friend could not have sustained the claimed injuries from those circumstances. I'm not sure, but I think the ruling went (erroneously?) with Dr. Rosso.

I sent him my books, Christmas cards, notes; nothing stirred him or Ellen to communication, so another of our real estate family dropped from view.

WALTER MANNING, R.I.P.

I met Mr. Manning while doing a market survey in Los Angeles on Harvard Boulevard. We were considering another foreclosed building in a more upscale Black neighborhood and wanted to get a feel for the area.

A slight man was tending to something outside a neighboring building. I approached carefully—always somewhat scared of angering someone who may have been dumped on by a whitey.

Walter Manning was his name, another super specimen of personhood. I thought he was the janitor but he explained that was what he wanted his residents to think, otherwise he'd hear too many sob stories. He cooperated courteously and completely then asked me if I had any buildings for sale he might buy.

So I got a new client and he bought three buildings. Two were in Baldwin Hills, an upscale area that had become predominately Black. The ophthalmologist bought a larger offering in the same neighborhood, which he subsequently sold to Mr. Manning.

Mr. Manning managed his buildings and I managed the doctor's. We went through a number of managers in Baldwin Hills. We had a delightful, personable woman, a terrific renter, but she was helping herself to the rent money. She swore she would pay it all back when things went better for her.

I went to the police anyway. Of course, they didn't want to act as a collection agency, but they did call her up which entailed two surprises for me. 1) She returned the call and schmoozed with the cops, and 2) I asked the cop if that was how you arrested people now—on the phone? He said they were often successful on the phone. But not this time. Much as I wanted to believe our sticky fingered manager, she didn't pay it back. The next managers were

Mr. and Mrs. Wells. Dressed to the nines for the interview, he told me frankly that someday he wanted to be me (he thought I owned the building). He was a man in his late fifties I believe, his wife about the same age. They were a successful team for a while, although their salesmanship did not seem to be in the league with their predecessor. After she stole she still netted more money for us than her replacement who seemed at that juncture to be scrupulously honest.

Until they weren't. The monthly rent report suddenly showed people who had faithfully paid their rent as not having paid. Mr. Wells assured me he would collect it. But it got worse. We took only checks or money orders so baffled with trepidation I visited the property one Saturday or Sunday morning and knocked on doors; when they were opened I politely, careful with the wording, asked if they had paid their rent.

Yes, they all replied and were able in most cases to produce receipts. In some cases they claimed not to get a receipt. I explained it would seem to us without a receipt they had not paid even if they had. Of course we would honor their cancelled check. Some of them said Mr. Wells asked for cash. No, they weren't suspicious, he was "the man."

When I asked (gently) Mr. Wells about these discrepancies he flared in anger. No contrite reaction from Mr. Wells. He was angry I snooped behind his back—it was as though I didn't *trust* him.

But I *had* trusted him—that was partially why we were in this fix.

"You'll get your money," he said, still trying to make me feel ashamed for asking. He just borrowed it because he needed it for some investments. He was going to be like me—if the banks turned him down because he was short of collateral, why he'd just have to resort to other measures. If they treated him like they should have he wouldn't have had to borrow from us.

I expect I told him I would have to go to the police. Probably mumbled—I didn't want him to shoot me. Or we made an arrangement giving him a short time to produce the shortfall before I went to the police (though by this time I realized it was mostly a bluff. The cops were too busy to go after this petty thief.)

Mr. Wells produced all the rents and deposits I realized were missing and some I hadn't. Either my records were faulty or his math was. Perhaps he was giving us interest on the borrowed funds.

Somehow we got someone else to collect the rents while he was moving out.

The next couple were "salt-of-the-earth" folks. A formidable, personable woman and a thin, almost frail-looking man. Their application indicated they were married a short time — perhaps one or two years. When I asked how long they had been married the woman said something like thirty-five years.

I noted the application.

"Oh," she said, "that's just this husband. I had two others."

They were competent managers, but again they didn't take in as much money as Mr. Wells — after his restitution — or our first thief after her theft. Perhaps there is an extra incentive when you know you keep some of what you take in.

If I'm not seriously mistaken, Mr. Manning took this building off our hands after it had given us enough experience to last a lifetime of property management. He also bought the doctor's property on Harvard after Doc had accumulated larger properties closer to home.

Mr. Manning was an extraordinary man for his time. He began his career in the Coast Guard. His wife produced for him several children and died before her time. To partially assuage his grief he began slowly and modestly buying real estate: first a duplex — they lived in one and rented the other — then an eight unit apartment, then to Harvard Boulevard — perhaps sixteen or so units — which was where I met him.

In the course of our relationship we invited Mr. Manning and his woman friend to break bread with us in our Palos Verdes home. They came dressed as though for something important, which I realized later it might have been. She of course was more "dressed up" than he, but is not this the nature of women?

Alas, she was anguishingly ill at ease. I had met her briefly on her own turf and she was pleasant and personable, almost outgoing, but in our digs she was visibly nervous, almost as though she were breaking some kind of sacred compact by eating with whitey. I tried my best to put her at ease, but if I succeeded it wasn't apparent in her reactions.

She owned a beauty shop so she was an entrepreneur like Mr. Manning—a serendipitous arrangement—more than had she only been a hairdresser.

The Manning saga ended with my attendance at his funeral. It was a dignified affair in contrast with the funeral of Mrs. Williams in Watts. The emotions were not so prominently on display. Perhaps because Mr. Manning had left all his children and grandchildren well off.

This was partially because his ambition was to pay off the loans on his properties. I mentioned the glories of debt as the path to wealth, but he was not interested. My father shared the free and clear mindset with Mr. Manning. Mr. Wells on the other hand, when he wasn't playing free and easy with the till was also a fan of debt, when he could get it.

Mr. Manning had a rich, full life. It could have been longer but he had some blood pressure issues brought on by a penchant for sugar—five pounds a week he confided to me.

Mr. Manning's son-in-law, husband of his beautiful, friendly daughter, had a respectable job as a fireman in Northern California. But as friendly and outgoing as Mr. Manning's daughter was, he was reserved, standoffish, guarded, even suspicious.

When Mr. Manning bought his last building from me, he wanted to put his daughter and son-in-law on the title. The son-in-law tried to talk him out of it, fearing the worst—he would be called upon to contribute cash from his pocket to resuscitate a failing enterprise. I felt he suspected me of taking advantage of them—it was, I thought, racially based. Racism goes both directions.

At Mr. Manning's funeral his grandson asked me if I would manage his properties—they had no experience at it.

As politely as I could I said I would give them all the help I could—either to manage themselves or recommend certified property managers in the Los Angeles area. But the properties were farther than I wanted to go from Palos Verdes at the time. I had by

this time owned my own buildings and managed for the ophthalmologist and the wife who had divorced him and stretching me further I didn't feel was to anyone's benefit.

He was disappointed—even angry at my response. Did he
feel I owed it to them because I sold them the buildings? Was his
attitude—ah—you take your money (sales commission) and run?

I still remember the graveside scene and have a twinge of
sadness about not accommodating this third generation. I couldn't
have done them justice.

I called him with the names of three certified property managers to choose from. I never heard from him again.

MANAGE GENERAL HERSHEY BAR IF YOU CAN

As with my memory of my choir experiences, the standouts in my memories of real estate management, are not the many wonderful people and painless transactions, but the less happy experiences.

The most dramatic to come to mind was General Hershey Bar. He was a guy I suspected would not see sixty again—his wife having left behind eighty.

Before you are too hard on me for hiring this bizarre character, I would beg you to understand how difficult it was to get competent, compos mentis managers in Hollywood. We did "luck out" as they say and had a few good ones. Of course they were mostly strangers to Hollywood and once they became acquainted, they flew.

General Hershey Bar had a real name which he didn't want to disclose. He also went by Calypso Joe. I suppose I ultimately got it so we could do a credit check and what have you, but I could well have been so desperate I took him with his alias.

He called in response to our ad and the woman who answered the phone reported he talked a mile a minute, proclaiming he was just the ticket to manage our building. Before you scoff, understand that the phone didn't ring off the hook for Hollywood managers. My recollection is it didn't ring at all. So, crazy as he seemed (borne out later in spades), he was apparently a sentient human being who actually wanted the job.

It was, I believe, at the interview that he hauled out his scrapbook with its myriad photos of him in his General Hershey Bar get up.

In my defense, if I have a defense, I was pretty new to the

business—and I like to think the best of everyone. Now if anyone mentions Hollywood, it's like ringing Pavlov's bell. I thought the circumstances cried out for compromise. It doesn't always work.

There *was* a General Hershey in currency at this time so it was a small jump for a creative mind like our General's to add the "Bar." Everyone thought he was a card—at least I thought so at the time.

What was not immediately apparent to me was our Hershey Bar came with almonds. More almonds than chocolate. At the time he seemed to be completely nuts.

He had an army cap with a bolt of lightning on the insignia in front—and there was a mushroom cloud on his uniform somewhere. He used to take to Hollywood Boulevard in his get up and stop people on the sidewalk and say, "Make love, not war." He was a real kick in the pants.

And he rented apartments. *And* he collected the rents, without pocketing any that I could tell. The building was on Afton Place, a short street that dead-ended into the Columbia movie studios perhaps a block or less from the property.

Gloria Swanson had lived in the apartment with Joseph Kennedy—the rightwing progenitor of the leftwing Kennedy boys: President Jack, Attorney General and Senator Robert and Senator Teddy—the latter the only one to die of natural causes with his boots on. Joe Kennedy reputedly had owned the building and his and Gloria's apartment was a real showplace—mahogany paneled walls, spacious two-story with a formal dining room and fancy plumbing fixtures. It is not reported if Rose Kennedy (Mrs. Joseph) ever tarried there. Word was she didn't like to leave her Massachusetts home. Lucky Joe. But the boys in the family sure knew how to have fun and now I read of a sexually uninhibited grandson via Robert with some fifty conquests under his belt while married to a harried wife. Could it have been all that Catholic upbringing and churchgoing and confessing that relieved them of their inhibitions? There can't be much doubt of my jealousy.

The General was aces for awhile, then he started to drift south. Why was I surprised? My phone rang at 2:30 or 3:00 in the morning. I had the flu. I answered. It was the answering service who put through an irate fella who stormed at me that the manager had violated his sacred space—his *HOME!* by entering it while he was gone.

How did he know?

The General had left him a note—a pay your rent reminder. He was angry and he wanted someone else to share his anger.

A chat with The General in the morning yielded the intelligence the resident was a bum who didn't pay his rent. He knocked on his door and there was no answer, so fearing the resident had flown the coop (not an impossible circumstance) he went in. He didn't touch anything, merely left the note.

In that area of town not everyone paid their rent promptly with a smile on their face—and with a check that didn't bounce.

I don't remember if he paid or moved. It would not have been unprecedented if he did neither. One of the games in the business was to use up your last month's rent, then linger until the marshal showed up, getting all the free time you could.

The second call was from a young woman with a story about The General letting himself into her apartment and offering gratuitous sexual comments about her underwear. She added he liked to hit on young girls.

To his credit, The General didn't deny this—calling it, rather, harmless fun.

Little by little things went to hell at Afton Place. I was finally forced to retire The General (with full military honors, to be sure, just without a pension.)

I met The General and the missus at an unemployment mediator's office. The Hershey Bar brought cartons of "documents"—doubtless a number of them testimonials from the Pentagon. They made their case that they were ideal managers and my firing them was capricious. The missus spoke up—one of the few times I ever heard her voice—he was in charge—make no mistake about that. Her contribution, "One minute he calls us geniuses, the next he fires us," as though that were an "impossible" inconsistency.

I might have riposted, "When you were geniuses, that's what I called you. When you slipped to disinterest and incompetence, I asked you to leave." The moderator, a nice enough young man (thirties) said he would take it under advisement.

When I later called him for his judgment he said in essence: those people came in here with three more boxes of stuff. He's a nut job and I want to get rid of him—he's getting the money.

The General in one of his getups.

Another early lesson in the easy justice of the marketplace.

Perhaps a mile or so northwest of Afton Place was our second (and mercifully final) experience with Hollywood apartments. It was on Wilcox Avenue and called something appropriate like Wilcox Arms or Legs or something. I had sold these properties to the doctor, so I was by agreement, bound to manage them.

Mistake. But in those days I was scratching to make a living.

Wilcox was a largely furnished apartment building. It was

occupied by a number of older people who had lived in Hollywood before it went to hell. At least I can't otherwise explain why these genteel old persons stuck around this sinking neighborhood in racial transition. We had a number of buildings in that circumstance, and I told all the managers since they lived in the building they could choose the people they wanted to live with. But if a Black was rejected and it turned out that was the reason for rejection and we were fined because of it, we would expect the manager to pay the fine. A shibboleth in currency was if Black people moved in, the white ones would move out. I didn't believe it—and it turned out not to be true. Not to say all Blacks are or were angels. A notable example of the opposite was Mr. Bailey. I don't remember his first name, I always called him *Mr.* Bailey.

He lived on the top floor, perhaps third or fourth. In summer the sun beat down on the tar roof, and un-insulated ceiling. The building was perhaps fifty years old in the 1970s.

Mr. Bailey was so discomforted by this climactic outrage that he took it upon himself to hightail to the roof, whereupon he unraveled the mandated fire hose, turned on the spigot and clumsily watered down the flat roof.

He did so much damage to the roof over his apartment that it leaked into his "home," and feeling we were responsible, refused to pay his rent.

Landlords are restricted in what actions they may legally take when a resident refuses to pay *or* move, as Mr. Bailey had.

I filed an unlawful detainer in court. Usually the occupant doesn't answer the complaint or show up. Some answer to buy time—free rent until the court date. Most of those don't show up in court because in fact they have no case to argue. Not having the money doesn't cut it. So Mr. Bailey answered—*and* showed up in court. His case was he offered the rent and we wouldn't take it. (If we had taken the money it would have nullified the unlawful detainer action and we wanted him out.)

The judge wouldn't put him out. Claimed I had screwed up the paperwork. After we left, I asked Mr. Bailey for the rent. He said he'd think about it. It must come as no surprise that his thinking went against us and he didn't pay.

Mr. Bailey, it must be confessed, had no visible means of support. Our speculation was he'd knock over a gas station or convenience store when he needed cash. Probably some unemployment/disability scam. Besides, the old women would come home from shopping and find Mr. Bailey in their apartment—doubtless to acquire some cash or negotiable artifacts.

He had, as it turned out, a multi-page rap sheet. For our next court foray we hired an attorney. We lost that one too. Our attorney was livid. There was, he said, no legal, moral or ethical grounds for our second rejection of a simple unlawful detainer. I always say the philosophy is simple: pay or move. I now wonder if in these post Watts Riots days some judges weren't intimidated by Blacks in downtown Los Angeles.

A kindly Black police detective dropped in the building from time to time. He was a comforting presence. I told him my tale.

"Don't quote me, but I'll tell you what I would do. I'd lock him out, tell him to sue you if he doesn't like it."

We did it. Mr. Bailey kicked in the door *and* sued us.

I spoke to a nice young attorney who was the representative of our insurance company. He had taken his law degree at USC and had a class with our friend Leonard Ratner (graduated first in his law school class at Cal). I asked what kind of teacher he was. He gave me an example of his classroom technique. He would ask a question, listen to an answer and say, "Well, I see your mouth moving, but I don't hear you saying anything."

I thought that was wonderful. I visited one of his classes and never studied law, but on hearing the students' responses I thought of that epithet. For the most part the answers seemed nonsensical.

I lamented to this gentleman the insurance company would throw money at the crook. He said, "It isn't going to improve his life one iota. It will be gone in a matter of days."

In fact, the insurance company wanted to offer Mr. Bailey fifteen thousand dollars, but they couldn't find him. Probably another notch in his rap sheet detained him elsewhere.

RELATIONSHIPS

*L'amour, c'est offrir à quelqu'un qui n'en veut pas
quelque chose que l'on n'a pas.*

Love is giving what you haven't got
to someone who doesn't want it.

—Jacques Lacan

Leave it to a Frenchman.

I was to have half a two-hour program to flog my book. As it worked out, I gave a pitch about my book (published) and a young woman gave her pitch about compatibility based on zodiac signs. Actually her schtick was fortune telling and an element of palm reading might have been present. And since this purported to be a book review program, the young woman had written a book on this very subject—it just hadn't been published.

So with perhaps an hour and a half left in the program and the floor and phone bank was open for questions, and they flooded in—every one about relationships. "I'm a Pisces, my friend is a Virgo. Do we have a future?"

"I'm an Aquarius. Can I find a relationship with a…?"

And the woman answered the questions in all seriousness. They were all the same. Can I find a relationship? Yet she managed to vary her single response (I see a relationship for you in the future—I can't say how soon…) so everyone felt she was speaking uniquely to them.

Theoretically half of the questions should have been addressed to me about my book (or my zodiac sign for that matter). How many questions was I asked?

Zero.

I've heard it said, "You can lead a whore to culture, but you can't make her think." It may even be true.

And of those questions directed from the other side, how many were about health? Would Timmy get over his pesky cough soon? Would Uncle Fred survive his cancer treatments? Or even Will I go on a long ocean voyage?

No! *Every* question was about finding a relationship. And every answer was some creative if mysterious form of the positive, often reached amid some torturous caveats.

I had to hand it to the swami. She said essentially the same thing to these acolytes for an hour and a half, but she made it with her individual tailoring, different. And, of course, my wild expressions were caught on camera. I thought they were embarrassingly over the top, but no one mentioned it. Which helped me to understand—people are preoccupied with themselves and no one is looking at you. To get noticed in that situation, I suspect I would have had to jump out of my seat, tear the microphone out of the hands of the speaker and shout something blasphemous.

Thankfully I kept my shenanigans short of burlesque.

The whole thing pointed up how preoccupied people were with their relationships.

So what is a relationship? What makes it tick? What keeps it alive? *Can* it be kept alive? Is that desirable?

Perhaps the first thought that comes to mind when you hear the word relationship is sex.

Valid and legitimate. But there are other kinds. Friendships that endure hardships. Teacher/student, instrumentalists with conductor and fellow musicians. Relatives. Some marriages endure without sex. But more likely the relationship of those monastic couples ends in divorce. And so many do. The percent continues to climb. Which brings to mind the newly sanctioned gay marriages. Without any real knowledge it seems homosexual couples endure longer than heteros. This could be because the homosexuals had to hide it and therefore were motivated to endure. Now that it is more or less accepted, I predict there will be more of it, and if it is easier to obtain, it might be easier to dissolve.

On a cruise I was at a table next to two men who fought like any good heterosexual couple. One was apparently paying the freight and was having little success browbeating the other with that intelligence. The guy in the inferior position threatened to get off the boat.

They were still together when I got off the ship perhaps a month or so later. They had moved to a table for eight so I lost the gems of their conversation.

I gave a speech about my books. They both showed up to swell an audience that was not exactly standing room only.

Whence the attraction of one person for another?

The focus here is upon heterosexual relationships which are still the most prevalent hook ups. But I speculate the basics of attraction are similar for homosexual unions.

It remains a major mystery to me. Looking over all the pairings I have known, I am looking for patterns. As someone once told me, the only pattern is there is no pattern. The closest I can come to an explanation is:

Proximity and Timing.

Obviously you can't fall for someone you don't meet. Yet there are legions of prospects we meet but who don't interest us. Why not? Or why *do* the few that *do*?

Timing. You have to be ready—in the market so to speak. For some anytime is right. Hormones rear and you rear with them. Others find ways to procrastinate; the more civilized the society, the more diversions there are.

Our ancestors seemed to take the plunge earlier in their lives. If your grandparents didn't go to college as mine did not, nor did Virginia's, there was a chunk of four years or so that wasn't fodder for procrastination.

My parents were twenty-four when they married. I was twenty-six. Our children were closer to twenty-nine, on the brink of that bugaboo threshold to spinsterhood of thirty.

My grandparents were in their early twenties. Our grandchildren may hold out into their thirties or pass up marriage altogether.

When I was a lad of formative years my Aunt Verna, Mother's younger sister, and my father seemed, if not convinced, fearful that I was a homosexual. Why? Because I liked music (classical), wrote music, belonged to the band and orchestra, and, this seemed to be the clincher for Aunt Verna, I had curly hair. I didn't get the connection. I didn't curl it—I didn't do *any*thing to it. It was just a little curly. A junior high school teacher, Miss Drucken-miller (imagine the day when we could stigmatize an unmarried woman by calling her Miss?), relieved herself of the wisdom to the seventh grade English class that she knew I curled my hair. Her theory was that in the rain it straightened, when dry I curled it? Or was it the other way around? Okay, a thirteen year old does not need to be humiliated like that. *Boys didn't curl their hair.* Not even sissies. But you couldn't come much closer to being branded a sissy than the general intelligence that *you curled your hair!*

I wonder now if Miss Druckenmiller thought I was homo...? She played the piano in the Sunday school band, and I sat there holding my cornet and made believe I could play it by blowing into it. Miss D was also the assistant organist and a member of the church choir where I also held the music—though I found singing more compatible than blowing into one of those brass horns and manipulating three fingers to approximate the required pitches at the right time and the proper duration.

Miss Schaeffer, the organist, was short of stature with one of those spine irregularities that made her appear something like a hunchback of Notre Dame, though I don't think she was a full-fledged hunchback. I expect she was in her sixties when I knew her.

Miss Schaeffer was the daughter of a minister at another church who had a pronounced Pennsylvania Dutch accent. He spoke of "sarvices" and Glarance and Villie. Did Emily Schaeffer have a close brush with marriage as reported—with a man whom the cruder folk referred to as a pansy?

She taught me piano and harmony and music theory. She was a better teacher than I was a student.

My lesson was usually her last of the day and she drove me home, a distance of a half-mile. She lived beyond our home on the same street.

I don't remember much of the conversation. I do remember my skills not keeping pace with my ambition. I wanted to play Grieg's Piano Concerto. She got me a simplified version; a crowning insult despite its appropriateness. Also I remember trying to boost her ego by a gentle degradation of her competing piano teacher. She would have none of it, gently suggesting the woman was doing good by teaching the piano and there was room for many approaches.

Whence my relationships? And why?

I remember feelings before I had the hormones to back them up. What were they? I don't recall physical excitement. Rather, I thought he was neat, had an engaging way about him. He was the third of five or six boys who lived near the town's only traffic light. I remember getting a nice feeling sitting next to him crammed in the back seat of a car with other fellas. Our knees touched and I wondered if it caused him some pleasurable sensations? Of course we would never discuss it. I didn't connect the feeling with anything sexual.

The first connection of that sort I felt while sled riding with a girl, Jan, I had a terrible crush on. I was perhaps thirteen years old. We sat on the sled, she behind me and wrapped her legs around me for stability. What else? But I felt her pubic bone against my back. I wasn't sure what it was, but it was terribly exciting. Of course there was no conversation about it—I—as I expect most are at that age—or were before the relaxing of the mores—was shy and reticent about intimacy.

I was too young and awkward to carry this excitement further. She began dating an older guy who had a vehicle with a rumble seat. Some sixty-five years after the sled riding affair, I asked her on the phone across the country if she remembered it—with a tiny chuckle she said she did. It made me feel good. I asked her what she saw in her boyfriend—who didn't go to college.

"He treated me like a queen," she said.

I wondered if I could have competed with that without a car. I didn't think so. But with relationships I was always thinking of the future—college—work—make enough money to start a family. Everything was just out of reach.

What was it about her? She had an engaging way about her. She was elected to every office she ran for—was pretty in a genuine sort of way—had a way of expressing interest in others.

In high school I remember confiding in her my father woes. I expect I was fishing for sympathy. She later referred to my father as "the menace" and it made me angry. Why? It is said we can say anything about our relatives, just don't let anyone else say anything derogatory. (Her father had been killed in an Air Force airplane crash shortly after the war was over.)

Some people refer to unobtainable others as "the love of my life." It was the timing part of the equation that knocked this re-lationship out. The proximity was unassailable—until it wasn't. Until she stayed in Pennsylvania to go to college in Gettysburg and I high-tailed it across the fruited plain to USC.

When Jan went to college she jettisoned the guy with the rumble seat and later began dating the guy she married. A guy who blessed her with five healthy, attractive, successful children, but also a guy who had an alcoholic breakdown, was institutionalized for years and I believe died in the institution. One of his children visited him every day in the facility. For her part, Jan had a nervous (nonalcoholic) breakdown and attempted suicide.

The question begging is had our proximity been in better sync with our timing and she and I had somehow married, would,

She have attempted suicide, perhaps sooner?
She have been successful?
I have attempted suicide?
She have had a nervous breakdown, alcoholic or non?
We have divorced?

Of course, I like to think that I would have made all the dif-ference and we would have been happy as clams. But it should be remembered that my own wife, Virginia, became clinically de-pressed after forty or so years of marriage to me and spoke of suicide. I wonder how many people contemplate suicide and *don't* speak of it? How much of a factor is the attention getting ploy of contem-plating suicide vocally?

My friend Bob Lindsey sent me his super autobiography which told that both his parents did the suicide dance—together when he was young.

Lest this recitation will seem too much like the ones who got away, I have had quasi-relationships where I was the one who got away.

I am reminded of the woman in the post office in Ketchum, Idaho who was an absolute bitch to her kids.

Seeing her a few minutes later across the street at a ski skating race, I was astonished at her transformation while she spoke to an apparently eligible contemporary gentleman. She had instantly transformed from wicked witch of the west into Snow White with an erotic edge. If they hooked up, how soon would it be until he was blasted with the western witch?

What is the optimal time for a relationship to show its true colors? Varies, no doubt. If someone starts to bore you, it could be your fault. Perhaps you don't inspire the best in the person, perhaps she loses interest in you and as a result makes no effort to enchant you. In any case, how long should the enchantment phase be good for?

It *is* finite. And the endurance of a relationship depends on many factors including the character, personality and background of the principals.

I spent the night in the hospital in Ketchum, Idaho after I fell off my bike and broke my leg. At three a.m. a lonely male nurse came to my bedside to chat. That was the result of the visit though I'm sure his rationale was to check on me. This I thought might more appealingly be done while I was asleep, but then I wouldn't have heard his story.

He lived, he said, with a woman for five years and everything was hunky dory. But she became restless to get married—legitimize the relationship so to speak, and wanting to make her happy, he acquiesced.

Within twenty-four hours, according to this nurse, his now legal wife turned into an absolute shrew who drove him crazy, the blessed union of souls soon terminated in divorce.

In the throes of passion, how long does it take for reality to set in? And why don't the folks who have experienced it set you straight?

Why? Because experience shows them it wouldn't be believed, wouldn't do any good. A man convinced against his will is of the same opinion still. Products of the worst, most acrimonious marriages often marry after swearing they would not.

Mores of society evolve. I had an attractive model who in one breath spoke of not having a boyfriend and in the next about tuning up her birth control. No, I didn't see this as an offer. She was twenty years old, I more than fifty-five years older. Vanity may have its attractions, but hopeless self-regard may not be among them.

We must not forget the view of these relationships at seventy-eight is much skewed from that of twenty or twenty-five when the heat Eros is in full sway.

All relationships culminate with Virginia—a woman whose commanding intelligence and level head bode salubrious for the long haul.

False starts in high school and college have been mentioned as has Joyce from the Navy year and slightly beyond. The first real love was stewing since our summers at National Music Camp in Interlochen, Michigan. My first kiss was there at the end of the season with June Lyon, who sent me to clouds one through nine, but who after a letter telling me I was the finest person she knew (we won't quibble about how *many* there were) disappeared. I often wonder what I did that seemed so fine. June didn't return to music camp, but Carol Bratton did. But Carol was music camp violinist John's "girl"—so I played it cool as only a sixteen year old can.

It wasn't until her father retired from the Anheuser-Busch company as a chemist (how much ongoing chemistry was involved in beer I never knew) and the family remains moved to Carmel, California in my bailiwick, did I get to know her with a smattering of intimacy.

I visited them in Carmel and Carol came to USC in the summer after classes. We went to San Francisco for the opera where we bought standing room for an endless Wagner opus—something from his "Ring of the Nibelungen" as I recall.

Too quickly it came time for my Navy air number to come up. I didn't want to leave her, but I didn't want to put my time in in a foxhole, so I did the honorable thing and honored my commitment—again, as far as you can get from Carmel, California in the continental United States—Pensacola, Florida.

We wrote, I asking a bunch of questions which she answered tersely without repeating the questions so I was at sea knowing what she was talking about. One of my subsequent questions while I was pining for her was, "How do you forget a person?"

She answered in excruciating detail as though she was a past master at it and had mastered it in our case. That may have ended the correspondence and the "relationship."

The last word on her was an invitation to John and me to attend her wedding to an economics teacher at some off the grid college. John and I pooled our resource to engrave a battered and broken tarnished silver tray with something goofy like: In loving memory of our hot times at NMC. We never got a thank you note nor heard from her again. I guess she didn't like it.

Many misguided attentions while at CBS are lamented elsewhere. But back to the germane question—what makes the difference between interest and non-interest? What attracts us to some and not others? There is the physical, of course. Experience teaches that beauty is only skin deep (but ugly goes right through to the bone). I don't think it is even that deep. I mean, what is it good for? Drawing the admiration and envy of your friends? In some cases it's jealousy. I have known so many women who were knock-out gorgeous—right up to the moment they opened their mouths. Dumb is not fun, not even for a couple of minutes. The converse is not true: ugly is not synonymous with intellectual brilliance. So something in between? Not always. When they ask people to rate the most important qualities in a mate, a huge number say a sense of humor. I don't quarrel with that unless she's laughing at me. Though if any female thought I had a sense of humor, I never saw it translate to interest. *Au contraire*, I also have it on good authority that girls prefer serious.

We can, verily, believe what we want to believe.

THE MASTERLESS BUILDER, PART TWO

Our next house, in Santa Barbara, was begun twenty years after the Palos Verdes house. Our daughter, Melora, was fresh out of college with her real estate license. She found us an eighteen plus acre bucolic hunk of ground at the northeast corner of the City of Santa Barbara.

There had been a small house on the property, but it burned down. I would build a *substantial* house that wouldn't burn. But just in case a fire came we would build a foot thick concrete wall as the north wall of the house with no breach of protection by any windows—only the front door faced north. Some eighty percent of the area fires came down the mountain from the north.

This wall rose from the ground to twenty-seven feet at its highest peak and on the vulnerable face covered the house.

In the unlikely event the fire came up the hill on the east, we had a masonry walkway ten feet in width and a water table running the length of the house. Behind the house was a stream with water traversing the southern exposure. In addition a fountain and swimming pool were on that exposure. We also fully sprinklered the property inside as the city required and outside as they did not.

A fire inspector came for final approval and told me, "Your house isn't going to burn. You did everything right."

Building the house was another experience. And verily, Confucius say all experience not good experience.

I knew building a house was no walk in the park. The upside is now I could afford to hire a contractor and I would be careful to see no contractors or subs got hurt.

It was not long before I saw the hole in that philosophy. It made me *more* vulnerable to being hurt by them. I interviewed eleven architects and nine general contractors. All the architects were amenable save one who lived on Mountain Drive, the rambling street on which the house was to be built.

When I visited his office he was doodling on something, for all I know it could have been a plan. If he ever looked up, I missed it. He said, "I design *organic* houses. If you don't want that go somewhere else."

I went. Not that I had anything against organic houses, God knows I favored organic food, I just didn't know what you could put in a house that *didn't* come from the earth without the aid of chemical fertilizers. Or did he mean one of those houses you buried so you didn't know it was a house? His own house did not scream, "*Look at me, I'm* organic."

I recall I gave the architect's plans to about six of the contractors. Only two submitted bids. One was a concrete contractor the other was an ex-school teacher/junior high coach. This would be his first real job. I called his reference for an addition I believe, and I would call her response positive for the most part if lukewarm.

Only one of the contractors hit me the wrong way. I was living in Palos Verdes at this stage of the planning and one of the builders insisted I make the trip (110 miles) to discuss the complex project with him.

This I did only to discover he hadn't looked at the plans, and when he did in my presence he announced that he wasn't willing to bid on it. He might consider some time and material arrangement where I could get hurt but he couldn't. He'd have to look at the plans.

"You mean you haven't looked at them?"

He had a mean deadpan. I don't believe he had smiled the whole time I was there.

"I wish you had told me that—saved me a trip."

Nothing from Mr. Arrogance.

I found out later he began his career as a house painter. Where he learned to carry on like a PhD from Harvard I don't know. He was so unpleasant I still don't know how he got any jobs. There is a theory that some people like to be abused—the rudest waiters intimidate the customers into giving bigger tips. I never understood that but perhaps that was this chap's bag.

In retrospect I guess one rotten apple in ten was not bad.

I signed up the ex-teacher in keeping with my fetish for the low bidder. He was so eager I think he would have worked for nothing. My first inkling something might very well be amiss was when a stranger sauntered onto the property and announced he was the supervisor for the builder I had chosen with the expectation that since he had no other work he would do the "supervising" himself. From my quick assessment of this supervisor he couldn't have been too expensive. Yet more than one hapless fellow has gone out of business by piling on the overhead before he had the income to cover it. I guess I thought that was not my problem.

But it was.

The architect had discovered a new technique for wall building known as Trus-Tek. It was supposed to go up in three days with perhaps another week for guniting it (a process for shooting concrete through a gun against some backing).

It was a steel mesh concoction with Styrofoam three inches from each side. The gunite was applied to this which left a six inch air gap for insulation and sound proofing.

So three days and one week. All ready in less than two weeks. It actually took eighteen months.

The architect told me there was only one guy in town with the experience to do it. I hired him. My first surprise was the mammoth footing which is required to hold those suckers up—wind loads and what have you.

Perhaps my first inkling I was not in the best of hands occurred when I saw one of the workmen hacking out the Styrofoam from the panels. It was no easy task to explain that without the Styrofoam we would double the amount and the cost of the expensive enough concrete.

Then after that hurdle was surmounted the fairly strange fellow who turned out to be the contractor's only gunite guy (who holds the hose and sprays the glop) wound up in jail. An inquiry into this mystery yielded the following reluctant intelligence: the chap had broken into some university girls' dormitories with the intention, apparently sporadically successful, of stealing the co-eds underpants. Someone apparently caught him and turned him over to the gendarmes who felt society demanded to be protected from this fiend by locking him up.

It was not an idea I cared to argue, but I needed a guniter. Surely there must be others who could do it.

No, said the wall contractor. He's the only one with the experience. It was not after all, a swimming pool.

Through all this it became apparent that neither my low bidding general contractor nor his site supervisor had a clue what to do to move this wall along.

Somewhere I replaced the contractor. I think he was relieved. I gave him some thousand dollars to help him out until he found a simpler house to build.

Ever the gentleman, he thanked me profusely and wanted me to understand when things got better he would pay me back. That was twenty-some years ago.

The guy with the jailbird guniter asked me to pay for work I didn't think was performed—so we sought the contractors' board for their opinion. We met and I was astonished to hear the fellow had no contractor's license. The arbitrator explained to him he couldn't rule for him since he was operating illegally. He said he was operating on his father's license, which I recall was in an unrelated trade. My 'contractor' stormed out spewing indignities—one memorable: "The next time you want to build your dream house make sure you know what you're doing."

I got all excited when my new builder called me to come to his house—a compact office on the lot where his walls were festooned with pictures of a grand house. He built that, he said. It belonged to Kenny Loggins. I didn't know who that was, but I was to hear the name ad nauseam, first from the bulldozer operator ("when I worked on Kenny Loggins' house") and on through the guy who sandblasted beams and an endless parade of subs in between.

My new contractor said he called me in to tell me the way the plan was drawn the house was going to leak. And that was the point of the meeting. I was disappointed he wasn't going to share with me his plans for expediting the construction and I am afraid I was rather demonstrative in my disappointment. I can peg our incompatibility from that moment, though it wasn't obvious to me at the time.

It was frying pan to fire. In the new builder's words I pushed all his wrong buttons. For example, if I asked how or why he did something, he responded, "My daddy was a doctor and he didn't teach his patients to be doctors, and I'm not going to teach you to be a builder."

We got a gunite crew from Los Angeles. There really were no companies in Santa Barbara with the equipment and expertise to accomplish this task. I blanched at how much it was going to cost—$175,000 in 1990, (I had planned on $40,000-$60,000) but we were past the point of no return on the wall.

My new builder was so sensitive about his height he wore short pants which allegedly made short guys look taller. He later expressed the secret aspiration to be a mail carrier because they had regular hours and could wear short pants in the performance of their duties.

He assured me he got three bids from all the sub contractors. Before I knew it, he was getting one bid, with the caveat no one else in town could do the job. A few more of our glitches with this supreme contractor:

After our two framers completed their tasks, our builder stalked the house with a level, marking various places he said were not level. Was I on the premises by accident or design? But the confrontation with the carpenter was not pretty. He blew up, told the contractor off and told him to get someone else.

Our contractor, rather than stand his ground, wimped his reply saying, "Well, if you don't want to fix it, okay. Just leave it." It was a turning of the tables our master builder must not have envisioned, and he became downright obsequious.

Somehow the guest bathtub plumbing was backwards. I asked to right it, reversing the showerhead and tub spout to the opposite wall where it should have been.

Couldn't be done, he said. One wall was concrete and the

other couldn't take the pipes for some reason—perhaps something
in the way. But there is all this room between the tub and the wall,
I suggested, couldn't you run the pipes in there?

"No," he said. So there he is the professional telling the am-
ateur something couldn't be done when it was plain it could be.
He had always been adamant about me not talking to the subcon-
tractors—only to go through him. Did he admit his position was
asinine, or did I go directly to the plumber? He did finally admit
he was wrong about that.

Another ethical dilemma: the grader was grading our front
driveway between the street and the garage. He told me he had
been told to grade the driveway what he thought was too close to a
large, perhaps one hundred year old oak tree explaining that if you
cut off access to rain water, the tree could die.

Like a good soldier, I called the builder. He didn't answer.
I left a message. I realized I could make the only sane decision without him but he was so touchy on the subject I at least wanted to include him—let him give the orders.

But he didn't call back. So I told the grader to do what he
had to to save the tree.

When the contractor found out he blew up again. I said, "I
couldn't reach you, did you want me to kill the tree?"

"I guess so," he said.

Thankfully the tree is alive and well and survived the Tea
Fire which destroyed the house.

I think the reason he was not available to take and return
my calls was that he had taken on a fourth job in spite of his promise to me he never took more than three. When I reminded him of
that he denied it.

He had gone long beyond our agreement to pay him any
money per month. He told me it wasn't his fault and I said I would
continue to pay his monthly stipend as long as I was satisfied with
his progress. He had three finish carpenters on our house, then suddenly there was one. He needed them on another job, he said.
Since he'd taken a fourth job he had three carpenters for four jobs.
I guess I was mathematically fortunate to get one.

And since I was paying him by the month, it was to his advantage to drag it out.

After I replaced this builder to do what I didn't want to—finish it myself—I hired five finish carpenters who took three months to finish the complete job. His one, a skilled man, but not greased lightning, would have taken fifteen months assuming he never got the sniffles or stubbed his toe.

Then I discovered through one of his carpenters that my builder had made an incentive agreement with one of his other jobs (or all of them for all I knew). He was to get a nice bonus for finishing by a fixed date. So that may have explained where my carpenters went.

There was of course more, but if I am getting weary of relaying it, I can imagine how weary you are getting of hearing it.

One final note: at the time I directed the South Coast Choral Society in the South Bay area of Los Angeles County. Our builder's mother lived in Palos Verdes Estates and came to one of our concerts. This widow of the doctor who didn't teach his patients to be doctors, was a handsome and most gracious woman and I enthused over her son whom I had just hired.

"He's going to be my savior," I said.

THE MIDLIFE

A celebrity is a person who works hard
all his life to become well known,
then wears dark glasses
to avoid being recognized.

—*Fred Allen*

THREE WEDDINGS
BUT NO FUNERAL

If you are lonely while you are alone, you are in bad company.

Si vous êtes seul quand vous êtes seul, vous êtes en mauvaise compagnie.
—Jean-Paul Sartre

We had three weddings in our immediate family. The funeral comes later.

Virginia, the distaff, made the arrangements with each of our three daughters in turn. She does not share my psychotic thrift, so no one objected to the arrangement. I'd served my time as Santa Claus, now it was her turn. My only restrictions were they could spend anything they desired as long as they didn't tell me how much it was. In exchange I promised not to tell them there wasn't enough in the bank to cover it.

Of course we had three lovely weddings which might only have been improved if the daughters had been sons and the in-law families had been on the paying end. It is the only time I can think of it is an advantage to have sons.

The first wedding of daughter Melora was in the unfinished backyard of our barely finished Santa Barbara house, cf. the Masterless Builder.

The groom was Jewish. One hundred percent so we had one of those little tents and they (or one of them) stepped on a glass wrapped in a napkin. So much for Jewish thrift.

We were informed the second groom was fifty percent Jewish—the third only a quarter—I expect if we had four daughters the fourth would have married a Christian. But by then religion was an afterthought. For the second and third we didn't waste any glasses.

The reception for Melora's wedding was at the polo club in Carpinteria. It was a nice rustic building. My father, who years before when asked how long he wanted to live said, "To see my first grandchild (Melora) married." And he made it. I am also pretty sure he knew he was there. In fact, he said he had been there before, giving my mother another opportunity to ridicule him.

To get our chaparral covered backyard and environs in reasonable shape for a wedding, our three gardeners worked steadily during the three-year construction process. The last month or so they worked seven twelve-hour days a week. So we invited them to the wedding.

Through the vagaries of the seating configurations they were seated at a table with the groom's cousin and other more remote relatives. The cousin, who we were forewarned was a trifle off-center, though certainly a respectable member of society (some job in the federal government patent office), was visibly shaken to have two of these just-as-respectable Mexicans at *his* table. As near as I could tell, they didn't put their elbows in the soup, burst into mariachi song nor make any untoward remarks about us gringos hustling them out of California in the nineteenth century. Perhaps it is poetic justice to see them quietly taking the state back.

I had them stand to laud their efforts in making the house grounds ready for the nuptials. The in-laws, liberal Democrats to the core, did not seem as overjoyed at this tribute as I had hoped.

THE SANTA BARBARA WRITER'S CONFERENCE
AND THEODORE ROOSEVELT

Art is too serious to be taken seriously.

—*Ad Reinhardt*

Barnaby Conrad (may he rest in peace) *was* the Santa Barbara Writers' Conference which I discovered toward the beginning of its run in the 1970s. His wife, Mary, a charmer in her own right, did the heavy lifting.

As with most accomplished women of her generation she worked behind the scenes and kept her accomplishments unsung.

A celebrity gadfly, Barnaby had had a watering hole in San Francisco where the elite met to drink—and by all accounts he was expert at the hosting trade. He certainly was a charming impresario of the Writers' Conference.

My first year I was obliged to be a little late. He was there to greet me (perhaps the a.m. after the opening the evening before). He made a fuss about the Theodore Roosevelt part of my name and was eager to know if I were related. Alas, I shared, the naming was more hysterical than historical—and the Second, rather than the more accurate Junior was the handiwork of the doctor, G.S. Backenstoe, who had a flair for the dramatic. (As had his father, Dr. M.J. Backenstoe.)

My father's father, Forest Gardner, worked in the local wire mill by day, and with nine kids to feed, served as a bartender by night at the North End Republican Club. Of course he was a Democrat. One story is the club gave him a gold watch, which depending on your faith in undertakers was buried with him — or not. The watch was to bribe him to or reward him for changing his registration to vote for Theodore Roosevelt.

He loved Theodore Roosevelt which should mitigate any thought of bribery — so much he named his seventh child (of nine) after the President — two or three months before the election. Perhaps that is why Theodore Roosevelt won.

But it was a passable subject for conversation. It seemed Barnaby Conrad claimed some relationship to one of those big time politicians (we call them statesmen when we are related), but I'm afraid I can't remember which.

The Writers' Conference was enchanting. Barnaby Conrad was an erudite guy (a *Yale* graduate) and a raconteur who could repeat from his fund of stories without getting too tiresome. My memory is I attended three years.

It was at the Santa Barbara Writers' Conference that I met the great Sid Stebel, teacher extraordinaire. I'd visited every class offered and his made the most sense to me.

Let us face it — writing is largely a vanity enterprise. I realize one of those Johnsons said anyone who writes for anything other than money is a blockhead, but the egos in writing classes are perilously close to the surface. Besides, millions of people write and only a handful are able to make a modest living by writing books alone.

The modus operandi in the "workshops" was to have participants read a few pages of some unvetted work of theirs, and let their workshop mates have at it. The edict was that before going negative, something positive had to be said so as to not demolish the (usually) frail ego.

I have always had trouble listening to someone read to me. Even from the time my beloved mother read Raggedy Ann and Andy stories to me, through school when my fellows read aloud my mind wandered.

Barnaby Conrad did not suffer fools gladly. And there were a passel of fools at the Writers' Conference each one thinking they were God's gift to literature—and a high percentage demonstrably wrong.

At the conference Barnaby (is that a *great* name, or what?) seemed to feel an obligation to be cordial—and no one was better at it. He had to fill the time in any case, might as well be a good Joe about it.

But if you ran into him in town when the conference was not in session you learned just what a fool you were.

He liked to tell how he got off the phone if he wanted to terminate a conversation. "Hang up when *you* are talking. That way the caller will think it was a technical glitch. Then leave the phone off the hook so they can't call back."

This came to mind when I saw him by chance in a now defunct bookstore, The Earthling, where his large caricatures of writers adorned the walls above the bookshelves.

I said hello and began some small talk when he darted away from me muttering something about his urgent need to consult some periodical at the rear of the store. Naively I followed along—being slow to grasp he didn't fancy my company. I imagine it must have been annoying to have so many acolytes follow you around like needy puppy dogs. Especially if it turns out they aren't related to Theodore Roosevelt.

As noted elsewhere, I am a slow learner, but that must not be confused with a *no*-learner. So, soon after we reconnoitered at the back wall I peeled off from my wingman position. He must have been relieved. No attempt was made to hinder my departure.

This scene becomes especially poignant to me after Barnaby discovering in some periodical a quote from Ernest Hemmingway about the annoyance of Barnaby Conrad making bids for his attention. Why did Barnaby tell this story? Surely not to make him look like a fool. Rather I expect to give him the bona fides of even being mentioned by the great Ernest Hemmingway no matter how derogatory.

GET A HOBBY

I worry incessantly that I might be too clear.

—*Alan Greenspan, Chairman of the
Federal Board of Reserve Board, emeritus*

Most of us, I suspect, have heavies in our lives and we may play the heavy to someone. For some years after he built his ten thousand square foot mansion not far from me, one of my neighbors was such a man. I'll call him Jack.

My first notice of him was his picture in the paper after he got out of prison. Some nuisance about his selling helicopters to the North Koreans—or one of those enemies. I remember him being quoted saying he wanted to put that unpleasantness behind him.

Well, duh, my kids would say. He didn't say what he would do with the ill gotten gains from the illegal transactions. There was no mention of turning that over to the government. Instead he built a ten thousand square foot mansion, which was, it turned out, not big enough to silence his incessantly barking dog.

I tried to be understanding—perhaps he was a devoted dog lover and he was deprived of man's best friend during his incarceration. Perhaps he was frightened of reprisals—some prisoner with negative chemistry perhaps. Or people he neglected to pay during his construction and after. I did a courthouse search (actually Lilli Rossi, RIP, did it for me. She had been the clerk or administrator or whatever they called her for twenty-five years.) The printed pages showed forty-two lawsuits against him for non-payment. I suppose if you sell helicopters to the enemy a little stiffing of a lot of people is pissant in the scheme of things.

Then I realized if forty-two people come after you, that's the tip of the iceberg. Does it equate to double that? I mean, how many people have the gumption to sue? Then if he hires people without licenses they can't prevail in court suits. Perhaps the stiff list is closer to two hundred—but who needs more than forty-two for a recommendation?

But you might wonder how he could continue to get people to work for him when these stats are public record. Two possibilities: no one suspects this magnitude of stiffs, or they see the huge property and elaborate architect's plans and think pot of gold and don't bother to investigate. How many people after all, make a religion of not making the last payment?

We want to think the best of our fellow man, and most of the time we are right.

People considering divorce could do a lot worse than borrowing a page from his book. He was married more than twenty years, had apparently made significant money—he owned eighty-four acres on our street which he divided into six or seven lots. He built his ten thousand square foot home on one, sold two others and the rest still have for sale signs on them ten years later.

In the records of divorce, he represented himself without an attorney—but I believe part of the final agreement was they would each pay their own lawyers. He got custody of three kids though I believe there may have been one or two who were already adults and living off campus so to speak. I wonder if he really wanted the kids or it was a money saving ploy?

He seemed to do okay. He had given, I believe, his wife a modest house and cash allowance of, was it two thousand a month for four years, or four thousand a month for two years? Whatever it was, it was a mystery to me how she could live on it—even while she was getting it. But when it cut off? A woman who had apparently devoted her formative years to motherhood? I didn't get it, but perhaps she was an heiress, and apparently she and her attorney accepted the deal.

The saga of the barking dog wasn't really settled until the

fire burned down the ten thousand square feet. Perhaps the dog was unattended and burned. Perhaps he died of old age. But it is blissfully peaceful in the neighborhood without the raucous, grating, continual barking of that pup.

When I wrote him what I thought was a consummately tactful note about the barking dog situation, suggesting if he didn't agree to peace from that quarter we might have the matter adjudicated, he responded in a letter saying, "Why don't you get a hobby," and he would meet any suit head on with the full arsenal in his possession and then added, "I warn you, my bite is worse than my bark."

It frankly scared me. I thought it was a physical threat. I called the police. I was right in my suspicion that they would do nothing. The letter, they said didn't rise to the level of a threat of physical harm. They suggested civil court.

I took their suggestion. Hired an attorney who said it wouldn't cost more than twelve thousand dollars. I thought if I got peace and quiet after, was it five years, it would have been worth it.

Good as his word, Jack fought the suit. When we met for the first time, required arbitration I believe it was, his young lawyer informed me that some dogs were better than some people. It is perhaps a tribute to my naiveté or obliviousness or both that I didn't think he was suggesting his client's dog was better than I was, so I mindlessly nodded my agreement to the proposition. When you consider the appeal of domestic animals in that they give unconditional love and never talk back, it is hard to disagree that there are *some* dogs better than *some* people. I just didn't think I was one of them. Of course, they thought differently.

We both tell our stories to an arbitrator provided by the court—in separate rooms. He goes back and forth so I have the privilege of paying my attorney while he whiles away his time while the arbitrator is off campus. During this time he is free to work on other cases as he demonstrated with his cell phone. When I pointed this out he laughed and said, "Yeah, I'm billing three of you for the same time."

I wouldn't swear he was joking.

The dog lover wore me down. All he seemed willing to

commit to was bringing him in when he barked, if he heard him.

By now my attorney bills had amounted to about $13,500 more than ten percent over his top estimate and we were nowhere. I reminded the attorney of his avowal the case would not cost more than twelve thousand dollars. He said, "Well I didn't know he was going to make a federal case out of it."

I had been worn down. If we went to court (the next step) my bill would easily double. My anguish was not assuaged with the knowledge it was likely costing my adversary more—*if* he was paying his bill. My inquiry of his lawyer, was he being paid? He gave me a big smile and said, "He treats me real well." Of course I didn't say anything about being wary of the final payment being met with any kind of legal tender.

We stood before a judge asking for trial with the sad news we had not come to an agreement.

The judge seemed put out. He recited all the things the attorneys had to do to get the trial underway—and I saw dollar signs.

It was around that time I threw in the sponge—I wasn't adroit at bluffing—and we set out to make an agreement to drop the suit.

I have to hand it to the defendant. He seemed willing to go down in flames to protect his dog's right to bark outside forever.

At some point the arbitrator said he had a solution.

What?

Ear plugs.

I thought that rather charming. In one simple stroke he could settle the case. All I had to do was impair my hearing with earplugs. I declined. This suggestion arose after we had visited the defendant's ten thousand square foot manse. A block long driveway snaked from the street. Two of the sons were standing by the dogs who may have been given tranquilizers for all I know because there was not a peep out of either dog—the raucous barker or the whiner. This latter sound was bearable—the hour on hour barking was not. Pity this attention could not be paid to the dogs when they barked at night.

Inside a beautiful young secretary sat at a desk close to the door. I'm still not sure what her purpose was. Perhaps a stature builder—gosh, he has a secretary at home? And a looker to boot.

Again we went in different directions and when the arbitrator came back you could tell he was smitten with this owner of this palatial house (some three times the size of mine). This was before he told me, gosh, the dog was an *outside* dog.

To which I retorted "and I'm an inside person."

"Yes, yes," he conceded, "and you're more important."

Did his kindness know no bounds?

Did the enemy suggest either subtly or outright, that a favorable conclusion to this grievance might result in further business with this attorney, who, since he took on this arbitration for virtually nothing must have hoped for some business from it. Since the defendant was being sued endlessly he seemed the better bet for the gold at the end of the rainbow. Besides, the arbitrator was a dog owner/lover which could have been a basis for my rejecting him, but I was eager to get it over with.

It was agreed the defendant's attorney would draft the agreement.

He came up with a document that made his client look like the proverbial knight on the shining white horse and me being the hind end of the same horse.

Under duties of parties pertaining to barking, mine were multi paragraphs. His were a couple of sentences.

This was the tenor of the opus and when I asked to take the dog in at eight p.m. they refused. Ten was the best he could do. I'd compromise at nine, he wouldn't.

The arbitrator had suggested I wouldn't be happy with a jury. I'd happily have settled for a judge, but the enemy wanted a jury. It was a harassment tactic, I said. The attorney agreed but it was his right and he would probably exercise it.

Now these jurors were just folks, not rich folks who should get hobbies and not tie them up on such a frivolous case. Court was for murder, not spats over barking dogs.

Most of them probably rented and here we were, two guys on eighteen and twenty-five acres respectively, who couldn't settle a dog dispute.

Of course, I thought I was in the right. I suspected there

would be more jurors who were bothered at some time by the barking of dogs than there were people who loved barking dogs and would defend to the death their right to bark at will.

I also, immodestly, thought I was a better salesman than this bull in a china shop and could garner more sympathy from the jurors. My record in acting as my own attorney was two wins, zero losses, but I didn't want to do it again. It was all consuming and I was aging sufficiently without another of those hassles.

But when I read the document his attorney had prepared I decided they thought I was decidedly stupid.

They were quite angry that I wouldn't sign. But this fellow who had stiffed forty-two contractors seemed willing to mortgage his house if necessary to run me into the ground. My hope was in letting it drift away. If it didn't improve and my spirits did, I could sue again.

But it *did* improve. The barking *usually* stopped around ten or ten thirty except one night he barked all night. I called the neighbor's phone he had given me. No answer. I left a message.

He called me in the morning to apologize. Gosh, he went to see his mother in San Diego (and you *know* a guy who pays attention to his mother can't be all bad). He plumb forgot about the dog.

Then our houses burned down and though I'd hoped to solve the grievance less drastically, when he rebuilt it was sans doggies.

Free at last. Thank God almighty, I'm free at last.

CONFORMITY

Always remember that you are absolutely unique.
Just like everyone else.

—*Margaret Mead*

Conformity never held any conscious appeal for me. I don't know why. I sort of liked being different.

Of course, in retrospect, how different was I, really?

I remember being the only male in my high school who did not wear jeans. I don't know why not—perhaps I thought they made me look like a farmer. But that's no disgrace. My mother's grandparents were farmers. Also my father's. I wrote music, directed it, arranged it—no one else did. But now I am scratching for some other differences that were my doing. There were still only a handful of professional families in our still small town. But that was not my doing.

It now occurs to me I didn't want to be different—rather I didn't want to be the same.

What makes one person a conformist and another not? And what makes a person so keen on having others conform? Does it validate their own persons? Is the opposite an invalidation?

I, and I expect people in general, don't want to stand out in the crowd as being so different to be bizarre—or even noticeable. It is a fine line between some conformity and clamoring to be noticed.

A venerable neighbor said: "We are ceanothus people here." With the strong suggestion I plant to conform. Or was it toyon people? Or both? Oleander?

Anyway, I discovered I wasn't a ceanothus person—though I planted it here and there. It was an effective ground cover—low water. Maybe even I could have become a ceanothus person, but I had additional aspirations—and planted my own botanic garden. Perhaps I am simply unobservant, but the fellow in question's property is up the hill from mine and I can't recall *any* planting there. I expect you can be a ceanothus person without planting it. Or rather that was the beauty of ceanothus. You didn't need to plant it. It grew wild.

I remember when I was a kid of marble-playing age. Third grade maybe? Fourth? A teacher confiscated my marbles—and I expect at that stage you were judged by the stash of your marbles. Could that have been the origin of the saying, "He's lost all his marbles?" I think this teacher was a friend of an older cousin of mine who may well have been babysitting me—in the course of which a visit to this teacher's house, a few doors up the street from her house, ensued. There was a kid perhaps a year or two younger than I was, playing with *my marbles*. A fringe benefit of the teaching profession?

I remember one marble that had a particular fascination for me. It was essentially clear glass with swirly red and green elements encased. I must have used it for a shooter.

The game entailed a drawn circle in the earth (or with a crayon or pencil on the sidewalk). You had to shoot your marble in the crux of your bent index finger, propelled by the thumb of the same hand. The object was to hit as many marbles as you could, knocking them outside the circle. Was the shooter immune from capture? I remember losing it somehow to Dick Loux or Terry Letterhouse.

My dim memory tells me I finagled something to get it back. I trust honestly, but I couldn't be sure. Perhaps trading for two or three others.

I was playing marbles with Dick Loux a few doors down Second Street from my home when a police car pulled up in front of our house and a policeman accompanied my father to the front door. I sought to divert Dick's attention from this embarrassment without success.

Dick asked why the police were taking my father home. This suggestion of non-conformity chagrined me. I think my father was District Attorney at the time and I hope I had the intelligence to speculate it was work related. The District Attorney and police worked hand in hand.

I can virtually guarantee I didn't have the wit for that response. I am sure I tried to underplay it somehow. The police never brought Dick's father home nor anyone else's that we knew. My mother reported they brought him home from a drunk driving episode either in progress or to forestall it.

I didn't want Dick or anyone else to know that. I wanted to conform.

I recently made the acquaintance of a woman—forty-two years old, mother of two, by all appearances a normal, educated, productive member of society. She came to my house in the service of her profession as a travelling notary public acknowledging signatures to be genuine. I like to write with, and sign necessary papers with a fountain pen, as I am now using to write this, which you are good enough to read. She preferred (mandated) I conform and sign with her blue ink ballpoint pen. I acquiesced. But this woman (notary), who was forty-two years old, had never seen nor known of a fountain pen! I couldn't believe it. She insisted—another wake up.

This is a woman who makes her living watching people *sign* papers. Thirteen years I believe she's been at it and has *never seen a fountain pen*. She asked me how it worked.

A conformist wouldn't use a fountain pen. At her insistence, I conformed.

My new home—and the run up to government approval and completion—was an object lesson in conformity. It puts one in mind of George Orwell's *Animal Farm* where the head pig posits: "All animals are equal, but some animals are more equal than others."

Neighbors, some, but not all of whom were in the neighborhood before I was, were people I assumed attracted to the hippie movement because they wanted to be nonconformists. Well and good, but that didn't seem to mean they could accept people who didn't conform to them.

The titular head of this neighborhood group came to kibitz along with an army of his fellows when our museum construction site visit was announced. How he who lives one and a half miles away got the notice and my neighbor who lives in the adjoining lot did not is a mystery to me. These guys haunt the halls of the building department and attempt to hold sway with the powers. I have no information that they ever prevail with their stop-building-progress, but I suppose they deserve some credit for their willingness to fight for their ideals, i.e. conforming to their norms.

This particular chap was president of a group of neighbors. He announced on my lot that his house burned also and had been condemned, "But I moved back in anyway." So this fellow who delighted in snubbing the system was attempting to work his will—through the system—on me.

We had a large concrete wall which was part of the house (see Masterless Builders) which burned to the ground, but the wall alone remained standing. He wanted it torn down—it had been standing there for twenty years. The Design Review Board said he should take his case to the city building department. If he ever did, I never heard of it.

Every step of the way these "neighbors" from one and a half miles away sought to hinder our progress. Their one triumph was in requiring we move the museum structure which was below the road—the roof at approximate street level—ten feet further down from the road. I estimated this little nicety cost us ten thousand dollars or so.

Finally they ran out of delaying tactics and we were given approval to begin grading and construction—four years later—six years from the onset of the planning and approval processes we were given final approval. I sometimes have to remind myself that the completed building is an actual fact and not an ephemera, miasma or delusion. It is woefully anticlimactic. Would the feeling be different had it been completed in a year or two or even three? I don't know. But six years later all the cells in your body have been regenerated and—physically—you are a new person.

With all our talk of honesty and integrity, some searching

in our past reveals all we are and have was based on a dishonest act, perhaps even illegal. It involved my father forging his birth certificate.

When he was a lad of fifteen years, he had a yen to join the Navy and see the world. Or, more to the point perhaps, get out of a house with eight siblings, two parents and himself—and it was not a large house. The hitch was, of course, he was only fifteen years old, not the required eighteen.

Looking at his picture in his Navy uniform I thought the lad was a passer: a believable eighteen. Though he had a pretty smooth face, I expect he was already shaving.

Is this an obvious example of situational ethics? Obviously he lied. Not a good thing. And to the U.S. government. They would not be amused. Yet could the recruiter really have been fooled by a birth certificate forged and aged by a fifteen year old in the backyard in the sunshine? One might think these circumstances in the service of avoiding serving would have a felony feeling more so than a kid who was itching to do his bit.

One must also consider the recruiting officer was not fooled, but had a soft spot in his heart for a kid who wanted to be older—to "serve his country."

What were the ramifications of this dishonest act?

Well, as mentioned, he got out of the house and had a so-so chance of seeing the world. He got as far from home as Bremerton, Washington where he was on a scaffolding painting the side of the ship. When it got underway without warning he fell from the scaffolding and plunged into the icy Pacific Ocean. He contracted pneumonia, pleurisy and an honorable discharge—the latter making him proud. But his pride threshold seemed pretty low.

It was a year or two he lost in school so he took the high school equivalency test, then got a scholarship to Muhlenberg College in his hometown, Allentown.

Then our father got a senatorial scholarship to the University of Pennsylvania law school. He delighted in telling how his introduction to the school was an assembly of new students addressed by the dean, "Look to the left of you, look to the right of you. There are three of you. Two of you won't be back." Theodore Gardner vowed that wouldn't be him and it wasn't.

Of the nine Gardner children—one of them graduated from law school (Theodore R.) and only one went to college, the same Theodore R. Could this have been because he left for the Navy at fifteen? Matured early? After graduation from Pennsylvania Law he set out his shingle—a gutsy thing to do in the depression.

Mother and father met in a play put on by some local group. *Kempy* was the name of the play—not Shakespeare, but it did the trick.

But check the timing. Had he not gone into the Navy and lost a year or two, this fortuitous meeting would not have taken place, they would not have married and six years later given birth to you-know-who. He didn't conform to the norm.

And it's no use speculating that the world would have been a better place if old Theodore R. Gardner, the First, had stayed in high school for to quote a former president, "It is what it is."

Judge Jimmy also met his first wife in a play.

There are those who would say I was *anti*-social. To this I respond I'm not anti-social, I'm just not social. I like people just fine. I just don't want them around all the time.

Why? What is the reason for this? It could simply be genetics. The Gardner side of the family sported a lot of shy guys. The mother of the brood of nine was considered a saint for obvious reasons. But she was *painfully* shy. Even when, as a little kid, I was alone with her.

I consider it a remarkable feat to be a wife and mother of nine *without* being depressed. I was told she rose out of her bed at four a.m. to prepare the breakfast for her brood AND TO IRON THE TABLECLOTH for the meal.

Surely this is hyperbole! These were not the idle rich—or she would have had a maid to put on airs. No, poor humble working people with eleven mouths to feed. Was this some kind of sociological statement? I could believe that a Sunday breakfast might warrant tablecloths, but *every* day!? Not to my knowledge did any of her children perpetrate this tradition.

Then there is the conformity of clothing fashion.

Some strikes me as downright silly. The idea of throwing

new jeans in a washing machine with stones and selling them as "stone-washed" jeans eludes me.

Pants already frayed or torn when you buy them? Cost more because fraying or tearing them is an extra step.

Why aren't those runway models smiling? Shouldn't some of this be fun? Dressing up like the Mad Hatter in *Alice in Wonderland*? And *none* of them seem to have gotten enough to eat. My current sculpture project is five or so rail thin models with sour pusses sporting outrageous "fashion" stuff that you never see in public (count your blessings). How could anyone not laugh out loud let alone smile if gotten up like that?

But the models don't smile. Are they being paid too much? Is it a serious business and any suggestions it isn't might be risky — maybe the emperor *is* naked? It might not do to have the audience for this audacity get the idea it is a farce. Especially if it is.

I remember Jenna Lyons, who made a mercurial rise to the top of J. Crew which is sort of a fashion house for the common man or woman as this case may be, when her name was Judith. At some point she let it be known she wanted to be called Jenna. No one argued with her.

At the time, I expect she wanted to be different. There were a couple of Judith's around, but I didn't know many. I didn't know *any* Jennas. Now I read about a Jenna now and then.

Jenna's mother is Barbara Lyons, divorced from her father Rory Lyons. I remember Jenna as a nine or so year old acting so grown up. And as an exceptionally talented artist. In a recent trip to the Santa Barbara Airport I perused a magazine rack in the book store and who was on the cover of the magazine I had not heard of called *Fast Company*?

The caption read, "JENNA LYONS has turned J. Crew into the Apple of fashion." The bold type headline down the left side of the cover, the length of her upper body says, "HOW J. CREW STAYS WHITE HOT (IT'S A SECRET)."

High praise indeed, and apparently true. On the cover she is seated in one of those wire chairs which after a time imprints little squares in your backside. Harry Bertoia? Saarinen? Mies van der Rohe?

She is all in white except a black belt and black shoes (or slippers?) and oversized black-framed eye glasses, legs crossed, right hand on her bare left ankle. The cuffs of her pants are frayed—threadbare. Her white shirt has flared cuffs and is adorned by a white bow tie. Everything looks brand spanking new except the pants which we are given to understand from a glance at the article therein, seems to be selling the new to look old.

What was her secret, promised on the cover? As near as I can tell reading the piece inside, is that she has good business sense, good judgment, super taste, and the good fortune to work for (run) a company not beholden to that great leveler of taste, the American stockholder.

In other words, she could not be classed as a conformist. (Nobody in the company seems to wear socks. This is attributed to Jenna, who sets the style.) I have tried wearing shoes without socks. It appeals to my sense of simplicity—of frugality perhaps. I don't like it. It doesn't do diddly for my sense of comfort. When it comes to wearing socks, you may put me down as a conformist.

Jenna's non-conformity, the article points out, extends to her personal life. She has a gorgeous young son—five or six in the picture where she is painting his toenails some garish color.

Jenna was married to an artist who graduated from Yale. An institution that famously turned a blind eye to my applications—three of them. It might be good to keep that fact in mind, to keep in perspective the opportunity for jealousy that could creep in here.

The photo of Jenna, her son and the toenail painting caused a minor furor. She was accused of exploiting her own child—The whole thing was so silly, I wondered if it could have been a publicity-garnering gesture. If so, it was a success.

I have a group picture of our daughter Abby's wedding in Santa Barbara with all the attendees spread out on a grassy area. Jenna and her husband-to-be are in the rear of the group, smooching—as they seemed to be at every opportunity. Fast forward to her apparently falling in love with another mother of three or four kids. Divorce!

Acrimonious! As homosexuality becomes more accepted, I expect we will see a lot more of it. As well as less hypocrisy. Or is it

a question of a person achieving so much seemingly effortlessly, becoming bored with the status quo and conventions of conformity?
If I see Jenna again, I will ask her.

PREDATOR AND PREY PRAY

Paradise Lost

The predator reigns in all of life—
While the prey's life is one of strife.
But, what if in some future day
Prey becomes predator, predator prey?
What will be that ultimate cost,
If this, our paradise, is finally lost.

—*HermiTed*

In my garden I have added a sculpture of giant flypaper (twenty-one feet tall) with a giant fly atop the trap that has ensnared numerous tiny human bodies. It is accompanied by the above verse.

This food chain is something I prefer repressing. We eat animals, but we don't have to see them being killed in the process. In fact, I am shocked to see anyone enjoying this spectacle.

Let me pump up my squeamish bona fides:

I have walked out of only one movie that I remember in my long life. I suppose I am an incurable optimist and I hope it will get better which I venture to say in reality doesn't happen. But hope springs eternal. It's the definition of insanity all over—using the same methods and expecting different results.

Or am I just so thrifty that I insist on getting my money's worth? Leaving in the middle of a seven-dollar movie is tantamount to making a $3.50 donation to a theater who had the temerity to book a turkey expecting Joe Public to pay him for it. The flick in question (notice how at ease I am with generation-spanning synonyms) had a name I have mercifully forgotten. Had I not forgotten it I like to think I would have repressed it. It opened with a brigade of fluffy coated white sheep corralled in crisp, clear air, their sheep herders prodding them into chutes you know presage their ends. Cut to a bunch of burly guys with full body, blood-soaked leather aprons. They are hacking away at the furry animals, cutting them into pieces, then when that task is complete, they toss the bloody carcasses on a pile reminiscent of one of those stacks of obsolete automobiles.

Okay, I should have left the theater then. I did become a vegetarian for a couple of weeks after that. It was the best I could do. But this blood and gore was before any story began. So I'm an optimist. However, the filmmakers passed the background test in spades. Hacking at carcasses was the perfect foreshadowing of the plot.

There were three to five young men at the epicenter of the tale. They were no-good-nicks, at liberty from any kind of productive work. They got by by mooching and preying on vulnerable souls—not above armed robbery were they.

One of these souls was an elderly woman—eighty-five or so—lonely, I suppose, and she took the chaps into her home where she treated them like royalty, whereupon they made their plans to kill her and take all she had. The boys were fawning over their weapons of choice—including a hatchet, as I recall—which tied so nicely into the opening scene, don't you see?

It was at that juncture that the scenario and I parted company. It is possible that I missed a gratifying denouement—say, the boys set about their business of hacking her in her sleep giving her in essence what the sheep got—but she saw it coming and pulled the pistol she stashed under her pillow and, dead shot that she was, plugged them all in the face.

On the other hand, I was unwilling to risk viewing what I expected instead, a hacking to death of their kindly benefactress no matter how tastefully the director shot it.

This sensibility carried, spilled, over to my witnessing a young, good-looking couple and their dog amid one of these food chain, predator/prey dichotomies. I fail to recall the exact venue of the episode—could it have been a national park? If I knew dog breeds or half-breeds I could tell what the dog was—but I don't have that expertise. Suffice it to say the dog must have been a killer.

This, I would say medium-sized, canine put on a display that pleased his patron mightily. He toyed with some small animal—perhaps a chipmunk or squirrel—then suddenly snatched the creature, perhaps one-twentieth its size, in his iron jaws to the immediate raucous amusement of the young chap in his charge.

As I recall he thrashed the furry thing who tried to resist hopelessly until it lay limp in his jaws. All this to the aggravating merriment of his handler. He laughed so hard with such shrill delight I thought he might explode.

All the while I witnessed this spectacle I tried to understand what this Homo sapien creature found so gut-splitting amusing. Here was the food chain at work, okay, but funny? I found it repulsive.

I looked at his female companion.

She didn't get the joke either.

THE BAR, THE STEINS, AND THE DRINKING

I like to behave like men….strong and childish.

—*Francoise Sagan*

My father used to repair to his basement barroom—euphemistically: rathskeller—I expect when his buddies were elsewhere.

He seemed at peace there with a beer and glass in front of him on the round cherry wood table. What went through his mind during those solitary sessions underground, I don't know. My recollection is it was beer only when he was alone. The harder stuff required a social setting.

It would not surprise me to learn he might have ruminated about his success in being able to afford these luxuries. A refrigerator stocked with more beer than he could drink, a bar with every kind of liquor you could imagine. If he entertained you, he had what you wanted. It was a point of pride. In his house on the alley his father permitted no alcohol. His father should see him now.

Perhaps that was what he was thinking.

Or could his mother have been the subject of his thoughts? I remember seeing him blubber at her funeral—loud, prolonged, uncontrollable sobs.

Our mother, who never passed up an opportunity to dig him, said his emotions poured out because he was ashamed he didn't do more for her. Was this a fair warning to me to test my allegiance to her—my own mother? If so I might have passed: I didn't cry at her funeral.

Just now I wonder from the perspective of a teetotaler what

this relaxant/stimulant alcohol contributes to the quality of a life which without it might be virtually unmanageable.

The Judge gave us several opportunities to witness these variations. He went "on the wagon" several times in my experience. The verdict seemed to be he *was* more likeable under the influence of alcohol. When he was sober he seemed tense, on edge, less able to cope with the vicissitudes of life with perhaps close to zero tolerance for the barbs and jibes from his wife.

In short, he was not a mean drunk—he was a happy drunk. Is this why prohibition came to a quick, ignominious end?

The basement table was originally cherry wood. I suspect some decorator took the situation in hand and recommend he antique the wood furniture with cream paint and goldish streaks in it to, I speculate, ape the knotty pine with which he covered the walls. The provenance of the table was I believe from Grampop Knoll's Broad Street Hotel after he sold it—about the time the Judge was furnishing the basement in his district attorney years.

Uncle Barney told Father that Grampop was mightily miffed that his prized cherry wood tables were defiled with paint.

At ceiling level, which coincided with the ground level outside, there were six or eight high windows that were set in window wells just below the surface of the grass. The only time I remember any of them being opened was when we took delivery of a truckload of coal while we still had a coal burning furnace. As I recall there was a lot of shoveling involved. This was, remember, in the days of the humanoids stomping on the garbage on the back of an open truck to compact it. So I don't think there were any fancy conveyor belts to hustle the coal up the hill from the street, an elevation gain of perhaps six to eight feet at the location. Because of the grade, the truck could not simply dump the coal into a chute because it would have had to travel uphill. Somehow the coal was delivered to the coal room a shovelful at a time.

In the wintertime I remember shoveling coal into the furnace to keep the house toasty warm. I don't doubt that made me feel important.

Perhaps it was after World War II that we converted to electric heat and had single unit air conditioners installed in the living room, dining room, and master bedroom, a relatively palatial room added to the back of the house with a second bathroom and a lengthening of the kitchen into a first class diner. The old dining room was incorporated to increase the living room, the old kitchen became the dining room and a garage was dug into the earth below the new kitchen—stairs were added. It worked out perfectly: one level of stairs brought us from the garage which was on street level. Retaining walls were added to the garage driveways.

Alas, there was no air conditioning in the front guest bedroom which I was obliged to occupy on my visits. The oppressive heat kept me awake many a night before I opted and could afford to stay in air-conditioned hotels.

Since the Judge eschewed debt, I expect he paid cash for this nudge upscale.

His steins circled the basement room now—on shelves he had built—two horizontal rows for maximum views. A lot of shelves, but you don't put five hundred or so steins on view without them.

He claimed to get great pleasure sitting among them, reminiscing about their origin stories. I suspect it was a badge of his success that he could do this. There was no room for this display in the house he grew up in on the alley, and very little left in this basement bar. And too, don't forget, his father had moonlighted as a bartender—a man who didn't drink and didn't allow his children to drink.

I think of him and these basement episodes when I walk through the garden and glory in the collection of plants and sculpture, many of which I made.

Lately I have added to my property a "museum," six years in the making, where repose perhaps twenty of my large bronzes and seventy or so bronze busts of authors. Now and then I sit in there and contemplate which puts me in mind of him in the knotty pine basement at the faux antiqued cherry wood table.

That, I suppose, is a genetic brush with immortality.

As a tribute to him, I compiled a list of his some five hundred steins, printed it in a book. A print run of perhaps three or four copies.

We presented him the book—

The Beer Stein Collection of
Theodore R. Gardner

while he still knew what it was. But we got it in just under the wire. During the process we took the notes he had made, using his numbering system and typed those we could read. When we couldn't decipher an entry he was usually able to remember what it said. Things like where and when he got it, a description of the scene depicted, notes on the lid, if any.

When it was printed and bound and given to him he was very gracious as he always was. He had very few compos mentis years left to him. As his mind was drifting from reality his doctor told us the Grand Old Judge was likely suffering from Alzheimer's and it would be good if we could talk to him and try to interest him in anything that he could relate to—like his stein collection.

I tried, but it was no sale. I'm not sure by that time he remembered he had a stein collection.

I didn't regret the effort we put into the book. It was, I thought, a point of pride to him while pride was still for him an operative word.

The stein collection was put up at auction. The hope of the Judge was someone would buy the whole shooting match after he was gone, but it was not to be. Stein collectors were around, but very few with the money to buy so many and/or the place to display them. So the collection was broken, sold piecemeal and if I recall, garnered a reasonable amount of money. Of course it was not about the money. Though he was not averse to telling how much his prized specimens cost or were worth, I don't think profit was his motive. He never sold or even traded one of them in his lifetime.

Each of his children picked one or two to have as keepsakes or souvenirs of his collection. I kept two—one was a library motif— books all around the vessel. Did it have Bismarck on the lid? Or was that another? I may have had three because there was a tall, valuable one that I fancied aesthetically.

They were all fire victims—but not victims of the fire, but

the aftermath when the plunderers came down the mountain above the house (or perhaps through the park behind the house) filled their knapsacks with what they would including one of my bronze heads, which I considered flattering.

What level of Dante's Hell should be reserved for creatures who profit from someone else's misfortune and misery? Surely it would be close to the bottom, hottest level.

I remember the Judge playing bartender to his buddies. It must have been a fantasy for him. There were four boys in the brood of nine. Earle and Ted were serious drinkers, John, the youngest, was not. Lester the oldest, I believe, died in his twenties and his alcohol relationship is not known to me. None of the five women were drinkers, though one married one.

My picture of the bar was the Judge was the bartender, his buddies sat at the bar as customers, and I don't think that arrangement changed any over his lifetime hours the bar was in service.

It was my uneducated opinion that our father didn't drink that much by volume. He said he was known as a two-beers Gardner in reference to the amount of spirits it took to get him inebriated. That much I witnessed. But once he had achieved that state, I lost track of what followed. Mother didn't share this judgment. She thought he drank a lot.

However much booze passed through his body, in his eighties he began to lose contact with reality and memory. He asked me who I was. Since I don't drink strong spirits, I want to believe that is what caused his Alzheimer's and the role of genetics in those particulars is negligible at best. Neither of his abstinent parents suffered from Alzheimer's or dementia, neither did my mother's parents, so I may make it to the end still more or less compos mentis. Anyway, we believe what we want to believe.

In my young years I would fantasize in bed before going to sleep that I was the owner and driver of a candy store truck. The interior walls stocked heavily with all my favorites which at the time must have included Hershey bars, kisses, peanut butter cups, licorice of all types, M & M's, saltwater taffy, Necco wafers, those little sugar wafers with fortune sayings on them. I may have branched out to ice cream. But it never took long with those pleasant surroundings to go to sleep. I don't imagine I used much restraint in depleting the inventory with in-house samples.

Now seventy years later, I make my own candy and ice cream and finally find it beneficial to use some restraint in its consumption.

Who knows, had I been a drinker, if I would be known as a one beer Gardner. I might have had a barroom, the walls lined with all kinds of liquor. But the embarrassments to his family of his excess did not hit me with candy and ice cream; though my mother-in-law posited that they were just as bad for you as booze. She was a drinker who lost her faculties at the end. I am approaching the years when she and my father sank to oblivion. So we will see…

DELIGHTFUL PRETENSE

I'm Nobody! Who are you?
Are you - Nobody - too?
Then there's a pair of us!
Dont tell! they'd advertise - you know!

How dreary - to be - Somebody!
How public - like a Frog -
To tell one's name - the livelong June -
To an admiring Bog!

—Emily Dickinson

I adore pretension in all its forms. I like to hear speakers say "close quotes" at the end of a quote. The utterance of "the discipline(s)" by some would-be erudite academic thrills me to the core. I began thinking about it some years ago while preparing a book about Lotusland, one of Santa Barbara's prime attractions—a lush botanic garden in Montecito—I'd say the heart of Montecito except that might sound pretentious when it is a small, albeit prominent collection of über properties housing the very rich. Perhaps when you are that rich there is no need to pretend.

Lotusland was formed from the dust of the ground by its creator, Hanna Puacz, an uneducated but rich Polish girl—rich through the auspices of four of her six husbands which unarguably demonstrated she knew how to pick 'em and entice 'em into marriage, she just didn't know how to hang onto 'em. But, perhaps she didn't want to, owing to her penchant for spiritual values when her crass counterpart was interested in sex. She was, in her prime—the era of four filthy rich husbands—astonishingly beautiful. This brings to mind the old adage "pretty is as pretty does." One might wonder what the men got out of the relationships. Was it perhaps the vicarious thrill of being linked to such a ravishing beauty? How did that make these important men seem more important? By all accounts she was not interested in the ever popular delights of the flesh that her husbands had crassly come to expect.

Hanna had, perhaps, the corner on pretension. Early on she decided she should be called Ganna Walska—the great waltzer and let it be known she should be referred to as Madame—not the whorehouse variety, the royalty kind.

There was a nice existing garden at her thirty-five acre estate in Montecito, California, she purchased for her sixth husband, the only American Buddha or some such pretension. He was by nature impecunious—for all the spiritual values aside, being a monk of any stripe was a hard dollar, and Brother Bernard's tastes were anything but plebian. To wit, this thirty-five acre estate in Montecito— which when Ganna Walska was in residence became somewhat stifling for the holy man. So he prevailed on his benefactress to buy him a pad in the mountains where he could get out of the house and away from said benefactress for his meditating.

Whether or not he was meditating at this juncture with some young things is a moot point.

He was twenty-five years Madame's junior and what would pass these days as a cute guy.

Ganna Walska began buying plants for her estate like they were going out of style. She was, if nothing else, in the words of one of her late caretakers, avaricious, an aggrandizer, and she built (from said dust of the ground) an eye popping garden. She never settled for one species of plant when a dozen would do. Thirty-five acres is a lot of ground. She employed four or five gardeners, but after she died the powers in charge upped that to twenty.

I was assembling my book, *Lotusland: A Photographic Odyssey*, which I hoped was a suitably pretentious title, when I came in touch with one Gregory Padgett, a young chap with surprising native photographic talent. Most of his pictures were taken with a box camera.

I asked to see some of his pictures he had taken when Ganna Walska was alive. He was, I believe, a lad in his twenties when he met Ganna Walska, then in her eighties—and proposed marriage to her hoping to land a slot as husband number seven which surely would turn out to be a lucky number (not as lucky as 77 perhaps, but lucky enough).

Though the details are somewhat murky, the union never took hold. Perhaps she was simply tired of mating—and who could blame her? Or she realized that his age and sexual orientation was not all that compatible. She was probably more comfy in her well-honed role as predator than as prey.

Poor Gregory met a premature end in his bathroom after hitting his head on the sink or bathtub or some like hard surface, after reportedly imbibing a surfeit of strong spirits, and/or pharmaceuticals.

Gregory, who instead of showing me his pictures of early Lotusland, came to our office with a slide projector and CD player in tow and proceeded to give a show of his slides with soft opera arias as offering background music. (One of Ganna Walska's pretensions was to be an opera star—which was in its way charming, except for the fact that by her own account, in spite of daily lessons, she couldn't sing and had debilitating stage fright.)

Anyway, it was Gregory who pronounced during the projection of one of his slide photos that one or another of Ganna Walska's conglomerations of plants and stuff was so "delightfully pretentious."

I never forgot it.

In the course of writing the Lotusland book, I talked with Ganna Walksa's niece Hunka which she changed to Hania after marrying Mr. Bacon. She said she didn't want to be known as Hunka Bacon.

I asked her if Ganna Walska would prefer an honest warts-and-all rendering or an idealized portrait. Without a second's hesitation she said, "Oh, idealized."

I considered the preference briefly—then did the warts and all. I'm too old for Santa Claus.

SUN VALLEY

I wish the rent
Was heaven sent.

—*Langston Hughes*

We built a house in Sun Valley, Idaho—in our humble estimation the premier ski resort in the good old USA. Clint Eastwood, Tom Hanks, Bruce Willis, Arnold Schwarzenegger, Ashton Kutcher and Demi Moore among others agree and put their money where their mouths are by building not so modest mansions there. That's the pretension. We actually built in Ketchum, Idaho, right next door, but without the cachet.

The process was somewhat memorable. At least *I* have retained it in the ever-growing sieve of a mind.

Mr. and Mrs. Hanks were sued by their contractor who seemed out of joint for being stiffed for around a million in changes requested by the missus—including moving the swimming pool after it was complete. The contractor won every penny plus interest and penalties. Hanks is appealing it. Noblesse oblige.

For some twenty-five years we had been coming to Sun Valley off and on for winter sporting. Some skiing, some ice-skating, sledding and I finally settled on cross country skiing which suited my metabolism. Soon after it entered the mix I took to skate skiing which may not have been all that compatible with my metabolism, but it was a heck of a workout.

I half kidded myself that building a house would be economical vis-à-vis renting condos. We had three daughters, the oldest already had two sons and the second oldest was married and threatening progeny.

So we threw up five bedrooms and a nice library off the stairway for me, and place under the stairway for my harpsichord (possibly the *height* of pretension).

En route we had to buy a lot or a house or condo. I looked at all the possibilities. We'd stayed most recently in The Wildflower Condos and in the process saw the swell, giant unit reputedly belonging to that bodybuilder *Ahnold* Schwarzenegger. We heard of a unit that seemed right for us. Called the broker who said it was no longer available or "off the market" in the parlance of real estate professionals. The next broker told us that was hogwash and he would show it to us, which he did. It didn't send our hearts a racing, so he showed us some houses and lots. Nothing lit any fires. When we returned to Santa Barbara he kept in touch and sent us lists with pictures. One of them seemed like it might work for us — with copious repairs and additions. We made an offer.

The response from the broker was the offer was okay, but since we hadn't seen the house we would have to see it lest we back out. I told the broker the offer was contingent on us seeing and approving it, but that wasn't good enough.

So, foolishly as it turned out, we made a trip to Ketchum. The broker at my prodding reassured us the sellers would accept the offer if we made the same offer *after* we had seen it.

We saw it and accepted it without me asking for any more concessions. Emboldened, the sellers changed *all* the terms. The broker seemed somewhat embarrassed to read to me the terms of his counter offer. I said, "You know you assured us the offer would be accepted if we saw the house and kept the offer the same." As though he were spaced on some controlled substance he was moved to read to me again the terms of their *counter offer* which he had apparently helped them craft.

I don't do business with dishonest people — if their offer is five dollars more than our agreement, I won't buy it.

Their counteroffer was couched in angry terms. "We *won't* do this…he *will* do that." Perhaps they had a military background.

My request to see vacant lots was met with the broker's intelligence there weren't any. I took a bicycle around the area of interest and saw six signs on vacant lots in twenty minutes. I called one, made an offer and we reached an agreement. Since I am a licensed real estate broker I could have kept the commission. Instead I called this forlorn broker and asked him to complete the transaction—a few minutes of paperwork—and told him of the many lots available, all in his multiple listing book.

He took us to the airport and thanked us for our patience with him.

I still wonder if he lied to me or just suffered from chronic incompetence.

We offered a nice builder a bonus if he finished the house by the following February so we might move in and enjoy the ski season.

A phone call came early on the day of our flight (it is an hour earlier in California than in Idaho). The house was complete but a pipe had burst at a faulty pipe connection—the plumber slipped up. His insurance would cover the repairs, which with the water damage were considerable. We got rooms in the Lodge apartments and somehow got in the house at some forgotten time.

Some interesting things happened in Idaho. Out riding a skinny-tired bicycle I had not ridden in twenty-five years, I had an accident.

Daughter Melora was riding ahead of me, and coming out of a plush subdivision I was about to rear-end her turning onto the bike path. I swerved onto the grass to avoid hitting her, and I did avoid hitting her, but I fell off my bike and because I had straps on the pedals, my foot stayed on. I heard the snap. A passerby called the ambulance which arrived in a gratifyingly short time. Double staffed with volunteers for the short ride (less than a mile) to the hospital where the sawbones on duty could not be located. I expect he didn't need another Medicare charity.

Dr. A. Herb Alexander to the rescue. A retired orthopedic surgeon from the U.S. Navy, perky and bristling with personality. I inquired after his experience in the bone line and he riposted that he was really a waiter at the Pizza Hut out for a lark.

But, bless him, he did the deed at eleven at night with a

tiny slice around my ankle into which was inserted a thin rod which was screwed to the errant bone in several places. The second break in a bone, I was informed, would right itself in time without any additional heroic measures from the sawbones.

When it was time to pull the metal rod out, I got to watch the procedure on a TV screen. It was a stop-motion thing that reminded me of an early, jerky silent film.

Alas, a few of the screws broke while the doc was attempting to take them out. This spooked me a bit and I asked if there wasn't something he could do to get them out.

Sure, he said, but it would destroy the bone. I settled.

NAME DROPPING

The writer's only responsibility is to his art. He will be completely ruthless if he is a good one....If a writer has to rob his mother, he will not hesitate; the 'Ode on a Grecian Urn' is worth any number of old ladies.

—*William Faulkner*

Another art almost as gratifying as pretension: it is the envy that results from an association with those who appear to be of a higher order of mankind.

In the early days of my dreaming unreality I sought to familiarize the same aforementioned mankind with my books. At the juncture in question, my first book of the subsequent thirty-nine was called *The Paper Dynasty*. It was a tome of doorstop heft that had garnered most gratifying reviews. I had visions of its becoming an overnight sensation with all the concurrent ego gratification many nascent writers have come to expect.

It mattered not that instead of this being my first book it was by actual count my tenth. I could hardly be blamed for that. The publishing world was too shortsighted to actually grasp the import and potential to rock the literary world on its very foundations of the first nine. This was *it!*

There is a quaint saying in the halls of pop psychology:

"If at first you don't succeed, try, try again."

To this chestnut a few words have been pragmatically appended:

"Then if you don't succeed, give up. There's no sense being a damn fool about it."

I must confess to some failings along this line. To wit not grasping when to give up—when to realize enough is enough.

So I sent *The Paper Dynasty* to 35 publishers—let me validate the veracity of this statement by spelling it out—to *thirty-five* publishers, before one offered to buy it.

Sort of. It was Zebra Press whose alphabetical position tells you something. But when the hunger for fame and fortune has been teased to its apogee one is loathe to quibble with the powers of publishers.

In this case, the editor said, "you write very well," an assessment a person never tires of hearing. Then explained she could make a small offer for my ten-year effort to the tune of $2,500—in legal tender backed by the full faith and credit of the U.S. government. Ok—that worked out to $250 a year for the effort or $5 a week. I should have been insulted.

I was delighted. I would be in *print*. It could not help but vault me to the stratosphere of literati.

There were a few conditions of course.

I had to cut it to 200,000 words from some 260,000 I believe.

I should "beef up the women."

The first of these I achieved with some relish. If I had to I could reduce 260,000 words to one sentence. If it meant after a ten year schlep getting in *print*.

Beefing up the women was more problematic. It was a story about a Los Angeles newspaper Dynasty going back 110+ years when women were seen but not heard in the business.

Zebra Press—the offeror—was a romance house. So I should make this book which they could see as a "family saga" a torrid romance. They had only one theme for all their book covers:

A woman with her dress slipping down – a man with his shirt off and a horse. I thought she was kidding. She wasn't.

Oh—and I should change my name to a woman's—"It is women who read these books," she said.

"I'd read it," was my sage riposte.

"You'd never find it," she said—"it would be buried in the romance section in the back of the drugstore."

This was ok, too. Faulkner had some germane words on

selling your grandmother if you had to. I sort of liked the sound of Theodora Gardner.

I asked to see the contract. The editor put me off until they were satisfied I had done my chores. After I cut the book by 25-30% (alas, not discernably to its detriment) I called her. Her response?

"Ted who?"

"Gardner. You made an offer on my book."

Short silence. Then, "That's impossible."

"Well, I talked to someone who sounded very much like you."

"No," she said. Pause. "What was the name of it?"

"The Paper Dynasty."

Sounds of her shuffling papers on her desk—something clicked and she remembered. She'd look at my revision.

Later she told me I had made a herculean effort of cutting—had she forgotten about the beefy women? I didn't dare ask—for the contract was forthcoming.

They would own the rights for twenty years whether they published it or not—and there was no obligation on their part to publish it at all.

Paranoia kicks in so easily. I opined 2500 smugolies to keep this out of libraries and bookstores might be a small price to pay for a hugely wealthy newspaper family.

Ms. Lafarge, the editor, said, "Oh, if you are going to nitpick the contract we shouldn't do it." But she suggested an agent and gave me the name of some authors they published who signed the contract.

I got one on the phone. She said in essence she was so eager to get published she would have signed anything.

The agent, who I had known years before, had been a story editor on a TV show I had submitted to at CBS, *The Twilight Zone*. He read the contract and allowed as how it was pretty tough. He had never seen anything like it. And he said he would see what he could do to liberalize it in my favor.

Nothing. Of course, nothing.

There was nothing for it except to form a publishing company with the lofty purpose of seeing this worthy book into print.

Especially since it had been legitimized with a third party, arm's length offer—a house that featured girls with their dresses falling down, fellas naked from the waist up—and the horse, don't forget the horse.

Voila! Allen A. Knoll with a goose for a symbol came to the rescue. And the A in Allen was at the *head* of the alphabet – take that Zebra!

We sold thousands of books—at a loss. Another charity is born. The imprint has published diverse books from various authors and is on the cusp of celebrating its twenty-fifth anniversary.

In the course of my brainless promotion I hit a bunch of bookstores in the LA area for signings. This was followed by a whirl-wind East Coast tour. It was not an easy sell—but I had made a decent living as a huckster so I knuckled down to the task at hand—and I made sales in every store—except one—where I was scheduled for Sunday morning. It was in a mall in Pasadena where no one seemed to darken the door before noon on Sunday. The store clerk was kind enough to stock a reasonable number of them which I signed, without a tremendous hope of them flying off the shelf.

Some time, not too much later, I got a call from Los Angeles County supervisor Mike Antonovich—no friend of the *Los Angeles Times*, the metropolitan paper that had gone from staunch conservative in leanings to staunch liberal—though they would try to deny it.

The County Board of Supervisors was represented by five districts—Antonovich's Antelope Valley et ux were conservative (ranchers and what not) as was the South Bay, off and on. The rest of the group were solid liberal as was most of California. Now there isn't a Republican in a major office in the state.

Antonovich graciously expressed admiration for the book, told me a friend of his had bought it in a Pasadena bookstore. I hadn't sold one copy during my signing. The supervisor had bought the rest to give to his friends and supporters. He was having a get together of supporters and would be pleased if I could join them.

Virginia and I hightailed it to some place in his district—Monrovia? Altadena? I had taken I believe my second book *Off the*

Wall and when we got to the packed hall with people seated at banquet tables we were greeted by the Supervisors Chief of Staff—I asked where I could leave the book. He said, Oh give it to him yourself.

We looked for an unassuming place to sit, thinking as far from the head table as we could get would be appropriate. Whereupon the guest of honor sauntered over. I asked where I could unobtrusively dump the book. He was most appreciative and it was dispatched somewhere. He then asked us to sit at his table, and when we got there, the only places were next to him. I thought there had to be a mistake and asked if this position of honor would not be more appropriate for an important constituent. No, no—it's for you he said.

I tried to hold up my end of the small talk when Antonovich went to the stage to give his warm appreciation to the assemblage he introduced me and praised my book and *recommended* it.

After that he invited me to be the M.C. at his big fundraiser at the Bonaventure Hotel. I had written all sorts of pithy and witty remarks, but when I attempted to deliver them there was such a din of conversation in the room I could not be heard. I thought it was my fault.

The newspaper in question had done a number on the guest of honor—lambasting him for helping his friends. I questioned what the Times would have instead, he should help his enemies?

Red Buttons, comedian—who I was surprised to discover was still alive—was the featured attraction. He was at an age where plastic surgery could have been beneficial—or it could have drawn attention to your age. He went without it. Or did he?

I gave him a flowery introduction and he began to complete silence in the room.

"Ted Gardner, he is better than a good friend—he's a perfect stranger." His talk was very funny and it could be heard—befitting his stature as a comedian who had earned his chops.

The supervisor sported Virginia and I to a room at the Bonaventure high up with a view. He continued to entertain me—at a dim sum restaurant—with notes—handwritten cards with pic-

tures of his new family – he had married a Doctor of Asian persuasion and sired a boy and girl—the gentleman's pair—and his cards
at Christmas time were festooned with numerous biblical quotes.

Before all this happened I went to a gathering at the Palos
Verdes library where candidates for the Republican nomination for
governor were "debating" the issues. There were too many of them.
Six? Eight? It was Mike Antonovich who impressed me the most
and I voted for him. Though I don't remember who won, it wasn't
super Mike. Pete Wilson perhaps? Whoever it was paled beside
Mike, but politics makes strange bedfellows.

Years later when this narrative took place I asked him if he
wasn't going to run for governor again.

He said he had a family now and had to devote his time and
attention to them for the time.

I'm convinced he would make a good governor—though
unless he switched parties he'd have an uphill battle to get elected.

PLUMP JACK

Life is too important to be taken seriously.
—*Oscar Wilde*

Gordon Getty wrote some good music. The fortune he inherited from his old dad, J. Paul Getty made him an enticing
prospect for performance.

I, myself, wrote him a fan letter, asking if he had anything
our South Coast Choral Society might perform. I must have had
visions of his laying a million or so on us in gratitude.

He had written an opera he marvelously called *Plump Jack*
after one of those fat English Kings, and it was not half bad. It was
kind of fun—proving I suppose, that wealth need not be a hindrance to creativity.

He was scheduled to speak at the UCSB music school and
to be introduced by the dean, a woman who will be pleased to know
I have forgotten her name. I'm sure she's forgotten mine.

Mr. Getty was at least 30 minutes late for his talk—more
like 45 minutes to an hour. Traffic and getting lost were his excuses—something I could relate to. As I recall he was coming to
Santa Barbara from Los Angeles and that could be brutal.

My feeling was the dean was ill at ease not only introducing
Gordon Getty, but simply being in his presence—giving him a plat-
form she perhaps felt she would not have done if he hadn't been so
damn rich and she couldn't help but salivate at the prospect of his
dumping big bucks on the music department adding a pleasing
feather to the dean's cap.

On the other hand, she had to be careful not to make it seem she was endorsing his ability or skill as a composer—at least until there was a substantial body of agreement among her peer group.

As one might suspect that validating was guarded, as anyone knew anyone that rich had to be suspect, talent wise. After all, even in those days, J. Paul Getty was worth north of a billion—and remember, a billion *is a thousand million*.

So the dean's intro was bound to be circumspect, not to say gingerly lest anyone get the slightest notion she was flattering him for his money.

So she spoke of grand plans the music department had for research or some such academic ephemera involving so many "disciplines" and hinted ever so circumspectly she was pleased to say Gordon Getty would be "helping" with this project (read: underwriting it).

Getty gave a talk—about *Plump Jack*, I believe—and perhaps sundry projects in his composing oeuvre. I was most pleasantly surprised that he was a handsome, personable, well-spoken and engaging fellow—in stark contrast to the dean who adored speaking of the "disciplines" as poster children for academia.

I don't think the dean ever married—she being preoccupied with disciplines of another sort—so imagine her shock when it was not long thereafter revealed that Mr. Getty had a second family and household in West Los Angeles in a union unblessed by the imprimatur of church or state. His philandering father came to be a serial monogamist at best. It is said children should outperform their parents in one or more ways—Gordon Getty was not going to make more money so he developed a musical composing skill that the old man lacked. As though that were not enough, it would be his lot to exceed him in the personal realm. J. Paul was well known for acquiring a bevy of belles, bringing them to the brink of marriage with all kinds of promises of putting them in his will, then dumping them as unceremoniously as possible, sometimes with a friendly stipend to cushion the blow.

Gordon, his youngest heir, saw no reason to be so callous, he would maintain two households, north and south. And support two wives and a number of children by each.

Why not? He could afford it.

But do you have to imagine the embarrassment this visited on the dean of the music school? A woman who from all appearances did not suffer fools gladly—a woman who, if she had any humor in her bones kept it there. I don't know—I have no firsthand knowledge, but my instinct tells me the dean felt possessed to cut off all contact with the scallywag, including the acceptance of any proffered funds for her dreamy projects. If any dough had been forthcoming, I wonder if she returned it with a terse note.

It was shortly thereafter that I was in residence at the distaff's abode in downtown Santa Barbara. She was apparently lending her house to a fundraising tea for the music school.

The dean made an appearance—gave a short talk about her beloved disciplines, wherein followed a personal encounter with the dean—it was hardly avoidable, the crowd being so small—but what I said to her does me no credit—instead it accrues to my everlasting detriment. It is a kind of proof that all of us have meanness within and consequently have a duty to our fellow man to keep it there.

Alas, I did not.

As the dean was taking tea and mingling with the guests in a manner no wise meant to suggest they were her betters, someone introduced me, I suspect with the preamble, "Do you know the dean…?"

"Oh yes," I said. Then I found myself incapable of keeping my mouth shut. "Gordon Getty," I added with impeccable timing, followed by a supercilious smirk.

She didn't comment, but left the gathering without a word.

THE DISTAFF

Melancholy is the pleasure of being sad.
—*Victor Hugo*

And so, at last, to the most difficult part to write. What is difficult is to do Virginia justice without being maudlin. But, I think we will both be better served with me writing about her than having to read what she would write about me.

Life, of course, is a matter of perspective. We do, verily, believe what we want to believe. Time passes and memories go with it. But my lasting impression, beginning perhaps fifty-five years ago, has been of a gentle woman of superior intelligence, even temperament who did her duty on the home front. Her grandfather whom she revered was a duty-doer. I would say Virginia was more even-tempered than anyone I have ever known. In hindsight it was a salubrious precursor of her later illness. I benefited from it for forty-some years. We lived together for forty-two years so I maintain no one was in a position to know her better.

She had her enthusiasms which could have been precursors—mini-manias you might call them. Virginia was a brilliant cook and superior mother. Devoted to her family in those vital, early, formative years.

She struggled against the academic bureaucracy at USC to complete her Master's of Library Science degree at night while I was on deck for babysitting duty. It gave her a get-out-of-the-home diversion.

Since we were without trust funds and not independently

wealthy, one of us had to work. That was me—and my real estate shop required daylight. To moonlight as I did as a babysitter required that the latter be performed in the moonlight.

The pool of available and affordable babysitters went to school themselves in the daytime. There was our conundrum.

But the head of the Library Science School felt unmoved at our request in the wake of her deciding it was necessary to have a good chunk of the class time toward the degree take place in the daytime.

We went into opera production mode. I wrote a letter to the USC president at the time, stating our case. Virginia had begun the course with assurance that the school could accommodate motherhood and the rug was yanked after she had begun and invested in the school's not-cheap tuition.

"What do you want for Christmas?" I asked Ginny.

"To be able to go to library school."

She had begun the course for a Master's of Library Science degree when the school switched the rules. The bait had been she was able to go at night. The switch was she wasn't.

I wrote my letter to the president of the university before I realized the role of the university president was to raise money. Since I didn't have any, I was not likely to attract his attention. I expect a secretary read a paragraph or two and routed it to whomever responded. It was someone sadly devoid of human warmth or empathy.

I wrapped the copy of my letter in Christmas paper and put it under the tree. That was the easiest part. The later response from the academy I'd rate between tepid and gibberish.

Somehow an audience was arranged with the dean of the Library Science school.

Ginny and I went together. The dean was put off her feed as though a thirty-something whippersnapper could conquer the august, sixtyish dean. She banished me from the meeting. Was it she felt outnumbered? Or it was none of my business? Or she had trouble defending against the logic in my letter—which had been given to her by the university as though the fire needed more fuel.

Virginia reported after the meeting a compromise was reached though it sounded more like a capitulation to me. Dean Martha Boaz had, Ginny reported (we called her Ginny in those days before she took the notion that Virginia was more grown up and dignified — like women reaching the age when they decide to cut their hair short) broken down in tears explaining her position which she undoubtedly had to do to her superiors, which humiliated her. She was only trying to maintain certain standards with an eye to coveted accreditation. That required *day* students. Night students smacked of trade schoolism — so she strove to get her daytime numbers up. UCLA did it (which was why Ginny, given the chance, chose the more expensive school).

Somehow we muddled through with the compromise. Ginny could take more night courses, but less than she'd hoped.

We had a dinner party to celebrate Ginny's Master of Library Science degree — at Hatsuni's Japanese restaurant in Redondo Beach. It was a favorite of ours — and when Hatsuni went back to Japan to stay, the likes of it was not seen again in the South Bay.

Margaret Ready (the early customerburger) sewed an apron with embroidery of "The Babysitter" signature which was on the invitations. I cherished the apron and wore it to a frazzle until it went up in smoke in the Santa Barbara Tea Fire.

The 'SC Library School itself went up in smoke, metaphorically, not long thereafter. I wonder if it was because of the financial strain of making ends meet after nixing the trade school operating method. Or was it a device for easing Dean Boaz to pasture? Who can know? Perhaps they just found it difficult to sell the product when the state supported institution across town was giving it away. (No more free lunch. UCLA's tuition is still less than 'SC, but substantially increased.)

'SC prided itself for being the first university to make money, turn a profit where the tuition paid for the operation. Of course, you can do anything with numbers but the "take away" thought was, they did all right.

So when the Library School failed to break even, those in authority opted to close it.

Though Ginny had worked part time in libraries to keep the home fires burning before she went to library school, she never did after obtaining her master's degree. The fun upside was we could count her a USC basher from among those who held degrees from the same institution: her husband and later our daughter Julia.

Now with the advent of the Kindle and books that seem to appear out of vapor and take zero shelf space, when the New York public library is shipping their books to storage in New Jersey, the 'SC library school reopens. Is there something bizarre about the timing or is it only me?

When the children were on what for the most part was the straight and narrow, Ginny eased into the business of selling horticultural and botanical books. This enterprise began when she took over some guy's hobby loss—selling books to one of a handful of small horticultural groups in Southern California, finally including the Southern California Horticultural Society which in those days met in Los Angeles's Plummer Park.

I always thought selling books could be a profitable enterprise as long as you worked for nothing and stole the merchandise. And found some benefactor to cover your expenses like gasoline and book carts and purchasing a van to transport the inventory to her various venues. This 1995 Dodge van, complete with automatic lift, is still doing yeoman service at my Hermitage almost twenty years later.

After she established herself as this book charity—she loved to make gifts of the books and discount heavily for some worthy customers, and, in time some not so worthy, she began going to garden shows where she was required to rent space. These rentals were not inexpensive and I don't think she was ever able to cover the rental with the concordant sales. She was, it turned out, in the service industry. And she *loved* it. Talking about her books to people gave her a real kick. A mini-manic you might say. Of course, as befitting any charity, this ability to jaw about her books mushroomed. And she *knew* her books and what was in them. There were hundreds, mind you, and she spoke with intelligence and discernment. She and her books toned up any garden gathering. But I suspect the only people that profit from those endeavors are those renting the real estate.

Ginny was voracious in acquiring inventory—multiple copies of new books along with a foray into used books with broad spectrum of rarity and price.

The most expensive acquisition (I don't think reselling it was a motive) was the Bank's Florilegium—a unique printing of some five hundred botanical plates made from drawings by Banks on a voyage to and through the South Seas with Captain Cooke. The plates are in the possession of the British Museum. The printing and sale of one hundred copies of the sets of hundreds of unique botanical prints was supervised by Joe Studholme and his London company, Editions Alecto. It was a pretty expensive undertaking (they were hand printed one page at a time on a reconstructed "original" press). He finally sold almost all of the hundred (plus a few "Artist Proofs") at six figures, though I believe contrary to his initial wishes, some of the last sets had to be broken up to sell them.

Ginny liked the attention and company lavished on her as she was considering the purchase. We stayed at Studholme's English country house where we enjoyed an English pot roasty dinner and free lodging for a night. This was high society stuff—Bunnie Mellon had one of the sets and Ginny's hope was this would open doors to new intellectual friendships—not the least with Joe Studholme himself. As I recall, as soon as the ink was dry on the final check, he tried to peddle his Audubon series and perhaps a few others, but Ginny was interested in plants, not birds. Perhaps when you hope to obtain friends by the purchase of their goods one can only expect it to work while you continue buying. Though Studholme was intelligent and personally engaging, business was business, not friendship.

Perhaps had I been more attuned I would have realized that her manic buying of books presaged her eventual condition. But in her new house is a two-car garage stuffed with books. People were hired to catalog them and put them in boxes.

She had some success selling some of them on the internet, but a significant dent in the inventory was not in the cards. Even booksellers to whom she offered them free were picky. God knows *they* didn't have room to store them. In spite of all yeoman efforts the garage is still heavily stacked with books, is still not home to her automobile…a sporty Lexus convertible.

Had I written this thirty to forty years ago, I would have been more reticent about personal considerations. But with age, inhibitions seem to melt—not necessarily a good thing.

Even so, I have not been so inconsiderate to blurt everything out. I am able to maintain a modicum of privacy through a remaining shred of modesty and/or convenient memory loss.

※   ※   ※   ※

They call her illness bipolar disorder. They used to call it manic-depression, but those are such loaded words; like the Welfare Department morphing into Social Services. Bi-polar means two poles, but they are non-descript. As far as some know the poles could both be similar. Arctica and Antarctica—our north and south poles—both are cold—one has more land than the other, but they are essentially the same—ice-covered wastelands.

Bipolar disorder's two poles are—if you will pardon the pun—polar opposites. From what I have learned reading about this syndrome after it hit her, it is not something you contract, rather a genetic glitch you are born with. It is just a matter of time before it comes out. Her father's came out in his early twenties. Ginny's her sixties. In a way we could count our blessings she didn't have to cope with it earlier.

That, at any rate, is my conceit. My friend Robert Lindsey said, "Anyone married to you would be depressed." I think he meant that kindly, but just in case he didn't, I continue to search for evidence to refute it.

I sometimes wonder if there weren't earlier symptoms I should have recognized, and, had I done so, the cure would have been easier to come by. That is the philosophy of some who posit the cure is easier in the young. Ginny's father's case might contradict that. With it all, it came on suddenly—full-blown with her expressed desire to kill herself.

I was in Idaho with debilitating bronchitis. Julia called me and gave me the news. Ginny was hospitalized. I never thought Ginny had the temperament required for suicide. To me suicide was partially attention getting—finally you have to notice me—but if you succeeded you wouldn't be around to enjoy the attention. And Ginny herself admitted she didn't have the courage to do it. I never thought of it as requiring courage, but rather cowardice—a fear of facing reality.

She was in Cottage Hospital's location for mental illness. I expect there was a euphemism, but I don't remember it.

Subdued and childlike were states that came to mind when I first saw her in her turquoise hospital get-up. I expect she was apologetic—it would be in keeping with her character. But just now I'm not sure that wasn't conjecture. Subdued she was but either they had incised the mania or she was simply in the subdued, depressive mode, her demons stealthily waiting to burst full blown into the manic phase—or the up, as we characterized it simply, as opposed to the down of depression.

There are numerous ways to cope with this for the loved ones: anguish, acceptance, anger, denial. But fighting it is futile.

Our daughters were stellar compassionate compatriots. There are options for reacting and handling a not-easy situation. They could have thrown her under the bus, rationalizing, not unfounded, that they had families of their own that had first call on their attention. But they all rallied to make the best of a situation. And they continue to support her psychologically.

We wonder what all this conglomeration of medicines does to her. I asked her latest, greatest psychiatrist what kinds of studies were available on the effects of the many variations of medicine combinations.

Dr. Nagy's answer? "Not enough."

So the burgeoning of drugs has outpaced our understanding. As a result I think it is a miracle they have not made her sick.

At this writing her condition seems much improved. She is on an even keel, has kept encouragingly active with all sorts of classes, bridge, even golf—and does yeoman service as a companion/babysitter for Abby's three children.

We believe what we want to believe, and I want to believe the worst is behind her. She will soon move into a cottage on the grounds of a non-profit, church-sponsored facility where her meals will be provided and her living space commodious but manageable. Where there are built-in friends—and she thrives on friendship.

THE GOLDEN YEARS

I scorn the doubts and cares that hurt
The world and all its mockeries,
My only care is now to squirt
The ferns among my rockeries.

—George R. Sims,
A Garden Song

THE EASE OF COPING
WITH NUDITY
THE SCULPTURE GARDEN

A man who knows he is a
fool is not a great fool.

—*Chiang-Tzu,*
In Writings

No. The answer is no. I have
sculpted about twenty-five female nude
models and two males in my studio. Add
another ten or so in sculpture classes. But,
no, I've never had any "romantic" in-
volvement with any of the models.

How is that possible? I salute and
share your skepticism. When I read that
the famous photographer of nudes, Hel-
mut Newton, said he never touched a
model—before my sculpture days—I was
skeptical. How was that possible?

Then I saw a picture of him pho-
tographing nudes with his wife seated
(fully clothed) observing the procedures.
She was, I would guess, as he was, in her
fifties. Her eyes were not on the nudes or
her husband shooting them, but on the
photographer who was shooting her and
the broader tableau.

She looked a serious prune.

The models were, of course, gorgeous.

How *is* it possible? How is it not? Once you get over the thrill of the societal taboo you soon settle into the business at hand—to wit: the molding of a hunk of clay to look like a human. In sculpture class we did bodies from the knees up to the neck— no calves, arms or heads. All the models in the class were in good shape—the theory being women who were unhappy with their bodies wouldn't pose nude. I managed to crack that inhibition with my *The Weigh of the World* sculpture comprising a five-foot tall runt of a fella holding up three obese women. But the pickings were a lot slimmer than they were with normal nudes.

The placement of everything is predictable—the breasts are never on the knees or shoulders, the buttocks are always on the top of the legs and in the rear, never on the breastbone.

So once you get the hang of where everything is, you learn to push and press the clay to mimic the human, you focus on pressing the clay in the right places. And it is a matter of lines and shapes—and there are only so many variants.

And clay isn't sexy.

After a session or two, I asked the models if they were nervous the first time. Most of them said only the first few minutes.

All I remember about the first model in my first class was she was not a looker. But she had all the stuff you needed to do the job.

The teacher, Storey Kornbluth, has a daughter named Day who went to Yale, if that tells you anything. And speaking of the ubiquitous Yale, I have just seen a delightful film by André Gregory and his wife called *André Gregory: Before and After Dinner*. In the section after the film, titled "Deleted Scenes," Mr. Gregory tells the story of his Yale rejection—he schlepped to New Haven to audition for the drama school. There he auditioned for the head of the school, whom he describes somewhat like Edward Noyes, the Chairman of Yale Admissions who told me I was like the car with enough gas, but no engine. This Drama School head told André Gregory he had no talent and should pursue another line of work. Does academia attract these demi-gods?

I remember these naysayers:

Ellis Kohs, USC Music Department Composition

teacher—"You'll never be a composer." Summer job disc jockey WHOL Allentown—station manager, Mr. Chambers—"I don't know what you want to be, but you'll never be a disc jockey." A fellow realtor—"You couldn't sell peanuts to elephants." Or the night course writing teacher at UCLA who shared with me and the class his considered feeling that I might be better served if I got a day job.

Teacher Storey took the new kids outside for the introductory pep talk—about buying clay, and tipping the models weekly. If there were any hints on how to sculpt I don't remember them.

So thrown to the wolves, we made a base for our sculpture to sit on.

Mine was cheesy. I suspect I was saving money as was my wont. The clay cost something like four dollars for twenty-five pounds, so the base ate up perhaps five cents, but you can't be too thrifty. That was the easy part. Trying to push and pull that clay into some representation of the scrawny naked female came at a higher price.

We had some weeks to accomplish our tasks and before the model flew the coop I had a sculpture—or what someone with scant artistic sense might recognize as an ersatz sculpture. I think this was a torso. Before long we did a whole seated body. The models changed with the poses.

The instruction consisted of the teacher moving from sculpture stand to sculpture stand, and horsing with the clay at her whim—so depending on how much time she spent with you, you might get a half decent piece out of it.

One of the students, a teacher in his own right, talked nonstop through the class to a younger woman whose position next to him was jealously guarded. More than one would-be poacher was sent packing. My guess at his age: sixty. Hers: thirty-five.

He disappeared for one model, and was moved on his return to explain he couldn't stand her—she talked too much.

The women sat, stood, reclined—we even had two together—and it was great fun.

There was a woman in the class who brought a photograph of her pony—was it a Shetland? Something out of the ordinary. She was doing a small version of the pony instead of the model.

"I'm tired of doing nudes," she said. But she was there session after session—was it for the camaraderie—some kind of collegial feeling—or perhaps the benefits of the few minute tutorial from the teacher?

I expect she never felt moved to tip the model. I never noticed.

Then there was the guy, a practicing psychologist, who set up next to me and proceeded to hum some unrecognized tune(s). I took my stand to the other side of the room. He liked to circle the room and look at everyone's pieces, offering suggestions when he felt compelled.

He stopped next to me and said, "Moved to get another perspective?" Was it less a question than a plea for reassurance it wasn't personal? I didn't like him for some reason? Perhaps he had body odor?

In another of those seemingly endless *faux pas* in a manner that suggest I am better off home alone, I responded, "No. It was to get away from the music."

Though I expect his training in psychology might have prepared him for such slights, and somewhat inured him to his personal reaction, I think he was hurt.

He might even have stopped the incessant humming.

Finally I wanted to do something larger, so for one of the full body sculptures I set out to make it life size. This had to be accomplished in sections, which I was able to bring off until I tried to put the sections together and the whole thing fell apart.

So many of my learning experiences stem from failures. Apparently it was a matter of a firm structural underpinning. About this time I left the class to strike out on my own. I always had grandiose visions and I got a yen to make what I thought was a majorette. The genesis was thus:

I saw a *Smithsonian* magazine feature on a sculptor named Jimenez who had done what I remembered as a majorette. It was painted fiberglass. We had a devil of a time contacting him in New Mexico, I believe. Then it took a year for him to quote a price: $85,000. That's not a misprint.

"Eighty-five thou!" I exclaimed. "I'll make it myself."

It was the time when the famous Kobe Bryant, basketball genius and the nephew of Patty, my sister-in-law's twenty-year boyfriend, got in all that hot water for forcing his intentions on some hotel employee. He said she was consensual. She sued.

So I thought it would be just the thing to have Kobe's wife—who reportedly had been outraged by his actions—to be the majorette, leaning back in the pose I remember with her baton up high and ahead of her—skewering the head of Kobe Bryant. What a wonderful idea.

So one of our gardeners made the armature out of galvanized pipe and galvanized couplings. I was on a ladder (she was one hundred-fifty percent life size, so about ten feet from floor to high point) finishing the top portion, her head, when the sucker crumbled—fortunately *away* from me. I would not be surprised if that ton of clay knocked me off my ladder to the concrete floor— would have killed me. A macabre footnote, Mr. Jimenez who did the original, met his maker with just such an eventuality. A huge mustang he was accomplishing for the Denver airport fell on him. R.I.P. I thought he was a wonderful sculptor—though not everyone agreed with me. He had an installation on State Street—our main street in Santa Barbara which drew the most astonishing criticisms. He had a magnificent steel worker which put me in mind of Rodin's *Balzac*. Some critics thought it was glorifying the communist party. I personally have some right wing bona fides and I thought that ridiculous. One of his horses with blue eyes connoted the same. The paper ran a full page of these carping criticisms. These representational sculptures were replaced by what passed for piles of dung. Was it a commentary on the prior criticisms?

I rebuilt the majorette and it fell again. Also fortuitously missing me.

That encouraged me to get a welder to do the armature right and completion was at hand. In honor of Sculptor Jimenez, we cast it in fiberglass.

Around that time I found a picture of Jimenez's *Majorette*. It was a bar girl with a raised glass of beer.

LOST

Amazing grace, how sweet the sound
That saved a wretch like me.
I once was lost, but now am found,
Was blind, but now I see.

—John Newton

In one of those Italian towns you wouldn't think was large enough to get lost in, I pulled it off. Was it Sienna? Padua? It was one of those places you climbed a hill after you parked in a "lot" at the bottom and did the tourist dance—descended the hill, got in your car and returned to where you were staying. In this case a distance of thirty-five miles or so.

The place was large enough for a bus and after I had separated from our group to forage on my own, I saw a number of our bunch waiting for a bus. They invited me to join them, but I had opted to do the town on foot. Was it a macho thing? Whatever else it was, it was a mistake.

We came up the hill from the parking lot on a bus, so I grossly underestimated the distance for my hike down on a different road. When I finally got down from the town I was shocked that someone had apparently moved the parking lot. But it had to be here someplace. We parked the car in a lot. How many lots could there be? I would just mush on. Eventually I would come to it.

As the time wore on (and I mean *wore*) it creepingly dawned on me there were apparently a lot of lots—none of which seemed to house our rental car. Of course it must be conceded I'm not that hot with cars. I can usually recognize my own which I've had for fifteen years—sometimes by consulting the license plate—but this was a rental car of a non-descript color, probably gray, but as for the make of the car, I was at sea.

We recently toured San Francisco in an SUV I was later told was a Mercedes. I didn't believe it. And I had owned two Mercedes myself so I was cognizant I could well be looking for a car I wouldn't recognize.

But, you know, the universe at the foot of the Sienna (or whatever) hill was vast and unending, with parking lots that seemingly could house every car in Italy. I expect you think I am exaggerating, but then you weren't lost in this vast wasteland that was *all* car-filled parking lots.

Now the space between the lots grew and I was still on foot—but I was mentally processing my options if I never found the car or its passengers.

Keep your head, I told myself, that's the first requirement here. You're in a strange city in a foreign country and you are, face it, lost.

I expect you will agree it was hardly my fault. I mean, how many cities have *you* been to where the cars were parked below the elevated population—where you had no city landmark for reference—where the whole area suddenly became on your return a vast sea of parking lots. Remember, after you parked you had every reason to believe this was *the* parking lot for the city. Before you enter the elevated city its as if you had no idea how many cars had to be parked to accommodate so damn many tourists. I could simply not fathom why all those people didn't just stay home. In the meantime, could I find my temporary home? Would I ever see my real home again? There are certainly worse things than perishing undiscovered in Italy—just at the moment I couldn't think of any.

So when no solution presented itself and I wandered this country road which had, while I was in the little town above, become a super highway with cars everywhere, I realized finally the magic solution was not presenting itself in any guise whatsoever.

This trip was somewhat in advance of the ubiquitous cell phone. Of course there were pay phones in Italy and I expected with some help I would be able to use one. If only I knew the number or even the name of the owner of our rental house and their city.

In the meantime I'd better do something—darkness would soon cover the earth and that didn't bode well for making my task easier.

I thought I could call our California office to see if they had the number of the place. *And* the conflicting time zones were aligned with lucky stars. And perhaps—just *maybe* someone would call the office and we might connect through messages.

Then I wandered into a taxi lot in search of a driver who spoke and/or understood rudimentary English—for I did not understand rudimentary Italian and my attempts at snowing them with my sub-rudimentary Spanish were laughable. At least I thought they would laugh—if they understood me. Somehow I communicated I was lost and looking for a car in an unknown lot. I'd just stand by the locked car until someone showed up. Of course, that presupposed I could identify the car *and* the lot.

I got in the taxi—in front—and we drove—and we *drove*. It was astonishing just how many parking lots there were. At least *I* was astonished. I expect the driver wasn't.

One by one I excluded them as not being right in one particular or another: geography, terrain, size, configuration. It was when we were at a lot on the upside of a road—that climbed the mountain which I *knew* was not correct—that I heard a scream. Could I help but look in that direction? It was part of our gang in I suppose our car, but how would I know? I saw our daughter Melora gesturing frantically, and was never so happy to see anyone. I told the surprised driver to stop—*alto*. He was confused. I explained I had found the holy grail or rather, it had found me—asked him how much and thrust a wad of bills in his hand without being bothered if the tip were included as it was in most places.

The driver seemed surprised. Either I gave him more than he expected or less. Either way he didn't say. I was so relieved I would have given him all I had.

I got out of the taxi into our rental—make still unknown to me—and I wondered how I was supposed to find the car if they were driving it around.

Then someone told me one of the group was stationed at the lot, should I turn up there.

You've heard the expression my relief was palpable?

Well, it was.

Dinner that night tasted especially good.

Whatever it was.

FIRE, LORD

Fire gonna burn my soul

—Langston Hughes

I didn't believe it was serious. When I got the call from Abby, our youngest daughter, I looked out the kitchen window and saw my potted bamboo blown horizontal and bending away from the house. I also saw the flames perhaps a mile or two away—the wind was directing those flames away from my house.

I took an overnight bag and stuffed socks and underwear, some manuscript to work on in my absence, the camera which I don't believe I have used since, and opened the electronic front gate. I received another alarmed phone call or two before I finally made my exit (it's heartwarming to know people care this much about you), expecting full well to be back in a day or two when all the hysteria died down. Hadn't that nice man from the fire department told me on his final inspection, "Your house isn't going to burn. You did everything right."?

It is a mile and a half to the next road to escape away from the fire. When I got in the car to leave I notice my driveway at the street was blocked with cars. I blew the horn and one of the drivers was gracious enough to move so I could get out. I must have wondered if these touristy types were coming into the area, why should I leave?

After I cleared the drive, the roadside was clogged with cars and lookers to the next street for escape. Dodging the lookie-loos, I headed for Virginia's house—she was on one of her many trips to

Japan—and it was sometime thereafter that the wind changed and blew the fire along with its full destructive capabilities to the huge, dry, chaparral covering Parma Park, behind my house—then somehow it changed course again to spew its red hot coals the length of a football field to imbed themselves in our wood siding—the eighty mile per hour winds keeping them alive until the ensuing flames engulfed the structure and took care of everything.

Inadvertently started by some students who trespassed on a posted private property, lit a campfire, thought they had extinguished it and apparently had not because wicked winds twelve or so hours later whipped it up into a frenzy of destruction which claimed more than two hundred houses.

There were nine or so in the party that trespassed, lit and did not sufficiently extinguish the fire, but their names were not released to the public. When they were finally arraigned in court it became obvious why the names were withheld. Several of them were Arabic and some of us might have panicked that it was terrorist based.

The fire burned out when it reached *Mountain Drive* and our neighbors across the street were spared.

Thus began five or six days of speculation. Virginia has TV reception, but I was unable to get any quick news of the homestead. There were a lot of flames and the house is almost midpoint cross streets and the local commentators didn't mention our neck of the woods—probably because no one could get close enough to see.

Near the end of the fire—we were still not permitted to enter—we saw a photo posted of my property on the internet. We contacted the photographer to see what he knew.

His news? He couldn't see the whole thing, but it appeared some of it was still standing. That turned out to be a gentle let down for us. *None* of the house was still standing, a fact we discovered (a couple of daughters and I) when we went through the park, driving as far as we could, then at the blockage walking the rest of the way—where, when we could see the whole property, it was obvious there was nothing left except the concrete wall which began in the ground and soared to twenty-seven feet at the pinnacle.

The metal "harp" of the grand piano was there but broken from the heat and falling perhaps. It now reposes in our museum as part of a larger sculpture. Some bronzes were left including the small chest of e.e. cummings, the head I surmised had been carried off by some looter.

Everything went including my music compositions, my manuscript to the high school musical *That's For Sure*, and a first draft collection of a dozen or so short stories.

Yet my thoughts were always only how to rise from these ashes. Since I couldn't get anything back I didn't yearn to spend time lamenting my fate like Minever Cheevy.

Miniver Cheevy, born too late,
Scratched his head and kept on thinking;
Miniver coughed, and called it fate,
And kept on drinking.
E.A. Robinson

Diane Wittry, friend and director of he Allentown Pennsylvania Symphony—a group that passed on my application for the same position—told me I may think it didn't greatly affect me, but one day it would hit me—hard.

It's been five years and I chose the only option I saw—and moved on.

Life is less complicated after a fire. The burden of possessions is magically lifted. I had fifty plus neckties, I replaced one of them.

Call me Mahatma Gandhi. I always admired his ethos. Though I suspect it wasn't always on the up and up—e.g. I was always amused at his professed quest for celibacy, and the conceit that he took nubile girls to bed to test his resolve, when, no doubt, he had wearied of his burgeoning wife. Posterity has not been rewarded with statistics on the Mahatma's success rate with this celibacy test.

AND YET MORE BUILDING WOES

Architecture is frozen music.

—*Goethe*

Next on the boards was the replacement house for the Santa Barbara fire victim. This time I hired our daughter, Melora, a lovely and efficient human being, to be the project manager of the replacement house—and a building exotic next door. Of course I am against nepotism unless it's in the family.

In our building process, we also hired super competent Rodney D. Utt to be the site supervisor. He blessed us with our best building experience to date.

Perhaps in boom times you are absolved of some of this uncertainty, but all times are not boom times. Feast or famine they say down at the pool hall, and famine is no fun.

The architect, Bruce Biesman-Simons, was arrived at thusly:

We own an office building in Palos Verdes— or precisely Rolling Hills Estates—wherein resides our southern offices for Gardner Management Limited. (I always love the Limited bit instead of the more prosaic 'company' because first and foremost, I love pretension.) The office next to ours is occupied by Tom Milostan, the architect who did such a fine job on the house we built in Ketchum, Idaho. Since he was a paying customer of our real estate enterprise, I thought to return the favor.

When I approached him about designing our museum (the house was still two years from burning down) he told me he was "six months out" on a project and he couldn't please me with the timing. He recommended a young fellow who used to work with him but now was in another architect's office in our building. Another shot at professional courtesy.

The young architect said he was complimented by the offer, but didn't know if he was in a position to take on such a large job — he would think and "get back to me."

He did with the suggestion he bring a colleague of his to Santa Barbara (from the South Bay). He thought the two of them in concert might fill the bill. His associate, Bruce, was out on his own having left the estimable Frank Gehry office.

Bruce later told me that he would go to Geary with questions and 'problems' and Frank would say, "Deal with it, Bruce." I thought that an honest, refreshing self-effacement.

But he was a modest, soft-spoken man who had moved to Southern California from South Africa and married a descendant of the Carter, Hawley, Hale department store empire. She was a Hale. They named their first of two daughters Bria because during the pregnancy Bruce asked his wife how bria was (feminine short for embryo). He brought a resumé of sorts, his accomplishments on his own were modest. He had remodeled his residence in San Pedro which in some ways put me in mind of the great Frank Gehry whose architectural fees for the Disney Hall were around fifty million dollars. Somewhat out of my reach at a fraction of that. When I expressed my surprise (disbelief?) at the number Bruce allowed as how it was probably true. Gehry had an office with a whole potful of architects that he charged out like lawyers with an astounding number of them working for six to ten years. I find it a superb structure on the outside, and the concert hall acoustics second to none — and a thing of rare beauty. The rest of the interior strikes me as somewhat more funky than functional. Forced into the restrictive spaces dictated by the arty exterior.

When I asked Bruce, who was the senior associate on the project for Frank Gehry, his appraisal was very much the same. It must have made me feel architecturally savvy and perceptive. On the other hand we could have both been wrong. But it seems when you work from the outside in you necessarily set yourself up for some disappointments. Anyway, Bruce Biesman-Simons was a definite link to greatness. He was also the project architect for the Guggenheim museum, Bilbao.

I have just seen Gehry's model for his submission in the architectural contest to select the architect for the Disney Hall. It seemed to me fairly plebian, uninspiring and nothing like the monumental structure that was built.

When selecting an architect for our first Santa Barbara house, I thought to have a contest—Don Sharpe, who got the job said he would be glad to make a submission because he always won contests. But he would advise against it as a waste of time and money. The houses that win contests never get built, he said.

To feed fuel to further digression, the architect on our inverted top studio, Jerome Landfield, had made some wonderfully creative plans for structures that were never built.

Bruce's proposed prices for my contract and himself were, I thought, eminently reasonable. Of course, hourly charges can be tricky. So I signed them up after he told me if at any time I was not satisfied with his work, progress, anything, I could cancel the contract unilaterally without any extra cost.

Somewhat into the contract he told me his wife thought he should have charged me more. I replied wives always think their husbands do not set a high enough value on their services. This I assume excludes the home front where a wife may now and again undervalue a husband's contribution to hearth and home.

I then responded, since an unspoken question was on the floor, would I have paid more? "Put it this way, if you'd said your services were one thousand dollars an hour we wouldn't be having this conversation."

He further expressed the opinion that his hourly charges would probably add up to a standard ten percent of the building cost. Of course, I had no idea his design phase would take eighteen months before our first appointment with the art jury, within a week of the day my residence burned down. So I thought I would build the museum and live in it while the house was being rebuilt. Navigating the city building departments and bidding added another six months.

No one disabused me of that nonsense. This museum, a five thousand plus square foot pile of books sheathed in copper and brass (no more fire victim) was miles more complex than the house we planned—a concrete bunker of 2,700 square feet or so (it is so difficult to compute curves) half the size of the private museum and infinitely less complex.

We were well into the design of the museum when I realized we should have built the simpler structure first. It took us six months to clear the design review process so approval was granted some six months after the house was lost to the conflagration.

Biesman-Simons didn't argue about the house being easier and therefore quicker, just asked for more time on this architectural wonder which would put him near the head of the line in architects' heaven. He had contracted with all these architects and engineers to solve the conundrum of actually building it so it wouldn't fall over.

All this he accomplished without putting any dimensions on the plans, and when confronted for real numbers politely but adamantly refused to supply any. It was all there in the angles and whatnot. It was the same on both the house and museum and I'm damned if I know how anyone was able to build them. I wonder if Disney Hall and Bilbao had dimensions.

A lot of gracious curves adorn this "piano house."
"Run to the round house, Nellie, he can't corner you there."

The architect tenant of our office building through whose auspices we got Biesman-Simons soon dropped out saying it was beyond his expertise and required more time than he could devote.

Though Bruce's hourly rate was eminently reasonable, the aggregate charges for him and his selected cohorts approached the ten percent of construction costs he predicted. This was likely aided by our fetish for the low bid, bringing in the final costs below his estimates.

In time we began designing the Piano House, the residence—so-called because it held my Steinway nine-foot grand piano, had a piano cut out in the wall between the entry and the piano. It also had a skylight and lid in the shape of a piano and lid, the lid closing in high winds. We were not so fortunate in a recent wind. It tore the lid off before it could close automatically—apparently a too-slow process. Some kitchen cabinets have piano-shaped glass fronts in blue and green.

The entry pad to the front door is black and shaped like a piano, and piano outlines are carved in the concrete patios at the front and side of the house as well as black concrete stepping-stones on the remaining sides.

At the time the Piano House was complete, eleven months after breaking ground, the Book Building was in its fourth year. Now, in its sixth year since inception, it is complete.

The book building (museum)
Six years in the making

DOCTORS I HAVE KNOWN

*"...an essentially private man who wished his total indifference
to public notice to be universally recognized...."*

—*Tom Stoppard on James Joyce*

Well, I didn't get to know the first one right away. Gerald
S. Backenstoe, M.D. was a friend of my progenitors and delivered
me. According to my mother it took an inordinately long time—
and I was a long-term baby. I like to say thirteen months, but I expect it was ten. Eleven was more like it. And some of that may have
been a miscalculation.

At heart I am a Christian Scientist. Virginia's grandparents
experimented with the faith and it trickled down willy-nilly to her
generation where it unceremoniously dissipated.

My faith was never strong enough to heal my broken bones
or to shun anesthesia. But I do like the idea of toughing out minor
illnesses. My mother used to say if you have a cold and take the
medicine you can lick it in two weeks. If you don't take anything it
takes fourteen days. I always thought taking too much medicine
would lower my resistance to medicine when I really needed it.

In the early days of our courting I went to one or two Christian Science meetings. Some say it doesn't matter what you believe
in as long as you believe in something. My memory is of a group of
people who looked like they never felt much pain, medically or
economically. They didn't have ministers or priests, but Readers,
who read the scriptures from the King James Bible and the musings
of Mary Baker Eddy who started the whole shebang. I have a vivid

memory of a well-preserved older woman reading these scriptures in clipped tones as though she were a competitor in the early stages of a diction contest.

"Fi-R-st Cor-*in*-thi-ans chapter sssix, ver-sss for-teeeen." She was a kick.

I expect some of the devotees fudged the rules a bit, and let credentialed medical practitioners hold sway over the Christian Science practitioners. I don't deny a positive attitude can be helpful—and we do believe what we want to believe—but it seems to me the miracles of modern medicine have vastly outpaced the Christian Science cures.

I got seventy-eight years out of my left knee until I went to titanium and plastic. The right knee, seventy-eight and counting.

I twisted my knee, tearing something called a meniscus playing tennis five or six years before. I hobbled around on that annoyance for some years before I yielded to an operation to trim that thin piece of goods that was now flapping between the bones at the knee.

When you trim the meniscus (which does not regenerate) you set up a bone on bone condition. Though I asked a number of times to explain how this worked, I never understood the answer.

I was initially told this operation succeeded in eighty percent of the cases. Then I saw that drop to seventy and after the operation sixty percent.

No matter, I was in the failed group, no matter how large that was.

Between meeting the Santa Barbara surgeon, Victor Tacconelli, M.D. who specializes in messed up bones, and the operation, I read that seventy-five percent of knee operations were unnecessary. I mentioned that to him and he didn't flinch. I suppose it had to be understood that this one was in the twenty-five percent. He did give me options for pills, physical therapy or wait it out. He'd performed three thousand of these skits in thirty years, and I guessed one more or less wouldn't go too far keeping the wolf from the door.

Soon after I had obtained my modest (not to say lowly) 'position' at CBS typing scripts on the night shift, our family doc Backenstoe enthused that I'd be the president of CBS in five years. Then he paused and opined, "Maybe I'm wrong. It will only take two years."

Sally Backenstoe was one of my absolute favorite people. Bright, quick, funny, amenable, though I don't expect she suffered fools gladly.

She flattered me by inviting me to her graduation from Hood College in Maryland. There in the girls' school environment I was pleased to feel for the first time the attentions and intentions of Sally's classmates.

When one of them heard I was just graduating from high school she said, "Oh, I thought you were older. I just began to get interested." At seventeen being mistaken for older is high praise to be cherished. Now closer to the end of the line, being mistaken for younger is the ticket. It seems the former was more prevalent than the latter.

In Frederick, Maryland I was invited to breakfast in the Backenstoe's room. Soft-boiled eggs were served. I don't remember if I ordered them or they just appeared. But here I was with the primo family of Emmaus, Pennsylvania—social structure-wise— and I was paralyzed with fear because I wasn't sure how to attack this white object perched majestically in its pedestal cup.

So I did what any well-brought up chap would do. I waited for a signal from the host and hostess. I would simply follow their lead. Do what they did.

So I waited.

And waited.

And waited some more. By now my thoughts have bifurcated as follows:

That the egg was going to be stone cold by the time I set my teeth on it.

Could the Backenstoe's be torturing me, making fun of my bucolic lack of notions *vis-à-vis* the consumption of soft-boiled eggs?

Finally! Mrs. Backenstoe made her move. Something about slicing the top off the egg and spooning the contents onto the toast provided.

Piece of cake. I managed to ape her actions without splattering cooling soft-boiled egg all over myself and the hotel carpet.

Strange what we remember. The above two highlights, the girl who was just beginning to get interested and the challenging soft-boiled egg, stick out in my bank of remembrances. I don't remember much else about the graduation or attendant ceremonies.

Doctor Backenstoe made house calls, as had his father M.J. before him.

In my selective memory several things stand out about these house calls. One was the placement of two or three fingers on my chest and abdomen whereupon the good doctor thumped his fingers of the other hand on the flat fingers which rested on my young body.

Years later in my late teens or early twenties I summoned the nerve to ask him what that was all about. He told me he was checking for swollen innards which would help in his diagnosis of what the problem was. It was a matter of sound. A hollow sound was apparently copasetic. When he thumped a dull dead-end sound meant your spleen or whatever was enlarged and could spell trouble.

I also remember my father having alarming chest pains. Summoning the professional, he performed his voodoo with the thumping and stethoscope and after listening to the symptoms opined that the Judge had had a mild heart attack or stroke, but we had an allotment of seven before they killed us, though the doctor had himself had five already.

I had some sort of disturbance while I was a working lad, lately out of college. Perhaps a rash or some skin irregularity. I was visiting the frozen East. We were going to the Backenstoe's for dinner.

Momma Baby who could be pushy, insisted I ask the doctor to look at me during their dinner party. I was aghast at what seemed to me gauche behavior. We went for society, not business. I expect my father agreed with me.

No matter, Momma Baby brought it up and the doctor was only too happy to leave the table and showcase his skill. We repaired to his office—on the other side of his kitchen in the large house.

Once there I insisted he send the bill to me—which would indicate I was already on my way to becoming president of CBS. He waved my concern off giving me the impression there would be no bill. This was a social evening after all.

He did the thumping dance, looked at whatever it was I had, then with one of those battery operated lights peered into my eyes. I asked him what he saw there, what he was looking for wondering how it was revelatory of my skin condition. Or was it an earache? At any rate it wasn't an eye problem. I had 20/20 to get me into the Navy flight program.

Well, he told me, you could analyze the whole body by looking into the eye. I don't remember his diagnosis, all I remember is my parents—not me—got a bill. Probably he thought he had a better shot at getting paid. But no secretary knew about the late night exam.

But why not? The current lust for government controlled health care is along this same line. Why do we expect doctors to be altruistic healers as though they didn't need to make a living?

Most of the country's legislators are lawyers. You don't see them restricting legal fees.

✳   ✳   ✳   ✳

M.J. Backenstoe, M.D.—M.J. for Martin John, I believe, and M.D. for medical doctor—was the father of Gerald S. Backenstoe, M.D. M.J. practiced in the era of *real* country doctors, making his house calls in a horse and buggy. He was a distinguished looking gentleman with a goatee and moustache, gray when I knew him. His son finessed the goatee and kept the moustache. And *his* son, Judge Jebby, shaved the whole enchilada.

My first remembered contact with Dr. M.J. was when I was perhaps four or five years old and I must have disobeyed the parental edict to not go barefoot outside the house.

I was playing on the edge of the school playground when I stepped on a monster piece of broken glass causing an almost two inch slice in my instep which was virtually the width of my small foot.

I was whisked to the doctor with my bleeding foot—it was M.J. on duty—his son was on a European jaunt with his wife Harriet, sailing across the Atlantic. That was a big deal in the 1930's. So big my parents and Dr. and Mrs. Rahn went to New York for a farewell sendoff. My father had obtained a movie camera for giving a speech somewhere and recording this event was one of his first times out with the contraption. In those days it was all about movement—people walking past the camera, waving, turning. How else did you get the result to differ from a still camera?

Dr. M.J. was old school, no nonsense and what he deemed called for were clips. Six, I believe, and if you've never had clips on the soles of your feet you can't imagine the pain. It is said we forget pain (lest everyone would be an only child), but I remember the pain. Perhaps M.J. was so old school he didn't bother with anesthetics. Perhaps there was nothing available in those days without going to a hospital. Who knows how the decision was made to stick those pins through that tough flesh that constituted the soles of my feet—genetically rendered tough to take the abuse on one's feet before they began wearing shoes, not so long ago in the scheme of things.

So imagine a "u" made out of a flat band of metal, perhaps one-quarter inch between the ends, with a hole in each end for a nail to slip through to hold the tough flesh in place. So you pinch the skin into this clip, then slide the nail through one end of the clip, then the cut flesh, then out the other end of the clip.

Excruciating. And he did it six times. The doc said I was a real soldier about it.

M.J., as he was democratically called, went on to bigger things. He wrote a book called *Triumphant Living*—not a modest account of his life—fictitious though it may have been.

There were two opinions: 1) it was largely baloney, and 2) wow, that guy was some rake. My father said it should have been titled *Girls I Could Have Had*.

I read the book with keen interest at the time. I was a hormone-pounding teenager and I was enchanted. I mean, this guy knew how to get the girls gaga. He had episodes of climbing fences, jumping out of windows to escape the husband who came home earlier than expected.

There was a mother daughter scene. I mean, name your fantasy, this guy lived it. So you can imagine what that did to an innocent teen. I believed every word. It was a forerunner of pornography. *Triumphant Living* indeed—and oh, how many opportunities he had as a medical doctor.

I confess to a smidgeon of disappointment when I heard the expressed skepticism of the adults. Maybe it was just jealousy on their part.

M.J. went on a cruise to Europe when he was in his dotage—about my age now, late seventies, perhaps even into his eighties.

On the cruise he met a woman we came to call Momma Maud. She was a wonderful woman who apparently tried to dissuade the doctor from pursuing these childhood fantasies, and who—bottom line—held out with that intimate stuff for the ring. She was in her late sixties, early seventies, if I recall correctly. The actual marriage was short lived.

When I went to my default college USC, the Backenstoes encouraged me to look up Momma Maud. She lived in Pasadena and had a cottage on the beach in Manhattan Beach for summer fun.

It was there I first met her. And what a time I had finding that place. It was on the strand in Manhattan Beach, perhaps around Second Street. But Hermosa Beach down the coast enjoyed the same numbers and the ocean was the same for both towns. Couple that with my atrocious sense of direction, which I have come to blame on being left-handed. So I landed with my old Studebaker on the alley that was as close as cars could manage. The strand was for walking, skating and bikes. No cars. So I am floundering in the alleys and am dumbfounded when I go lower in numbers not to find Momma Maud's number. A few inquiries later (before cell phones—a chore) I discovered I was in the wrong town and the numbers started over after Thirtieth Street or whatever. I finally found her.

I visited her many times in my four-year stint at SC. Her house in Pasadena was easier to find. She said she slept only three to four hours a night and I saw no ill effects of that deprivation. I always wished I could get by on so little. So much more could be accomplished. She lived into her nineties, I believe. Probably as long as she wanted to.

She had some connection to the prime lumber family in the area, though I don't remember if it was her family or a late husband's.

When I saw Doc M.J. after my time with Momma Maud, he asked if she told me what a bad actor he was. I replied honestly I never heard an unkind word from her about anyone. He didn't seem convinced at first, but later I sensed a feeling of relief, proving again the sensitivity of even the loftiest members of society to their reputations.

❖ ❖ ❖ ❖

Dr. Rink afforded me the first opportunity to slice into my flesh for repairs—a herniated intestine in this instance.

His office waiting room was tricked out like a sitting room in the early days of the century (the *twentieth*). I think I mentioned it, something like, "You have a unique waiting room," and he said, "Thank you." Then I realized it wasn't a compliment. I did compliment him on his receptionist who was cheerful and made you feel loved and at ease.

He said that was good to hear because he had just gotten free from the receptionist from Hell who had been there fifteen or twenty years. I asked why he kept her. He said how do you rid of someone like that? I said terminate them. It seemed to be a foreign notion to him.

It occurs to me so many doctors have wretched receptionists. Several reasons come to mind: doctors are like gods, and though most of them can do passable humility, their employees often take on the airs for them.

Or doctors are so preoccupied with healing patients they

have no judgment in hiring help.

The walls between the waiting room and examining room were paper-thin and I heard every word of Dr. Rink's gentle berating of a woman for her weight. He couldn't operate through so much fat.

When she returned to the waiting room she said to the woman waiting for her, "He's on me 'bout my weight." I didn't tell her we heard it all. She looked like she had more fat on her than was necessary, but she didn't seem obese. I wondered at the doctor's standard.

After I was ushered into Dr. Rink's examining room, I was surprised to see him when he came in. I'm sure there is a rationale for putting the patient in the room before the doctor—a doctor should never be kept waiting. A doctor should not be surprised by a patient. It wouldn't be good PR to have a doctor cooling his heels waiting for a patient and all the variations of the above. But I was surprised on the border of shock when he came in. My father's dictum sprang to mind:

Do as I say, not as I do.

Dr. Rink sported a good deal of superfluous flesh. I expect if questioned he would say, "I am doing the operations, not the operee." He did have a belly on him that he might have lamented had he been a patient.

I asked him how many of these hernia operations he had performed.

"You'll be my second," he said without missing a beat, without cracking a smile.

In the same vein, without a beat dropped, I said, "And the first one didn't turn out too well."

If he laughed I didn't see it.

He told me he had played football for Columbia and had he not gone into medicine he would have been a coach.

Perhaps there are similarities that I miss.

After the operation I was sent a questionnaire asking about my pre-op and post-op visits by the surgeon and the anesthesiologist.

The latter showed up for both.

The former, the surgeon, jollied me up a bit before the surgery, but was not in evidence when the anesthesia wore off.

He was probably out celebrating the success of his second operation.

I liked the guy and wrote him a letter of appreciation and offered to take him to lunch. This was after I told the truth on the questionnaire about him not being there after the operation.

I never heard from him.

*   *   *   *

I had an exam by an acquaintance of our daughter. She, the skin doctor, said it didn't look like I needed anything but they would send stuff to the lab to make sure.

The next contact yielded the info that I did in fact have some nasty whatever they were and her partner dealt with those critters.

A visit to the personable, chatty partner yielded the intelligence that I had a number of these pesky growths and we should excise those that were cancerous.

Cancer? I was alarmed. I *have* cancer?

Now, I imagined she was on the spot. The idea, I assumed was to sufficiently alarm me ("Cancer!") without sending me to jump off a bridge.

It was a form of cancer, she informed me. Not fatal now, but if left to grow there was no telling what might develop. The only way to tell for sure if these growths were malignant or benign was to extricate them, then put them under the special scope which in X number of minutes would tell me which it was.

I signed up for the first of was it three visits? She could only do three at a visit, she said. The routine was I showed up, was ushered into a room where I was given local anesthetics for each "cancer," the head woman sliced the skin at the offending growth—melanoma I believe they were called. Scary enough, but "cancer" was still worse. After the incision and extraction of the little glob, it was rushed to the room next door where a time consuming process was employed with the little bugger (not to be confused with booger). Some machinery was apparently involved—scanning scopes, what have you—a picture of your cheek when developed in the inner sanctum told if they had gotten all of the offending gel. If not, further cutting was called for.

While all this voodoo was being exercised, (I never witnessed it) the patient was deposited back in the waiting room. The process was repeated as needed.

On my next visit (all had been benign from the first visit) I thought to ask just how many of these little buggers had killed people in her experience, had they been left to fester. The doc had told me she had removed perhaps ten thousand of the melanomas, I was eager to know the life-saving statistic.

Instead she gave me a good-natured lecture on how she would counter her Hippocratic oath if she knew the answer to that. When she saw a melanoma, she was professionally bound to take it out. It would be malpractice not to. I pondered that.

I'm still pondering. So if I get it and I am the first to admit I often don't get it—she has never examined someone and told them they had to remove a melanoma where the patient for whatever reason didn't do it, and died from it—or lived.

"But why do I have all these growths?" I asked her.

"From the sun," she said.

"But I have been religious about sunscreen and hats…"

"But it goes back to when you were a kid. We never thought about it then."

She was right about that. Every year I burned to a crisp—red as a lobster.

I thought she was very attractive—perhaps forty-five or fifty years old. And she said she was interested in me—for her mother.

Everyone needs a reality check from time to time.

Personally, I could do without them.

After I'd had the growths all removed with none of them being malignant—an assistant confronted me on my way out with the intelligence that I needed to make more appointments.

"For what?" I asked.

"For the other ones you have."

"Other ones? Why wasn't I told? Why weren't they taken with the initial group?"

"Well we don't want to do too many at once." Then the whopper. "I told you there would be others."

Since I had never seen this woman before I knew that was false. I told her I had never spoken to her but she insisted I had.

"How big is it?" I asked referring to one she said was especially large on my back.

"Pencil eraser size," she said.

"At what rate does it grow?" I asked.

"Varies."

"A range? Will it double in two weeks?"

"No."

"Or ten years?"

"We don't know."

I said I'd think about it and call if I wanted an appointment.

A few days later one of the contractors on rebuilding my house that had been destroyed by the Santa Barbara Tea Fire said he was on his way to the doctor to have a melanoma removed.

I inquired which doctor?

He mentioned the male member of the practice.

Was it a racket? Was it perfectly legitimate or somewhere in between? I never found out. I didn't go back and I'm still alive with no gaping holes anywhere on my body that indicated the ravages of a neglected melanoma.

I did, incidentally notice on the subsequent bill a charge for $365.00 for wart removal which consisted of a few seconds blast with some cryogenic contraption handled by an assistant. It was unsuccessful so I removed it myself with a five-dollar kit from the pharmacy.

DENTISTS WHO KNEW ME

I have come to several general conclusions about dentists. Male initially, then females who effortlessly encroached on this male purview.

The men were unabashed upbeat glad-handers—hale fellows well met.

The women were beautiful but also paragons of happy salesmanship.

Dr. Carl Graul had been a fraternity brother of my father at Muhlenberg College, Allentown, Pennsylvania, Phi Kappa Tau. I remember them memorializing a fraternity song in Judgie's knotty pine paneled basement barroom. I wonder if this had been a childhood fantasy—being a bartender to friends.

> We are brothers now and ever
> Until the day we die.

A little gloomy perhaps, but those are the only words I remember.

Then there was faux religion:

> Running oh-ver running over,
> My cup is full and running ohh-ver.
> Since the Lord saved me I'm as happy as can be.
> My cup is full and running ooooh-ver.

The Grauls, Dr. Carl and Audrey, were family friends until

many decades flowed under the bridge and the relationship disintegrated in the saddest way.

I have had one of Dr. Graul's fillings in the top of a front tooth for sixty-plus years. Still as perfect as the day it was put in.

I once asked him how often he changed his injection needles.

"After the third complaint," he responded quickly, deadpan. He was an original understated comic and I was crazy about him. He did me the honor of being an usher at our wedding.

One of my early attempts at novel writing featured a couple not unlike *Momma Baby and Judgie*, with some of the abusive dialogue he sent her way. I expect I gave it to Momma Baby to read, hoping for some of the praise she was so good at. If I got it, I don't remember. What I remember is she apparently gave the book to the Judge to read—or perhaps only a section that made him look bad. He must have read it without comment. But some time later, *much* later as I recall, he had done something to show him in a good light. He said with serious mien, "Put *this one* in your book." It took me awhile to catch on that he had read the derogatory stuff and was stung by it. There was simply nothing in his background that prepared him for the subtleties of the written words of fiction.

He ("Uncle" Carl) and "Aunt" Audrey—honorific not relative titles—came from their Philadelphia home to visit us in Emmaus, Pennsylvania for a number of weekends. It was always an exciting time for me. I loved to listen to the light-hearted banter between them. It made me feel grown up to sit in our basement barroom with those two serious drinkers, where my father and Uncle Carl, who I can't remember showing the effects of booze, hung out to schmooze.

The Grauls had no children. I was only too happy to act as surrogate. He took me fishing on his ocean-going boat. I played on the boat as a kid visiting the Grauls' rather nice house on the Jersey shore. Their Philadelphia digs were more modest. They had a weimaraner dog to which I seemed to be indifferent.

Both the G's—Gardner and Graul—belonged to a hunting and fishing lodge in the Pocono Mountains, perhaps forty or fifty miles from home. It was called Lehman's Lake. Uncle Carl toned that up calling it 'Lehmans on the Lake.' I think it was the only place where I was served canned chicken. I'd like to say that was the worst of their offerings, but I fear that would not be accurate. But what they lacked in the quality of cuisine they made up with quantity.

There is a saying, "Enough to choke a horse." But no self-respecting horse would have choked on this fare. He would have turned his back on the vittles long before he got to the choking stage.

I was six years old for my first Lehman's experience, deer hunting, which began in early December that year.

Cold.

The joke was it was so cold in the lodge which, in a tip of the hat to the Spartans, had no heat, that you left the windows open because the arctic outside air was warmer than inside. The premium room was the one over the kitchen where one might luxuriate in the accidental ambient heat from the wood-burning kitchen stove. But that wasn't much. We slept in our hunting clothes under every blanket we could muster.

Five below zero was my memory. And that was Fahrenheit.

But the breakfast *was* bountiful. The table was creaking with ham, bacon, fried potatoes, scrapple, mashed potatoes, coffee, tea, hot chocolate, oatmeal, dried beef in cream, you name it, we had it.

We arose for this feast in the pitch dark, perhaps four a.m. We had to be in our places in the woods away from camp before daylight so the deer wouldn't suspect us hiding in their forest.

And hide we did.

And freeze. We didn't have the advantage of movement to add to our body heat. There were the flushers who moved through the woods in an attempt to scare the deer into lunging toward the shooters in their foxholes or holed up behind fallen logs. I wondered and still wonder, how one group keeps from shooting the other.

Indeed, my cousin Pete's wife Jean's father was killed in just such a hunting accident. But his survivors kept hunting in another triumph of hope over experience.

I don't know how long we sat there freezing to death, but the thing I marvel at is these guys did this for *fun*! I found no fun, was mightily disappointed no one shot a deer, yet mightily relieved that no one shot me. Not only did we not leave the five below zero cold without venison for the freezer, but we didn't even *see* a deer.

It was my first and last hunting experience.

Fishing was more desultory. Meaning my first experience at a river in Philadelphia yielded a tug on my line. With help I reeled in a slimy, slithering eel which I thought was a snake. Not even knowing what an eel was, there was no thought of eating it, so we threw it back. Deep-sea fishing with my Grampop Knoll was next. Also empty handed at day's end. There was the other experience with Uncle Carl and the grand old Judge (who was not yet a judge) in the blue Atlantic where I sat with my line hanging over the side of the boat. I couldn't then, nor can I now see the fascination in this inert excuse for sport or pastime. To me it was a big bore. I was cured of hunting and fishing, those he-man endeavors, before I was ten.

After I was at SC, Uncle Carl was the editor of his dental fraternity magazine. He commissioned me, a would-be writer, to write something about the group. I visited, had a meal, and wrote two articles and received fifty dollars each (a week's work at CBS). The articles were fawning, hyperbolic drivel, but I suspect it made me feel important. I could honestly put that I wrote for magazines on my resumé.

Uncle Carl's tenure as editor of the Psi Omega Dental Fraternity journal was one of lighthearted, creative journalism—I suspect it was a benchmark among fraternity magazines.

When I was a boy, sub-teen, and the Grauls visited us I would bring their suitcases into the house and be lavishly rewarded with a twenty-five cent tip (about five dollars today). I lived for those visits.

Sometime between the twenty-five cent tips and the fatal breakup, my father told me he had written a new will for the Grauls and though he shouldn't tell me this because it was attorney/client privileged information, Uncle Carl was leaving each of the Gardner kids five thousand dollars in his will.

For perspective, that was the equivalent of about fifty thousand dollars then. I remember my excitement at the thought of getting that much money handed to me.

Alas, Uncle Carl died first after spending a lot of his estate on the nursing home, and Aunt Audrey required extensive, prolonged care and by the time she approached her maker the funds were shot.

It was another lesson in the expectations of getting something for nothing.

It was perhaps fifteen years after that news of the will when events transpired at Lehman's that destroyed the perhaps fifty-year relationship between the Gardners and Grauls. I was not present for this demise. And I don't regret my absence. I expect I was settled on the West Coast as a young husband and father when I got word of the blow up.

My sister was a high school girl at the time, fixing my age at twenty-six to twenty-eight. She and a friend took an ill-advised outing to Lehman's. It was a heavy drinking environment.

They went to bed and later that night, feeling no pain and, perhaps depending on the turn of one's liberal nature, disoriented, Uncle Carl crawled into bed with my sister's friend, scaring the bejesus out of her.

My father said Uncle Carl was an incurable joker, which he was, but some of the received wisdom at the time opined that this joke, if indeed it was, was not funny. This old rake with a teenage girl. Nothing untoward transpired, but the trauma level around the place was lofty enough for the grand old Judge to strongly suggest Uncle Carl apologize to the girl's father. Aunt Audrey inserted herself into the mix and strongly advocated her husband, and my father, let the matter drop. It was surely an innocent prank, he hadn't touched the girl, so why self-perpetuate the thing and blow it out of proportion? Who was Ted Gardner—a man famous for not being able to hold his liquor—to pontificate in this holier-than-thou charade and insist that his friend apologize, *de-*

mean himself (and I suppose Aunt Audrey by association) by apologizing for *exactly nothing!*

Uncle Carl apologized. I can only imagine the scene: the girl's father wanting to be one of the boys without sweeping the incident under the rug would listen to Uncle Carl tell the tale of his drunken mistake. He had no intention of compromising the girl, and in fact, didn't touch her. He was sorry it was all misunderstood.

The girl's father (one of the boys lest we forget) would say, yes, yes I understand, but she is a child and could have been traumatized. She certainly didn't understand.

How much Uncle Carl actually remembered about the incident I couldn't guess. He had probably drunk so much, so long, been bone tired and maybe *did* fall into the wrong bed. It wasn't his familiar home, it was a hunting lodge. The rooms tended to run together.

But Aunt Audrey was so embittered by the incident, the friendship collapsed. Soon after, Uncle Carl was put in what is euphemistically called "a home" where he was to end his days receiving some mysterious treatment for a mysterious psychological malady. Since Aunt Audrey was incommunicado with her former best friends, we never found out what he was being treated for. Alcoholism was a possibility. Schizophrenia?

I spoke to him on the phone once and he sounded his old self to me. He was overtly grateful for my call. I asked who was watching the store (his dental practice). He said "Miss Tober" (his dental assistant since he began practice perhaps thirty years before), "but it's half-assed."

✻   ✻   ✻   ✻

I was very high on my dentists. Princes among men, princesses among women.

My first Santa Barbara dentist of some twenty years, was such a princess—not in the derogatory sense of the spoiled young woman, but a genuinely nice person. She even came to a book signing of mine and bought books. The epitome of public relations savvy. Which, if you thought everyone in business would have, you'd be wrong.

This delightful woman had many siblings in the manner of an old fashioned Irish Catholic family. She hired two of them in her practice as well as her husband and one or two dental assistants. The hygienists I expect used her office on a percentage basis. But anyway you slice it, she had a horrendous overhead. In addition, she had some medical procedure that eventuated her prolonged absence from the office, during which she installed a dentist from the USC faculty (ninety miles to the south). He wore a skull-cap, was from New York City, and perhaps in his early sixties.

I asked him how he liked New York.

"Oh, we *loved* it," he said. He had lived there all his life.

"So why did you move out here?"

"We had an opportunity to escape and we *took* it."

But I wondered, who wants an opportunity to leave something you love? I didn't have the sophistication to frame that question, so I dropped it.

The dentist's two sisters at the front desk were pleasant enough, one more than the other, but never caused problems.

My wife, Virginia, went to a different dentist whom she adored. He was less expensive and I considered changing—never being averse to saving money. But I suppose I was still enchanted by my female dentist so inertia kept me in place.

Her staggering overhead was in the back of my mind. The erosion of time had worn down my front teeth and she sold and I bought caps—or some process where the tooth was restored to its original state. She told me those should be good for five years and then have to be replaced. It made me marvel at Uncle Carl's filling in the top of the front tooth that had lasted by then some forty years.

True to her prediction wear began to show—not so much perhaps to prevent me from becoming a movie idol, but *some*.

In my next exam my lovely dentist, returned from what must have been a very expensive hiatus, must have been looking to recoup some of her losses. Being the good soul that she was (this is more characteristic of women in my experience) the truth slipped out. The x-rays were good but this one particular tooth was showing signs of stress cracking and we should cap it.

This was pretty far short of a call to arms to correct a disastrous situation, and the old flag of suspicion crept over the hill.

At the checkout counter I was told the estimate for the required work was $5,500 or thereabouts. I made an appointment for five or six months hence which carried me over to the new year.

Before the scheduled appointment I got a call from the dentist's less gracious sibling to tell me that they raised their prices effective the first of the year—to more than six thousand for the work.

I said, "You mean you aren't going to honor your quote?"

In the iciest tones I can remember she said, "I *said* we *raised our prices!*"

I thought it was time to get a second opinion. I made an appointment with my wife's dentist, Dr. Dart.

He did the x-ray dance, stuck the mirror in my mouth, poked around and said, "I wouldn't do anything."

Of course, I balanced that wisdom with a possible ploy on his part to lasso my business. Time will tell, I thought. He did praise the dental work I had had done—calling it excellent. He further praised my dentist as being a terrific dentist. The fault, we silently agreed, lay elsewhere, with all the people she was supporting.

Time told. As is my penchant, I gravitated to one of the female dentists on his staff, a Kelly Kendall. She has been examining me for the past six years or so and is yet to discover those moneymakers in my mouth. So the $6,500 in dentistry that had to be done to protect my teeth has yet to kick in.

THE MODERN SALON

What is best in music is not to be found in the notes.

—Gustav Mahler

Some of our grandchildren are musicians, some are athletes, some both.

A young man — just turning double digits — is both. He is on a champion baseball team and he plays a mean piano. I am moved to go to his recitals, which number two per annum. I might be better served with one, but my vote doesn't count.

Let me hasten to add, I do not regret going to his recitals which consist of twenty-five to thirty young 'uns playing one or two pieces each for an elapsed time per person of forty-five seconds to a few minutes playing time. Some of the times are expanded due to memory lapses. All told a program of an hour or so. Our grandson Nathaniel's portion perhaps a minute.

Equal time is portioned to his brother, Owen, born at the same time as Nathaniel. His recitals are similar, except with violins rather than pianos.

The venue is an hour, round trip from my home. The whole thing puts me in mind of young Mozart playing for his father's friends or some command court appearance.

Nathaniel acquits himself well at the piano. I hear from Virginia he also does smashingly at his baseball games. Since a slower sport is unknown to man — unless you want to consider chess — I excuse myself from those contests, though they are closer to home, they take longer. Virginia, who has more patience than I, attends.

Her mother was a Philadelphia Phillies fan at the end so perhaps it is genetic.

I admit, after hearing Nathaniel play his piece—*Clowns* by Kabalevsky—on Mother's Day at his house, our daughter, also his mother, allowed as I could skip the performance since I had heard the piece. I riposted as any hero of the hour would, I considered it over and above the actual hearing of the piece, it was the tribute my presence would pay to the young lad. Carrying the flag, so to speak.

When I compliment him on his playing I ask how he felt about it. He is always positive which is a tribute to his nature. Some hardliners might nitpick a note or tempo here or there, but not Nathaniel.

When in the back of the auditorium, Nathaniel returns to the bosom of his immediate family, so to speak—three-year older sister, Emma and a brother Owen. I hear his father's hushed voice, "Thank Grandpa for coming."

Which he dutifully does without complaining. Now, at these semi-annual events I am forced to observe our fellows in the audience. Most of them are considerate to a fault. One family excepted. Heretofore there have been five of them: a mom, a dad, two boys and a girl. They look like nice people—well dressed and scrubbed—perhaps prosperous. But they can't shut up—and dad applauds his kid only. Does this small effort take too much out of him? Is he saving his energy for his forte response for his own little performer? Does he think that adding his applause to the appreciation of others will diminish the relative volume of the accolade for his?

The troop has the look and feel of entitlement about them.

I got him this time. I didn't clap for his little boy. You can see the level I have sunk to in this regard.

As soon as the music begins this family has much to talk about. I have been behind them for two or so recitals to date and the pattern is predictable.

My guess at the ages of the principals—the performer about eleven, his older sister perhaps thirteen, the little brother sevenish. Parents late thirties or forties.

The seating left to right from behind: stylish mom, little brother, big brother performer, dad, daughter who is generally snuggled up to her handsome dad. The conversations fly every which way, except only, of course, when their darling is at bat at the grand piano. Though his playing is nothing special, the house is silent as never before.

The baby of the family is easily bored and allowed to go outside and come back at will, crawling over his family to get back to his seat between mom and his big brother. This while another student is performing.

The mystery to me is what causes this avoidable rude behavior. These people do not appear stupid or uneducated—just insensitive to others. Is this the product of the technological age? Genetic impairment? Or am I (and the rest of the audience) out of step with the mores of the age?

The fact that they can cut off their remarks when their kid plays leads one to believe that it is possible to lend the same respect to the other kids. They just seem incapable of bringing that modicum of consideration off. I wonder if Mozart suffered these indignities when he was a kid?

After the darling has played his rendition of the Pachelbel's *Canon* and the program grinds on, a gray haired gent in a Hawaiian shirt saunters in while someone is playing and takes his place beside what must be his granddaughter, still in her proprietary embrace of her father. Now the old guy (my age) lends his voice to the family conversation.

That settles it. This inconsideration is all genetic.

THE REAL VESTIBULE

I'm not going to his funeral—
he's not coming to mine.

—*Grampop Knoll*

THE EARLY STAGES
OF THE LAST STAGE

Life begins when a person first realizes how soon it ends.

—*Marcelene Cox*

Our oldest daughter has the power of the plug—to pull or not to pull. This it would seem is not a power you would want to bestow on a spouse.

I am in Ketchum, Idaho, down market Sun Valley, where we enjoy a second home twice a year. In February 2013 I pick up an *Art Forum* magazine dated January 2011.

I leaf through the publication and am somewhat surprised I don't remember anything I am seeing.

Perhaps it's a fluke. Maybe it came when I wasn't here and I really never saw it before.

Then I look at another issue of the same magazine, and it's just the same: I don't remember anything.

And I'm not even seventy-nine yet.

Ambition is not a negative but failure should not be a disgrace.

Just as it is better to have loved and lost than to have never loved at all, so it is better to try and fail than never to have tried at all.

The joy, after all, is in the journey, not the arrival.

If there is perfection in the world, it has passed me by.

Life itself takes funny turns. Well, turns, certainly, whether or not you think them funny, as I do. But then I've always had a touch of crazy.

A time comes when you might, as I do, contemplate the end. I have just read a poem (by Daniel Halpern) that says,

> Breathing's generally wary
> Labored, as they say, when
> The end is at hand.

Years ago (forty or fifty?) I saw a movie with—was it Paul Muni?—rising up in bed in anguish, dying of a horrific heart attack. Never forgot it.

I wonder if it won't be a gradual weakening just like going to sleep with a fading consciousness. That seemed to be the fate of a friend, who, after deciding against yet another operation to delay the inevitable, took to his bed and with the humanitarian aid of products so designed by the pharmaceutical industry, got groggier and groggier while his heart and lungs hung on as if in defiance of the cancerous reality until he fought no more.

My friend, Mr. Manning—c.f. the five-pound sugar per week guy—said, "Everybody is scared of dying. I don't care who they is, they is *scared!*"

Que serra, serra. Whatever will be, will be. I wouldn't want to miss the experience (if I *had* a choice), though I imagine, the briefer the better.

Yes, everybody goes. How terrible it would be if some were immortal and others not. The only distinction is how long before it kicks in.

A number of my contemporaries have expressed the desire to bring the whole bloody mess to its inescapable end. Sentiments from, "I'd commit suicide in a minute," to "I *want* to die," to "I'm ready—I've lived my life—no sense hanging around."

The thought of being incapacitated or physically, mentally helpless is daunting and many reach out for the alternative.

I have never considered suicide an acceptable course. Why would you if you still get a kick out of life? Therein, perhaps, lies the rub. We may reasonably assume that those who still get a kick are not among the end seekers.

Insurance stats indicate all the healthcare dough is blown in the last two months. That might be the time to consider shortening the allotted span. But by then it's probably either you are not compos mentis enough to know what's up (my father at eighty-eight), or your faculties are so impaired you can't communicate any wishes you might have (my mother at ninety-one).

The question is sometimes asked would you trade your lifespan for Mozart's (thirty-five) to accomplish what he did? Or Stephen Vincent Benet, Dostoyevsky? My answer is always no thanks. Life is too sweet—fame seems more desirable when you are younger.

And I expect Mozart didn't spend a lot of time thinking about fame. He was too busy grinding out the music in his unending quest to make a living. And J.S. Bach, one wonders how he had time to *copy* out all that music, let alone *write* it. And when he died in 1750, of all his obituaries that lauded his skill as an organist, only one even mentioned he was a composer.

It was seventy-three years after Bach's death that Felix Mendelssohn discovered through a gift from his grandmother the music of Johann Sebastian Bach. Five years later he saw to a performance of Bach's monumental *Saint Matthew Passion* and the passion for Bach's music unfurled.

When I contemplate this finality, I sometimes think it will be disappointing because I will not be able to record it for posterity—not that posterity will be broken hearted.

See: I didn't forget everything.

THE DEEP BLUE

I am deteriorating faster than
I can lower my standards

—bumper sticker

From time to time I get something in the mail that reminds me of my mortality. These missives are from an enterprise called the Neptune Society—the deep blue sea—get it?

They'd apparently like to know if I wouldn't fancy winding up there via one of their relatively inexpensive urns.

They'd like to have my phone number "to determine which plan fits your family's needs." What is that? The sooner the better?

What plans? How hot should the flames be? I have heard of these operations where the bodies pile up because they don't have the resources (after graft and theft of deposits pinch the operating accounts) to see them through to their promised conclusions. What metal for the urn? Pewter or gold?

I may not consider myself old enough for these crass appeals to those who seek to deny their obvious mortality, but in the spirit of merchandising, I see their point.

A lot of us who live too long begin to experience dementia, Alzheimer's or just plain inability to cope with reality—before reality ends completely. So it behooves these hucksters of death to make hay while the sun shines. To get the signature on the contract before we forget who we are, what our name is, and how to write it.

I am, they assure me, under no obligation. But the envelope hinted the burning would be free. No wonder so many unburned bodies pile up in back of the garage.

The second pitch inside the envelope is a little vague on the free part. I do note I can win a prepaid cremation like Johnny Thompson did last month. And if I don't believe them I can send a *stamped* self-addressed envelope and if I do it before June 30 this year they will (cheerfully, I surmise) send me a list of the winners or the official rules for entering as Johnny apparently did. But apparently not both. Perhaps that takes a second stamp.

Atop the page that touts the prepaid cremation contest is a picture of three kids and two adults playing ring-around-the-rosy. The shot was taken in blurry sunlight (heaven?) just before the *all fall down* part. I divine the dramatis personae to be the children, their mother and grandfather—the latter being the obvious candidate for the services offered by the Neptune Society. If that is so, there is no daddy in the ring. Perhaps he has already fallen down— out of sight. Perhaps this is rather a nod to the modern family makeup.

Though I do notice the woman (the mother in my reading) is on the hefty side, bust and bottom-wise, and she could well be the first to "fall down."

At the bottom of this page is appended a cute quote from the ubiquitous Eleanor Roosevelt, known to the candidates preferred by the Neptune Society. I notice she was precisely my age when she was returned to ash. Makes you think.

I briefly wondered why they chose Eleanor for this part of the pitch:

> "Yesterday is history, tomorrow is a mystery,
> and today is a gift;
> that's why they call it the present."

I don't know about you, but I think that is darling. Especially if you are a Democrat. But what was the rationale for using a polarizing political figure? It could just turn off Republicans.

Then I thought, perhaps cremation is favored by those of a liberal bent and fuddy-duddy Republicans favor the venerable horizontal planting in a wooden box to give the worms a leg up.

So it was a calculated risk on the part of the Neptuners to appeal to those most likely to opt for being fried, if only finally, to show the fuddy-duddies that Mrs. Roosevelt (and God knows how much she suffered) was right after all.

Was *she* cremated? They don't say, which I expect they would have had she have been. No, I see her laid out for a heralded viewing—one of homo sapiens more barbaric customs—if for no other reason than to demonstrate to her manifold enemies that she was completely dead.

In the interests of political equality—not to say *correctness*— I expect the next pitch from the Neptune Society to bear a quote from Ronnie Reagan.

AGING

Too many pieces of music finish too long after the end.

—*Igor Stravinsky*

What does aging mean, and how do you know you are no longer an active member of the earthbound fraternity?

It sneaks up on you. You may say your years to yourself or others, but it has no meaning until you feel it. Little things go wrong—but you don't know it's happening. You may deny it for a while, but when it doesn't go away you suspect you are there. Suspect? Or deny. Denial is a convenient crutch. Notice how we all get shorter? Say you ride a bicycle as I do. You smile and say hello to riders coming toward you. They smile back and you feel a friendly connection. Then one day you notice some of the smiles are askew. They may not be smiles at all, but the early stages of laughter at a guy your age still peddling as though he were their age. Then you start looking and you don't see anyone your age or older on a bike. Or you note in competitions of hundreds of riders segregated by age there is only one in your category: seventy-five and older.

Body parts give out.

You have been taking off your glasses to read the piano music, when suddenly (it *seems* suddenly) it is clearer with them on.

Then a knee gives out and you watch knee operations on the internet. Slice it open, pull the skin revealing the sub-standard knee. Saw the tops of the femur and shin, glue on some titanium and plastic interlocking parts, sew it back up. Like an advanced root canal.

It is said we are close to copying and replacing the complete human body with artificial parts.

The reaper is stalking. At seventy-eight what percentage of my life is left? Less than one-third, probably twenty percent or less, one year for every four I have lived. But nature takes care of its own. At seventy-eight you've seen a lot of stuff. A lot of it many times over. How much is enough?

There is a story of an avid golfer who goes to heaven and plays golf every day and, as befitting heaven, every day he plays a perfect game. The ball lands at the same spot day after day. Always perfectly placed. You know before you hit it where it's going to go. Fun for a while, but how long before it gets boring? Two years? Two thousand? Two hundred would seem a stretch, a blip in the time-line of infinity. Life is finite but so are interests. So when an interest fades it behooves us to replace it with another. Sooner or later you land on something at which you are not half bad. This is perhaps the upside of dilettantism. Well, it's exercise you might say. But you don't *need* exercise, you're dead. My friend Jerry Moss said he used to think he was *especial*. But then he considered himself quite or-dinary. Does that observation come from seeing too much of the same thing? Or seeing too many others who think, with scant evi-dence, *they* are *especial*?

I have just read a piece by ninety-three year old Roger An-gell who first had a piece in the *The New Yorker* in 1944. That's sev-enty years ago if your math is shaky as he is and we are becoming. In an engaging piece called "This Old Man" in *The New Yorker*. He posits one of the difficult things for him is watching home movies, he speaks of being invisible at gatherings where if he finally contributes a mite to a conversation the gaggle of invitees stop in their tracks. Then when he has exhausted his pittance of a contri-bution return to their conversations as though he weren't there — hadn't spoken at all.

I don't often put myself into those social situations and hence am seldom annoyed by anonymity. In fact, I rather like it.

I met a woman who responded to the ubiquitous question, "What do you do?" with, "I'm an artist." For me that required some courage—self-assurance perhaps or self-delusion?

For me to say, "I'm a writer," seems to require the same, so I am reticent about it. I can more easily say, "I write books," than I am a writer, which might elicit the response, "Oh, really? What have you written that I might know?"

I think, hey, I didn't say I was Steven King, Grisham, the Harry Potter lady or the Clancy guy—or I didn't say I write best-sellers, just books—and she might think—hey, don't get all defensive about it—

So I have given to mumble I manage (or "have") some apartment buildings.

"Oh, where?"

"Over Southern California."

At last, something I can answer.

Inhibitions fade with advanced age—but they don't disappear. With the fading inhibitions goes strength and resolve saving society from a bunch of geriatric perverts.

Everyone wants to be well thought of, so perhaps that adds to the containment of inappropriate actions. Perhaps with enough time all inhibitions would disappear resulting in chaos. But how long? Fifty years? Two hundred? Five hundred?

We all have to confront death sooner or later. Later is better for most. Some crave the reaper but don't get him. (*En garde*, feminists. This terminal actor I cannot imagine as a woman. A benevolent God, perhaps, but not the hooded guy with the sickle. But, who knows, the feminists are taking over everything …matter of time.) Ceasing eating may help.

The fear can be truncated by a sudden accident. What do people going down on a plane think? Communiqués from passengers on 9/11 hijacked planes would indicate most of them are matter of fact. Time, which is always finite, compresses. It goes faster if you have a focus, like calling home to say goodbye. Not everyone is blessed with that opportunity. Some lucky ones will reflect on past pleasures. Some will wallow in self-pity. Some few might take a moment for self-congratulation for some accomplishment, real or imagined. Then the end. Final and irreversible.

So what is so great about eternal life? Already a lot of it is wearing thin in three score and ten plus eight.

Even eternal paradise must seem suspect. It always seemed to me the concept of heaven was dubious. First, where is it? The stars in our galaxies are *trillions* of miles apart. Is it in our galaxy? Then to accept heaven as a reality one has to allow for a place for all those souls who don't make the cut—and voila! hell is born. A distinctly unpleasant place. But by the same circular reasoning, if there *were* a hell, there wouldn't be a heaven because everyone would fail to measure up with pure thoughts and exemplary earthly behavior. Most religions, sects, cults have handy explanations for this, fudging the requirements, but my money is still on hell.

I have known several people who profess to believe in God and heaven as an insurance policy, in case there *is* a heaven they don't want to be excluded because of unbelief. Is there a deity that would be snowed by that tepid reasoning? If he were that easily buffaloed, how great could his stomping grounds be?

In my humble opinion one of the main attractions about being dead is that you don't know it. Sleeping every night gives us a perception of that unconscious state.

Those who think they will know they are dead and will love it are I think setting themselves up for disappointment. But if they don't know they haven't reached nirvana, how can they be disappointed?

It's failsafe.

In my time traversing Mountain Drive on my bicycle, I have seen a number of older folk who have since disappeared. The ultimate in aging, you might say. Those I remember:

A couple. Hale and hearty—she, perhaps more so than he, for I remember him trailing her on their trek. He was an author of California lore and I didn't succeed in completing the book of his I began. Fault mine, not his. He disappeared first, then she.

A woman who seemed to keep a brisk pace. She told me one day homeless people were living on my grounds in my collection of painted Volkswagens. I told her the painted cars were art. I don't think she was sold.

A neighbor. An architect mentioned before, under the influence of strong spirits. He muttered a hello, I said hello, he apparently didn't hear me. He stopped in his tracks, fixed me with a withering glare that you know can only come from an important person. "I said *hello*," he said. "Why don't you answer?" I said, meekly, I had.

A fellow sculpture student who lived a mile from me.

All gone — as are others less memorable.

(How to Act Really Old)

Should it behoove you to seem really old, whether for increased deference, sympathy or veneration, here are some suggestions:

Display some difficulty walking. The old equilibrium ain't what she used to be. Blips in your balance make you seem unsteady on your feet.

Make believe you can't remember the simplest things. Then, if it serves some purpose, recapture with a bravado announcement the meaningless tidbit.

The cliché is, "I can't remember what I had for breakfast." Does anyone *care* what you had for breakfast? Do you even care? But most of us have the same thing for breakfast daily. Shouldn't that be pretty easy to remember?

People's names are plentiful fodder for this activity. There are so many of them to forget.

There seems to be a general misconception that people don't want to get old, but many are glad to be out of the fray.

On our fiftieth high school reunion questionnaire we asked if the respondents would like to have another chance to live their lives over. The overwhelming majority said once was enough.

You have this opportunity, and it is a *great* opportunity, to have the experiences you have from cradle to grave, but once you have done it, you realize once may be enough. A passel of suicides might indicate for some, once is *too* much.

As one ages, faculties soften, weaken or disappear. One is

prone to lament those normal failings and without fail the hearer of those perceived sad tidings will say something reassuring that all is well, "It happens to me also," someone thirty years your junior will attempt to reassure you. Of course, it doesn't. Nor does it fool you. It is well intentioned and therefore appreciated as a nicety of social grace.

Verily, it is said if you have the flu and you hear of someone else having it, it doesn't make you feel better.

The easy fatigue is a foretaste of the welcome ease of eternal rest. The deference of the younger creeps up.

I have arrived at an age where I notice I am receiving excessive deference from our children and others. Surprisingly I don't find it patronizing or annoying, but rather endearing.

A recent *New Yorker* article on Alzheimer's disease indicates some of us may look forward to the body outliving the mind—a time when there *is* no short-term memory—a time when we don't remember how to dress ourselves.

Science has increased lifespans with antibiotics, vaccines, public health and other miracles and is working on doing the same for the forlorn mind.

In 1900 the average American died at forty-seven. Today the average lifespan is seventy-eight. Guess who is still seventy-eight?

If age indeed mellows, one has a better chance of being posthumously well thought of the longer one lives. Ambitions of youth may appear antisocial, abrasive. With the waning of the ambition, peace arrives. With shorter memories one is liable to forget past unpleasantness and remember the sanitized present.

Shakespeare said in *Julius Caesar*, "The evil that men do lives long after them, the good is oft interred in their bones." But his reasoning must be suspect since he was speaking of a relatively young man.

THE OBIT

There's never anything new about death, to be sure,
except its improved publicity....

—Roger Angell
The New Yorker

Newspapers falling on hard times have spurred economic genius in the selling of space for obituaries. It seems more and more people are availing themselves of this service to mankind.

Myself, I'm too cheap. With aspirations to anonymity. So I have left instructions somewhere not to pay for any obituaries. And as I think of it now, I am not at all sure I have any lust for any kind of death notice. I mean, what is so great if you die? Everyone seems to do it. Oh, I expect some would welcome the news for whatever the reason, I expect not all of them unfounded. One is bound to tick off a couple people if one lives long enough and it does get you out of the way. If one could eavesdrop after one's demise, I expect one would hear a mixed bag of comments from, "he wasn't a bad guy—annoying at times," "He sure did some crazy stuff," to, "I wonder what ever became of old what's his name?"

So how do these paeans to mediocrity begin—mediocre-ly usually—where and when born (Allentown, Pennsylvania, July 20, 1934—though I won't be expecting any birthday cards). After that it gets more difficult. The mention perhaps of a smattering of clubs and associations the deceased belonged to—it could help some fellow member place him. The high Potentate of the Knights Templar of the Sons of Rebecca. The best I can do is an Eagle Scout in

Troop 38 of the Boy Scouts of America. BS for short. I outgrew that
at sixteen. Oh, I was in a fraternity at USC (λXA) but that didn't
amount to much. For the rest of my life I experienced a dry spell
organization-wise. I suppose it was by choice. But that does leave a
gaping hole in the old the obit.

You could say how much I loved hunting and fishing—but
I don't. Oh, there may have been some people I wouldn't have
minded shooting, but that is so antisocial. Hunting animals (a reputed lower order—albeit significantly less offensive) is blessed by
the state, but I've got nothing against dumb animals—or smart ones
for that matter.

What else? Some statistics: one wife—going on fifty-three
years. Lived together for forty-two of them. Three daughters, Melora
Scharf, Julia Forester, Abby Schott. Eight grandchildren: Jordan
Gardner Scharf, Jeremy Gardner Scharf, Mason Gardner Scharf—
whose middle names are a snap for me to remember; Maxwell Tarik
Forester, Grant Knoll Forester; Emma Louise Schott, Nathaniel
Gardner Schott, Owen Samuel Schott. Is the naming of children
a mirror into the parents' personalities?

Jordan is the first in college: UCLA. Myself the arch rival
USC, 1956, by default. Of course, we had to pay. Jordan is so smart
they kicked in virtually all the tuition, room and board and sundry
niceties thanks to the taxpayers. Before Governor Reagan made a
show of making ends meet by charging tuition for state colleges,
we used to call UCLA Taxpayer Tech.

Navy flight program, Lieutenant Junior Grade USNR—
until I was no longer able to hide I really had no aptitude for flying.

Worked three years for CBS Television before they caught
on and hinted they would be happier if I went elsewhere. The verdict: definitely not an organization man.

Wrote two episodes of *Rawhide*—a horse opera starring
Clint Eastwood—the cultural highlight of Friday night.

Choir director, North Long Beach Methodist and Westchester Christian.

Worked in residential real estate. Founded Gardner Company and Gardner Management Limited in 1967 specializing in

apartment sales and management. The name of the companies
were snaps for me to remember. And two! Pretentious enough for
you?

Founded and directed and funded South Coast Choral Society. Thirteen years in the making, until the move to Santa Barbara, vastly relieving the loyal membership.

There might be some mention of a beloved pet who may
have predeceased our subject, or not. One can only rest assured
that the survivor will sorely miss the absentee.

I was six years old when my "pet" bit the dust. Saying it left
a vacuum in my heart would be a stretch. My mother and father
didn't even remember the dog.

Many of these sacred tomes are written by the survivors
who, let it be admitted, never come off poorly in the telling, no
matter how fraught with anger, disappointment and despair the relationship wore on.

A member in good standing of AARP—except I've never
given them a penny. I feel somehow AARP dates you.

Later in life when most of his peers were coasting on their
laurels, Ted became an avid composter.

I must confess I am writing this obituary template from
memory, and am sure I am missing *beaucoup* features—so I must
look some up to refresh my memory, which unlike some cheese
does not improve with age.

Okay—so now I am in possession of a boatload of obits—
and I am sorry to report (probably not news to you) that there is a
numbing similarity to them.

We may not be as special as we think we are. We're all com-
posed of the same chemicals for starters. So when we say we have
chemistry with someone—or no chemistry—what do we mean?
We're all the same chemical elements, yet some people attract us
and some repel us. And it isn't always mutual with the same couple.
I'm sure I'm not alone in aspiring to understand this phenomenon,
but I still don't grasp it. It brings to mind the supreme court justice,
Potter Stewart, I believe, who famously said he couldn't define
pornography, but he knew it when he saw it.

In fact, as I peruse these down home attempts at literary

pretension I am wont to wonder does anybody care one guy was a "die-hard" SD Chargers fan? Since the cost is six dollars a line ($6.35 on Sunday), perhaps the writer hoped to save six dollars ($6.35 on Sunday) by not spelling out San Diego. It is something I might have done if I hadn't lived long enough so I no longer needed to.

And speaking of saving money, here is a guy about whom they are at no pains to edit for economy. We are not only told that he worked for Lockheed Aircraft for thirty-three years, but that he was primarily in the Engine Accessions Group of the Propulsion Department of the Flight Sciences Engineering Division. There follows all the departments he worked in—five lines of type or $31.75 plus $25 for the photo.

You might be pleased to know the gentleman conducted functional and performance analyses of propulsion, mechanical, electrical, and fluid accessory systems including auxiliary and emergency power units and pneumatic, fuel, cooling and fire protection systems.

Somebody has to do it.

On the web page for the paper there is a guy who died in an accident, unspecified, who was widely praised for his bear hugs.

No one seems to save on the photo. One bought two, the pair showing the ravages of the aging process. I'm sure she was worth it.

What is the goal here? The hope of catching the eye of one of his Lockheed buddies from fluid accession systems or rather a sop to the survivors who could revel in his manifold accomplishments?

One of the guys reputedly loved to make people laugh and the picture of him furthered that goal. He is sporting a black cowboy hat and a black bowtie and a black pencil moustache. There's what appears to be an orchid on the lapel of his tuxedo or black jacket. For this fellow "no one was a stranger for long." More's the pity?

The breakdown—Tuesday—four men, six women, all smiling except one man who in the photo looks bewildered as though he were asking why me? Or why now? He may not have lived long enough (58 years) to get a really smiley photograph.

"Passed away peacefully" seems to be the opening gambit along with the date. Perhaps at the end, if we live long enough, our only option is a peaceful passing. None of these obits even suggest anyone fighting every step of way. No, eternal rest promises peace like no other condition.

To sum it all up the most you can do with a life after it is all over is to tell it like it was, and that is painfully mundane. We have avid readers and avid gardeners and tedious renderings of names and relatives and survivors (some of whom, of course, wrote these testimonials).

We thank the old folks home staffs for their love, kindness and professional help, with now and then thanks to a doctor who did yeoman service in the situation.

"It broke our hearts to lose you, but you did not go alone, a part of us went with you…"

So, we are given the statistics: birth, death in reverse order, occupation(s), social groups, hobbies, interests and the reassurance that the end was peaceful.

Who could ask for anything more?

I used to know a guy who wrote obituaries for the Allentown (Pennsylvania) Morning Call. He lived in my grandfather's house—a paying customer. That was sixty years ago. These obituaries were written in advance, ready to run when the old cork popped—and if too much time passed between the writing and the croaking they could be quickly touched up at the last minute. Perhaps in the intervening years she had joined the daughters of Rebecca, or he won some local pinochle tournament.

Now obituaries are a vanity press enterprise processed (well, not all of us are *writers*) by a survivor and *paid for* by the same entity.

And with all the infinite varieties of people, the numberless gene combinations, these posthumous tributes are numbingly similar. Change a few dates and sports teams and what you get are interchangeable souls.

ON THE ROAD TO RICHES

One realises that one never arrives at anything,
but must just go on fighting every day as long as the strength lasts.

—T.S. Eliot

And so, here we are on July, 20, 2013, my seventy-ninth birthday, ringing down the curtain on book number thirty-nine, one year to the day of when I began this first rough draft. Though it is not as rough as some, it will still warrant some horsing around before the second and third rough drafts, and being set in type and put between covers as the final rough draft.

I am at my desk in my library (remember how I value pretension) and this paper that is graciously, uncomplainingly accepting this fountain pen agitation and leaking green ink on it, sits atop far too much stuff:

It is perhaps a tribute to the paper industry that most of this "stuff" on my desk is paper. I am somewhat behind the curve on technology. Though I realize the prodigious benefits of the computer, my chemistry is with the fountain pen, ink and paper.

Piled on my desk are typewritten chapters of this book, pages that had no changes, as well as edited pages. There are pages of a contract to buy an eighty-four unit apartment building in Oxnard, California, abutting a marina near an enormous base that houses Seabees and navy and marines, even army. So if you must pray for peace, and far be it for me to discourage that, I only ask you don't pray very hard.

There are birthday cards, five by actual count to be opened

and savored after my bicycle ride up and down Mountain Drive. Imagine people taking the trouble to address a card they had to purchase, find a stamp, affix it, put it somewhere for a postwoman or man in tight postal markets? It is very touching. I also got a clever computer card from the Palos Verdes office of Gardner Company that somehow incorporated my face in the animated cartoon. Also a card from daughter Julia with an original, albeit heavily edited poem. There are also pictures printed from the internet of the most outlandish women's fashions you could find for yet another sculpture project of five or so of these fillies bedecked in what passes for fashion on the catwalk, though I don't think even rich Chinese would wear them in public.

Also littering my workspace are a Thomas Guide—quite a useful map book and enormously successful and lucrative enterprise, before the internet horned in and not only mapped the earth but provided aerial photographs of the area of interest rendering this heretofore indispensable map tool virtually obsolete—everything you need to know and lots you don't need to know is encapsulated in that ubiquitous tool the size of a flattened cigarette pack which functions, in addition to this storehouse of information, as a cellular telephone.

Coincidentally near the top and partially in view are my birth certificate (copy certified by the state of Pennsylvania) which was used to obtain a passport replacement for its predecessor perished in the fire.

Also a draft of a letter to all employees explaining the proffered healthcare plan. Though we have not reached the fifty-employee plateau, we decided to be good sports and offer it anyway since they would be obligated to buy it themselves. We had been putting ten percent of everyone's pay into retirement accounts. I don't know of another company that does that, so we are financing the not inconsiderable additional cost by reducing that somewhat, by paying a portion, by adjusting the yearly salary increases, by eating the difference on older employees whose health care hit is more than ten thousand each, annually. Do you wonder why there are layoffs of long time employees—and the difficulty they have in being hired again?

And here is a color copy of a painting by Willem de Kooning known as Woman V, a copy of which has been sent to a company in London that reproduces in oil masterpieces of art (and I suppose not-so-masterpieces if you are willing to pay for them).

Four bottles of ink—velvet black, supershow blue, "Naples" blue and sapphire green. Notes for future books. The beginnings of a novel about a young woman who worked for Virginia, nabbed for helping herself to fifty thousand dollars from an immobile employer. The girl was young (twenty-one?), cute and very pleasant with a nice way about her. She was able to return the lucre, and was given a light prison sentence in gratitude for her new attitude. Recently arrived New Yorker and Bon Appetit magazines. A myriad of pens, fountain and a few ballpoint, and pencils. Still I manage to run perhaps six or seven pens dry between refillings. This green I am dipping in a seriously depleted bottle, too low to successfully fill the pen, but a surprising number of words can be formed with one dip. Remember Shelby Foote, The Civil War: a Narrative, wrote millions of words dipping a quill pen in ink—at the rate of three words the dip. I get a good page (250 or so words) out of one dip. Foote says three words a dip nicely conformed to his metabolism. Mine at seventy-nine is somewhat brisker. So if there were any justice in the world, I'd sell as many books as he does.

Unopened envelopes from the Neptune Society (yes, yet another) the folks who want to entice you to get burned up, and the Metropolitan Museum of Art in New York. Files lately stuffed with ideas, notes and detritus miscellany. Most of which I will never look at again.

There is a setup or two on senior housing apartments—the wave of the future—if more labor intensive than unfurnished apartments.

Back from my bike ride where I encountered fifty or so runners spread across the street as though no one else had dibs on the street. I expect they were out in celebration of my birthday—and it wasn't just mindless knee-crunching-to-exhaustion exercise. At my first turn around point the runners congregated at the many cars parked there. I was relieved to be free of them so I turned around perhaps one hundred feet earlier than usual, pleased that I would have the road to myself for the return leg.

But no — feeling they had not celebrated my birthday adequately they too turned around and I encountered their admittedly thinned troops after my next turn around and on the way home. Since there were fewer of them and more spread out from fatigue, it was easier to transit the mob, many of whom seemed to be gasping for breath or sending auditory signals to the reaper to open death's door.

Not me. I am comfortably seated on a bicycle and I expect my ultimate transit will be as cushy.

And now my pen leaked all over my fingers of both hands. It is the price of writing with fountain pens. Green ink. My late friend and early benefactor (who treated me so handsomely when he sold me three properties at friendly prices and terms), Jerry Moss, wrote with green ink exclusively. I just now wonder if he ever got ink all over his hands and under his fingernails.

His wife Violet just died this year in a Santa Barbara nursing home at one hundred, perhaps five or six years after she told me she wanted to die. I have often said we live as long as we want to, but in her case it was a lot longer. To think of all the futile motions she went through, eating, bathing, toilet, etc. after life's offering ceased to enchant her. Is there not another solution?

It is a universal truth that everyone wants to be well thought of. The crucial element in this equation could be the thinker. What does he think and why? And what is his or her opinion worth? Do you want to be well thought of by strangers? Is that why writers write? People who know you don't need evidence of the written word. They have you in the flesh for their assessment.

I may have written this memoir in the nick of time — while I can remember anything. Just now I get an idea and by the time I get to pen and paper I've forgotten it. Or it is crowded out by another idea which I subsequently forget.

This book is the product of the remnants of those lapses. Or the lapses of those remnants, as the case may very well be.

Some might ask for advice from the culmination of a life: Do your best, and do it every day? Live life to the fullest? If your interests change, change interests? Create? Or perhaps most germane:

don't take any wooden nickels—unless that is all you are offered? Or my favorite: There are two kinds of fools: those who give advice and those who take it.

As they say in the movie biz on the completion of filming, "It's a wrap!"

Almost.

✻   ✻   ✻   ✻

I have a fax machine which prints faxes via a medium called "toner." This black powder is housed in an expensive cartridge and when this toner runs out the cartridge must be replaced. About a year ago a light went on and a message on the screen was received that it was running low on toner and this pricey cartridge should be replaced. But I noticed no drop in the quality of the type. The first few times the message appeared accompanied by the flashing light, I took the cartridge out of the machine and shook it—replaced it and the light went out—the message disappeared and it was business as usual.

Now the light stays on and the message appears, but there is no discernible drop in the quality of the product (the type on the page).

So I am wondering—I have perhaps gotten a thousand pages since I was told in no uncertain terms that the goods were depleted and it was time for a rejuvenation. But by god, that old cartridge just kept chugging along, spewing out legible type like there was no tomorrow.

There could be a metaphor lurking in there somewhere. Was I operating, perhaps, beyond my sell by date? Did I need a good shaking?

And as long as it is so much fun, I'll keep spewing…until my toner really zeros out.

And now, a few months after writing this, with no change in the toner, the screen is flashing.

WARNING!! TONER LOW
LESS THAN 50 PAGES

But I have printed *more* than fifty pages since this scary message first appeared and if there is some difference in the quality of the type on the page, I don't see it.

I keep thinking how sad it would be to put all that unused toner in the landfill, secure in its coffin-like cartridge—like burying people before they are completely dead.

✳   ✳   ✳   ✳

I opened the birthday cards. Since I got my start on the road to riches sending birthday cards to my high school classmates, I hold a special spot in my heart for those who bother to send them. We do see that our managers are remembered on their birthdays with cash and a card, and all our residents get a card and a small gift hand delivered by the manager. Lalana Kotkin, née Debra, whom we affectionately name my "personal assistant," is a sucker for the paranormal. Her card shows a gypsy fortuneteller, cards spread out before her, her right hand raised to neck level. The title says:

> All those who believe in
> Telekinesis raise my hand.

Doing the lion's share of the typing and proofreading of this manuscript is Elizabeth Hanning-Yu with typing help and editing by Abby Schott—our thirdborn.

And those birthday tributes exhibit a huge amount of love and praise that was heretofore given, if at all, somewhat more guardedly—but the closer one gets to the end (so my theory goes) folks may think it could be their last chance to say something nice—before it's too late for the subject to hear it. I would expect that would taper off if one hangs on too long.

I realize I could have said more about my wife, Virginia, children Melora, Julia and Abby as well as the assorted grandchilluns mentioned elsewhere. I adore and cherish them all and if pride didn't goeth before a fall I'd say how proud I was of all of them.

They have been unfailingly generous with their attention and good cheer.

Melora writes beautiful notes with positive reinforcements and copious praise. As mentioned, she spearheaded the last two building projects, the replacement residence and the museum (six years in the making).

Julia ran the real estate and property management company expertly for sixteen years, never once raising her voice to me—in spite of what I suspect were numerous provocations.

Abby is the publishing company, through whose efforts the books I write appear better than they were after I had written them. All are super moms. Is there anything more important?

I had always said I'd like to have six kids. Virginia humored me, being the wiser soul she must have realized I would brush up against reality sooner or later—preferably sooner.

And that is what happened. When we discovered each of our children was worth two, we had our fifth and sixth with the third.

But my instincts told me this thing was getting a little long. So let them write their own memoirs.

Do we end with a bang or a wimper? You decide.

I don't think I overlooked any opportunity to make myself look good, though I may have inadvertently stinted on or thoughtfully repressed those few instances where I did not appear the swellest fellow who ever came down the pike.

If you make believe I'm not here—before you know it you won't have to make believe.

July 20, 2013

Also By Theodore Roosevelt Gardner II

fiction
The Paper Dynasty
The Real Sleeper
Flip Side
Give Gravity a Chance
He's Back
Voyage to Oblivion

essays
Wit's End
Off the Wall

children's
Something Nice to See

nonfiction
Hermitage Santa Barbara at Twenty
Lotusland: A Photographic Odyssey
Nature's Kaledioscope: The Santa Barbara Botanic Garden

memoir
Momma Baby and Judgie

Writing as David Champion
The Snatch

(All Bomber Hanson Mystery series):
The Mountain Massacres:
Nobody Roots for Goliath
Celebrity Trouble
Phantom Virus
Too Rich and Too Thin
She Died for her Sins
Easy Come, Easy Go
To Die For
Bomber Bombs

Writing as Alistair Boyle
(All Gil Yates Private Investigator Novels)
The Missing Link
The Con
The Unlucky Seven
Bluebeard's Last Stand
Ship Shapely
What Now, King Lear?
The Unholy Ghost
They Fall Hard
The Ice Maiden Cometh Not

Writing as Alexandra Eden
(All Bones and the Duchess Mysteries)
To Oz and Back
Holy Smoke
The Duchess to the Rescue

Writing as Margaret Nicol
Enemy of the Average

Writing as Anonymous
The Two-Step Diet Book

Writing as A.T.R.
(A Con and Sindy Detective Series)
His Warranty Expired When He Did

Celebrating
25 Years of
Publishing Excellence

ALLEN A. KNOLL,
PUBLISHERS

ALLEN A. KNOLL, PUBLISHERS

Established 1989
We are a small press located in Santa Barbara, Ca,
specializing in books for intelligent people who read for fun.
Please visit our website at www.knollpublishers.com
for a complete catalog.
Call (805) 564-3377 or email bookinfo@knollpublishers.com to receive
a paper catalog and/or be kept informed of new releases.

Allen A. Knoll, Publishers
200 West Victoria Street
Santa Barbara, CA 93101
www.knollpublishers.com
(805) 564-3377

CPSIA information can be obtained at www.ICGtesting.com
Printed in the USA
LVOW11*1742090115

422090LV00002B/3/P